With or Against the World?

With or Against the World?

America's Role among the Nations

James W. Skillen

ROWMAN & LITTLEFIELD PUBLISHERS, INC.
Lanham • Boulder • New York • Toronto • Oxford

Published in cooperation with the Center for Public Justice

ROWMAN & LITTLEFIELD PUBLISHERS, INC.

Published in the United States of America
by Rowman & Littlefield Publishers, Inc.
A wholly owned subsidary of The Rowman & Littlefield Publishing Group, Inc.
4501 Forbes Boulevard, Suite 200, Lanham, Maryland 20706
www.rowmanlittlefield.com

PO Box 317
Oxford
OX2 9RU, UK

Published in cooperation with the Center for Public Justice

British Library Cataloguing-in-Publication Information Available

Library of Congress Cataloging-in-Publication Data

Skillen, James W.
    With or against the world? : America's role among the nations / James W.
Skillen.
      p. cm.
    Includes bibliographical references and index.
    ISBN 0-7425-3521-5 (cloth : alk. paper) — ISBN 0-7425-3522-3 (pbk. : alk.
paper)
    1. United States—Foreign relations—2001– 2. War on Terrorism, 2001– I.
Title.

    E895.S58 2005
    327.73'009'0511—dc22   2004018458

Printed in the United States of America

♾™ The paper used in this publication meets the minimum requirements of
American National Standard for Information Sciences—Permanence of Paper for
Printed Library Materials, ANSI/NISO Z39.48-1992.

For
Samuel James Skillen

Contents

Preface

The United States combines odd elements from a long Western lineage. We are a federated, constitutional republic, but also a nation with a global mission more expansive than that of the Roman Empire. We are among the most secular of modern states, but a nation with a civil-religious identity stronger than that of any state with an established church. Our military is positioned throughout the world, yet when we engage in battle, we believe we do so only in defense. The United States now exercises the dominion of an empire, but we are uncomfortable thinking of ourselves as anything more than a super-power that promotes freedom.

This is America, humble colossus, proud republic, now preoccupied with terrorism and an unruly world. For our own security and that of others, we are prepared to stand *against* the world of evil wherever it rears its head. Yet, in the way we have tried to fight evil since 9/11, we have raised doubts about our trustworthiness in standing *with* the world of democratic allies and the international rule of law.

The primary aim of this book is to try to understand America's often ambiguous ways of standing "with" or "against" the world. In the process of seeking understanding, the book's secondary aim is to explore how the United States might contribute constructively to the world of the future. Chapter 1 suggests that 9/11 did not change the world, although American foreign and defense policies shifted dramatically because Americans thought the world had changed. In the second chapter we begin to probe the historical and ideological depths of radical Islamism and American exceptionalism, depths that are largely unknown and unexplored by Americans who live in the present and look to the future. That preliminary probe is sufficient to show why we need to go back to the beginning, to the sources of the Western and Muslim traditions, in order to make sense of America's self-understanding, its view of the world, and the way Americans reacted to 9/11.

The next three chapters—chapters 3 through 5—focus on key developments that led to the rise of the modern West and particularly the United States. America's sense of itself as a new Israel, God's chosen nation, a city on a hill, is a corruption of the biblical story. The structure of the United States as a constitutional republic has roots in Greece and Rome and late medieval Christendom. The triumph of the modern state as the dominant institution of governance throughout the world today can be explained only by tracking what happened with the rise and demise of western Christendom between the eleventh and the sixteenth centuries. And western Christendom cannot be fathomed without understanding its triangular conflicts with eastern Christendom and Islam in the struggle for control of the territories and cultures of the declining Roman Empire.

What is perhaps most difficult for us to understand today is the religious character of America's political mission since the United States is a "secular" state. Chapters 6 through 8 try to account for this reality as well as for our difficulty in grasping it. Renaissance and Enlightenment visions of a revived humanity that is capable of creating its own bright future joined forces with Puritan new-Israelitism to produce an American civil-religious dynamo imbued with a world-historical mission. Only by understanding the peculiar relationship between America's grandiose messianic mission and its constitutionally restricted state structure can we make sense of the recurrent patterns of isolationism and internationalism, of realism and idealism, of reluctant engagement and aggressive warfare.

Chapters 8 through 10 take up current developments and future prospects. The range of issues and questions is vast and this book represents only an initial exploration. Nevertheless, an examination of President George W. Bush's National Security Strategy in the context of current events opens the way for a critical evaluation of America's global hegemony, or what Niall Ferguson calls America's informal, liberal empire. Chapter 9 turns the spotlight on the question of war, when it may be justified, and why justifiable warfare depends on just governance. In this chapter we also give attention to a growing American movement of Christian pacifism.

The final chapter draws together many threads in arguing that the great underachievement of the West's design on the world must now be given priority attention. The West invented the state, but it has not yet adequately answered the question of how to achieve international and transnational governance. The challenge for the United States and other states today is much bigger than fighting terrorism and encouraging people throughout the world to restrain their violence and to build their own democratic states. In the face of globalization, the growing interdependence of peoples throughout the world, terrorism, failed states, and a market in highly destructive weapons, the unavoidable responsibility of states today is to build stronger international institutions for the better governance of the world. The question is whether the United States will stand with or against the world in rising to this challenge.

Acknowledgments

The books, essays, lectures, and commentaries of so many people influenced and encouraged me on the subject matter of this book that I cannot remember them all. To those I do remember, and with whom I have enjoyed rich conversation over the years, I want to express heartfelt thanks.

Thank you, Rockne McCarthy, Bill Harper, Stanley Carlson-Thies, Justin Cooper, Bob Goudzwaard, Case Hoogendoorn, Keith Pavlischek, Luis Lugo, Don Kruse, Paul Marshall, Mark Noll, Jean Bethke Elshtain, James Turner Johnson, Jonathan Chaplin, Tracy Kuperus, David Koyzis, Steve Meyer, Dan Philpott, Mark Amstutz, Ron Sider, Serge Duss, Max Stackhouse, Jeanne Heffernan, Bruce Wearne, Keith Sewell, Roy Clouser, Bill Stevenson, Alberto Coll, Jim Ohlson, Clyde Taylor, John Bernbaum, Brian Fikkert, Carol Hamrin, Judith Dean, Myron Augsburger, Dean Curry, George Weigel, John Hare, Stanley Hauerwas, Richard Hays, Herman Keizer, Adolfo Garcia de la Sienra, Ron Mahurin, Roel Kuiper, Johan van der Vyver, Jason Kindopp, Alan Storkey, Craig Bartholomew, Stephen Lazarus, and early mentor Bernard Zylstra (1934–1986).

Special thanks to Jack Boeve for his editorial help on many fronts.

James W. Skillen
Annapolis, Maryland
Memorial Day, 2004

CHAPTER ONE

~~

Did 9/11 Change the World?

The enormity and utter surprise of the destruction in New York, at the Pentagon, and in Pennsylvania on September 11, 2001, shook Americans to the core. People across the world were stunned. On that day and in the weeks that followed, it was easy to imagine that the United States might be threatened with more assaults and that the next ones might involve the use of biological, chemical, or even nuclear weapons. Fear of imaginable, worst-case scenarios intensified precisely because the public had not imagined the possibility of 9/11. Yet, the fact that the suicide killers entered the United States without causing suspicion—some having lived and studied here for quite some time—and used no military weapons in their assaults tells us that the shock of the events was due more to their surprising nature and destructiveness than to any threat to America's military defense capabilities.

In response to the attacks and conscious of American fears, President George W. Bush quickly set the country on a course that met with both enthusiastic support and sharp criticism. The criticism mounted particularly after civil liberties groups began to digest the Patriot Act, which Congress passed before the end of 2001 to tighten homeland security; after publication of the administration's new National Security Strategy in September 2002; and after the decision early in 2003 to attack and destroy the Iraqi regime of Saddam Hussein. The president and most of his defenders, as well as many of his critics, believed that 9/11 had changed everything and that the United States would have to reorient its foreign, defense, and homeland security policies in a fundamental way.

1

But did 9/11 really change the world? Or was it only that Americans were shocked into thinking that the world had changed? One premise of this book is that the world in which 9/11 became possible did not change in a fundamental way on that day. Nor did the Bush administration's response come from out of the blue. It reflected enduring patterns of American foreign policy and sprang from deep sources of American self-understanding.

Aggression and Response

The 9/11 attacks were unprecedented in American experience,[1] launched without warning against innocent people by foreign conspirators willing to commit murder and suicide to accomplish their mission of hijacking airplanes and flying them into highly symbolic buildings. The immediate aim of the aggression was dramatic destruction of life and property, as had been the case in earlier attacks on the World Trade Center in New York, U.S. embassies in Africa, and other American and Western targets. The larger purpose (of which most Americans were unaware) of those who carried out the attacks was to intensify a modern Islamist form of jihad (holy war) against the West's barbarian idolatry and materialism (*jahiliyya*) that has for hundreds of years been corrupting the true meaning of life as manifest in Islam.[2]

The acts that Americans experienced as terrorism and that the perpetrators intended as an intensification of a divinely mandated cleansing of the world were designed to help bring about the collapse of all that the American empire represents, both inside and outside Muslim lands. In lauding the 9/11 assaults, Al Qaeda's Osama bin Laden said in one communiqué, "We hope that these brothers are among the first martyrs in Islam's battle in this era against the new Christian-Jewish crusade led by the big crusader Bush under the flag of the Cross; this battle is considered one of Islam's battles."[3] In another statement bin Laden made clear that "the highest priority, after faith, is to repel the aggressive enemy that corrupts the religion and the world."[4]

The 9/11 terrorists were not the military force of a foreign government, though we learned soon after the events that the Al Qaeda network of which they were a part had some military capabilities through its bond with the Taliban regime of Afghanistan. Moreover, the hijackers targeted innocent civilians, not American military forces. Given our government's responsibility to protect its citizens and to punish and stop violent aggression, American federal and state governments were obligated to respond, as they were after the Timothy McVeigh bombing of the federal building in Oklahoma City and other acts of violence committed within this country. The immediate response of the government was to try to thwart future attacks by strengthening domestic and international security and to capture and punish any living conspirators who helped to commit the crimes or who might initiate new attacks. Furthermore, as soon as President Bush learned that the attacks originated with the Al Qaeda organization, he was right to demand that the Taliban regime stop Al Qaeda in Afghanistan and bring it to justice.

When the Taliban refused to cooperate and even made clear that it was complicit with Al Qaeda, the United States was justified, on internationally recognized grounds, to identify the Taliban government's complicity as a casus belli—a cause for justifiable warfare. In other words, if the Afghan regime continued to harbor and protect Al Qaeda operatives intent on committing murderous acts in the United States, then the American government had sufficient reason to treat the Taliban government as a military enemy. However, in terms of the moral reasoning of the "just war" tradition, a decision to go to war requires more than a just cause. It requires right intention, which may not be revenge or hatred; it must be a decision of last resort, after other attempts to redress the grievance have been tried; and it must be made with the expectation that victory is possible and with the obligation to help establish peace after winning the war.

The president did, in fact, send the American military into Afghanistan with the aim of destroying Al Qaeda and rooting out the Taliban, though he did not ask Congress for an official declaration of war. The Taliban regime was relatively quickly routed, and most of Al Qaeda's training and supply operations there were destroyed. Yet, we know at the time of this writing, more than two and a half years after 9/11, that even with Western military forces still active in Afghanistan, Al Qaeda has not yet been eliminated, and a new government has not yet taken full, constitutional control of the country. In fact, the rapid growth of opium production and trade since the end of major fighting, together with the continuing hold on power by regional warlords, raises questions about the legitimacy and long-term success of the American and allied intervention as measured by just war criteria.

However, even if we judge, as most Americans and many foreigners have done, that the *undeclared* war against the Taliban and Al Qaeda in Afghanistan was justified, what is the meaning behind President Bush's explicit and repeated *declaration* that the United States is at "war against terrorism" and against "rogue states" that support terrorism? Is his use of the word "war" merely metaphorical, like President Lyndon Johnson's declaration of war against domestic poverty? If so, then in what sense is the fight against terrorists throughout the world like or unlike the American military engagement in Afghanistan and the 2003 war against Saddam Hussein? Or is none of this really war in the traditional sense of the term? And if none of it has been real war, then what is it, and how should we evaluate it? On the other hand, if the president really means that the United States is at war with terrorists and rogue states, then should we assume that the military engagement in Afghanistan, the war in Iraq, and the intelligence and policing efforts conducted against terrorists at home and abroad are all expressions of a single, all-encompassing war?

In a review of eight books on terrorism, war, security, and civil liberties, Ethan Bronner writes that the president's phrase "war on terrorism" is not, in fact, being used metaphorically. It is not like the war on drugs or crime, which is "a marketing slogan aimed at connoting seriousness of purpose. It is a legal term of art. The long-term struggle against Al Qaeda and other radical Muslim groups has been cast in military terms—war—for a specific reason," writes Bronner. "The enemy has made the entire world the 'battle-ground,' the administration says, so anyone we capture in 'battle' can be labeled (by the commander in chief) an 'enemy combatant,' meaning someone with few rights under our Constitution."[5] "This is true," says Bronner, "even if that captive is an American citizen caught in the United States. . . . As [Attorney General John] Ashcroft said, 'The last time I looked at 9/11, an American street was a war zone.'"[6] Is it correct, however, to describe the streets of Manhattan on 9/11 as a war zone while describing the streets surrounding the bombed federal building in Oklahoma City as a crime scene? If the president and the attorney general do intend to speak nonmetaphorically of "war" against terrorism, and if the whole world, including all of the United States, is now a war zone or potential war zone, then what lines can be drawn any longer between policing and military engagement?

One consequence of the fact that the 9/11 attacks were spawned by Al Qaeda, whose cells had spread throughout many countries, is that the United States could not (and cannot) by its own declaration of war defend against or destroy Al Qaeda and other terrorist groups. For the United States to launch its own "war" against such terrorists in all countries, without regard to the responsibilities and capabilities of the legitimate governments in other countries, would be to commit multiple acts of unjust aggression that would undermine rather than reinforce the legitimacy of the U.S. government's authority. And the entire tradition of just war decision making (as well as much international law) depends on the recognition and exercise of legitimate authority. Why, after all, would the United States send its military to make war against Al Qaeda operatives in Germany or Italy, two of our allies in NATO, rather than seek the cooperation of the German and Italian governments to bring the terrorists in their countries to justice? The United States did *not* launch its own military assault on terrorists in those countries but instead asked for and received the German and Italian governments' cooperation in tracking them down and rooting them out. In fact, one of the most important and obligatory steps the United States took in the months after 9/11 was to lead in promoting a *cooperative international police and intelligence campaign against the terrorist conspiracy* by means of which all cooperating governments increased their efforts to uncover and destroy the cells of organizations plotting to commit acts of criminal violence against Americans and people of other countries.

The point here is that a judgment about undertaking justifiable warfare depends on a prior judgment about whether certain violent acts actually amount to a cause for war, a casus belli. And it is not self-evident that the 9/11 attacks were acts of war rather than criminal acts as these two are distinguished in Western law. Did the confusion about war rhetoric begin, then, not with President Bush's call for a "war on terrorism" but with his administration's prior misidentification of the terrorist attacks as acts of war instead of criminal acts? And did the president make that mistake because he accepted at face value bin Laden's use of "holy war" language to characterize Al Qaeda's attacks? If so, there may be a common thread running through the criticism from American civil libertarians and from many foreign governments directed at the Bush administration's conduct of a "war" on terrorism. Civil libertarians fear that the heightened security measures of the Patriot Act may allow the government to run roughshod over long-established constitutional freedoms of American citizens that are not supposed to be infringed upon by American military or foreign intelligence agencies.[7] Foreign governments object to American actions that appear to overlook or ignore the difference between war and policing and that blur the lines between an American war to defend itself and what should be a cooperative effort among many countries to protect themselves from terrorism.

The United States is, after all, not the only state in the world with a legitimate (de jure) government. It does not face terrorism alone even if 9/11 did hit Americans at home. The United States is a state defined by the context of a nearly five-hundred-year history of similarly organized states that together have developed many practices and international laws by which to relate to one another and to hold one another accountable. Among those laws and practices are the ones that distinguish domestic police and intelligence responsibilities from military and foreign intelligence responsibilities. Mutual recognition of the multiplicity of states in the world implies a mutual obligation of the governments of those states to recognize one another's domestically policed territories. Neither the United States nor any other government has the right, unilaterally, to declare the territories of other states to be its own war zone, for that implies that it is at war with those states. Persisting in an indefinite American "war" against terrorism, therefore, may cause long-term damage to U.S. relations with friendly states and allies, something that would be directly counterproductive to stopping terrorism.

Different views of what constitutes war are not, however, the sole cause of a divide that has emerged between the United States and a number of its allies and friends. Robert Kagan contends that the United States is facing a "crisis of legitimacy" in the eyes of other nations for a reason that has less to do with specific Bush actions—even war actions—than it does with different views of how the world should be ordered. "A great philosophical schism has opened within the West," writes Kagan, over the question of legitimacy— "not the legitimacy of each other's political institutions, perhaps, but the legitimacy of their respective visions of world order."[8] The question of how the world should be ordered is the one that concerns us in this book. And one of the most fundamental questions about world order has to do with who has the right to make war, for which cause, and in which way. With its self-declared "war" against terrorism and rogue states, is the United States signaling that it intends henceforth to decide how the whole world should be ordered?

My hypothesis is that the international effort since 9/11 to mount a cooperative international police and intelligence campaign to stop terrorism is *not* war and that the Bush administration and the media should never have called it war. The campaign to track down and stop international criminals of the Al Qaeda type may require some revision of laws governing domestic security and intelligence gathering, including a revision of laws governing immigration and travel.[9] But the Bush administration has not made the case that the fight to stop international terrorism must be a war effort rather than a cooperative international police and intelligence campaign conducted in accord with domestic and international laws of criminal behavior and punishment. This is not to say that American military intervention in another country can never be justified on just war grounds. American military responses to the collusion of the Taliban and Al Qaeda in Afghanistan and to Iraq's invasion of Kuwait in 1990 could be so justified. For every government and alliance of states has a right to defend itself against attack. But terrorist networks like the ones that launched the 9/11 attacks will be stopped, punished, and eliminated only if many legitimate governments adequately police their own territories and cooperate with one another both within and beyond their territories to capture and punish such conspirators. This is different from governments fighting wars against other governments by military means.

Fareed Zakaria says that in a "metaphorical sense" it may be legitimate for the president to speak of "war" against terrorism, because "the magnitude and urgency of this struggle go far beyond mere law enforcement." However, Zakaria continues, "to speak of a war also distorts thinking by suggesting there is an easily identifiable enemy and an obvious means of attack. The vast bulk of anti-terror operations, in America, Europe or elsewhere, is aggressive deterrence and prevention at several levels done by police, intelligence agencies, and other nonmilitary bureaucracies."[10]

There is another important factor to consider here. Warfare, according to the just war tradition, has an end in view—a goal of expected victory and conclusion—at which point peace is established in the defeated country, requiring some kind of adequate government. However, by describing its entire response to the evil of terrorism and rogue states as "war," the Bush administration has committed the United States to what could turn out to be endless warfare with no peace and no conclusion. This approach calls for serious criticism in the light of just war principles. Moreover, the administration's approach may actually hinder the fight against terrorism because such "warfare" is likely to continue indefinitely and will generate resistance even from friendly countries. George Soros voices this concern.

> The war on terrorism as pursued by the Bush Administration cannot be won. On the contrary, it may bring about a permanent state of war. Terrorists will never disappear. They will continue to provide a pretext for the pursuit of American supremacy. That pursuit, in turn, will continue to generate resistance. Further, by turning the hunt for terrorists into a war, we are bound to create innocent victims. The more innocent victims there are, the greater the resentment and the better the chances that some victims will turn into perpetrators.[11]

Returning for a moment to Osama bin Laden's use of "holy war" language, Lee Harris has another reason why Americans are mistaken to let the word "jihad" stand for what we have traditionally meant by war. Bin Laden and his associates, says Harris, are acting out of a zealous "fantasy ideology" akin to a form of "magical thinking," not out of the logic of a military strategy. "The issue facing the U.S. [after 9/11] was not whether to accept or reject al Qaeda's political demands, which were nebulous in the extreme. Indeed, al Qaeda did not even claim to have made the attack in the first place!" We are, says Harris, "fighting an enemy who has no strategic purpose in anything it does—whose actions have significance only in terms of his own ideology. . . . [For the radical Islamists] it matters not how much stronger or more powerful we are than they—what matters is that God will bring them victory."[12]

The Bush administration's decision to go to "war" against Islamist terrorists also ran the danger of confirming bin Laden's view of America and giving him a stature that he does not deserve. "An undefined war on terrorism will look like a return of the Crusades to many Muslims," writes Philip Heymann. "Even if it is plainly addressed to a particular organization, Al Qaeda, it grants that organization the dignity of parity with the United States and spares it the condemnation that the terms 'terrorism' and 'crime' evoke."[13]

There is a big question, then, of why President Bush decided almost immediately after 9/11 to insist that the United States was at "war" with terrorism rather than choosing to call for a major international campaign to dismantle the Al Qaeda "crime syndicate," inviting close allies and friendly governments to join the United States in a cooperative policing and intelligence effort. A very specific war against the Taliban regime might indeed have been necessary and justified, but it would then have been situated alongside the much wider international police and intelligence campaign against terrorism. How can we explain the president's decision and the widespread American support for the "war"? Do Americans, even today, believe that our "war" against terrorism and the jihad of the radical Islamists mean the same thing?

A Wider Range of Questions

These introductory comments and questions about terrorism, war, and policing in the immediate post-9/11 period open the door to other important and closely related concerns. Think, for example, of the words "state," "government," and "sovereignty," which we take for granted without need of an explanation. Where do these words and the historical realities they represent come from? Why do Westerners have such a different attitude toward the state than do people in much of the Muslim world? Why do Americans assume that the sovereignty of the United States is a self-evident truth, that our national sovereignty should not be restricted in any way, and that any infringement on our sovereignty most likely calls for a military response? Moreover, if the sovereignty of our state and that of others is so sacrosanct, why have powerful states like the United States nonetheless helped to build international organizations like the United Nations? Don't such organizations merely dilute or undermine state sovereignty? Does the existence of the modern state comport well with the just war doctrine, which was developed hundreds of years prior to the emergence of the state? Why did just war reasoning come about in the first place, and should we continue to assume that it has validity today?

There is another important line of questions. What if Al Qaeda and similar organizations are *not* conducting what we have traditionally called war but are instead doing something else? Does it make sense in that case for us to consider them a "war" enemy? If Western judgments about the evil of terrorism make sense in Western terms but not in radical Islamist terms, is it wise for us to continue to try to fight terrorism only by reference to our own criteria of judgment? Might that restriction keep us from understanding the motivation and aims of our attackers and from figuring out how best to stop them? What is the origin of Al Qaeda, and what is its relation to Islam as a whole?

Many other questions follow. Why, in the face of terrorist assaults and continuing threats, has the Bush administration acted with such confidence and sense of rightness about its cause, even as it has frustrated and alienated many traditional allies and aroused growing anti-Americanism around the world? What are the roots of the American conviction that the United States is the vanguard of democracy and freedom in the world and that its causes are certainly good and not on the side of evil? These and many additional questions press upon us as a result of 9/11 and its aftermath. If we are to be able to make sound judgments about how the United States should stand with or against the world today and in the future, we must try to answer them.

The events of 9/11 did *not* change the world by significantly altering the world's different cultures and religions, or undermining American military superiority, or changing the structure and responsibility of states and their governments, or making the just war criteria obsolete, or obliterating the important distinction between war and policing. As a consequence of 9/11, however, American foreign, defense, and security strategies have shifted remarkably—and may still be shifting—to an extent that has led two critics to call President Bush's foreign policy a "revolution"[14] and another to identify the United States itself as a "rogue nation."[15] Arguing strongly to the contrary, Charles Krauthammer says that 9/11 simply awoke America to what really is new, namely, "the emergence of the United States [ten years earlier] as the world's unipolar power."[16] And what the United States should do now, according to Krauthammer, is to take advantage of its unique position as global hegemon to advance democracy worldwide. "Call it democratic *realism*," says Krauthammer. "And this is its axiom: *We will support democracy everywhere, but we will commit blood and treasure only in places where there is a strategic necessity—meaning, places central to the larger war against the existential enemy, the enemy that poses a global mortal threat to freedom.*"[17]

Who is correct in assessing America's responsibility in the world today, and how shall we decide what its role should be?

CHAPTER TWO

∽

Forgotten Depths

"History matters to Muslims. By contrast, Americans usually ignore history."[1] If it is true that Americans ignore history, it is not because their memories are unusually poor compared to others on this planet. Rather, Americans discipline themselves to be forward looking, confident that the future will bring progress because their aims and hard work are progressive. The past belongs to habits and patterns that don't need to be remembered because even greater achievements are still to come. If some people and nations are living in the past, well, they shouldn't be. "We are the nation of human progress, and who will, what can, set limits to our onward march?"[2]

The last quotation is not from George W. Bush, or a contemporary geneticist, or Bill Gates. It comes from an editorial by John L. O'Sullivan titled "The Great Nation of Futurity," published in 1839 in his newspaper *The United States Democratic Review*. As Richard Gamble explains, O'Sullivan applauded the fact that "America was an original nation, a new thing on the earth," oriented only toward the future, "unsullied by the past."[3] Forgetfulness of history, in other words, is as old as America, and now that the United States has become the most powerful nation in the world, perhaps we should celebrate O'Sullivan's prescience. If America's pragmatic, scientific, technological, economic, and political orientation toward the future of freedom is what has carried us to the top of the world's power pyramid, then why shouldn't we assume that our success represents God's confirming blessing, offering all the justification we need to continue our pursuit of the future, which will also be the world's future?

Yet, posing the hypothesis of "futurity" this way seems to hint at Jean Jacques Rousseau's judgment that some people have to be forced to be free. In a conversation with some leading American journalists, Samuel Huntington described the American mind-set in just those terms: "I think in our culture there is the assumption of universalism, the assumption that everyone else in the world is basically like us in terms of culture and values. If they are not like us," Huntington continued, "they want to *become* like us. And if they don't want to become like us, then there is something wrong with them. They don't understand their true interests, and we have to persuade or coerce them to want to become like us."[4] Yet, if American leaders shape foreign and defense policies, as well as economic and educational policies, on the basis of this conviction, do they not position the country *against* rather than *with* the world? Or is it that they position the United States only against those in the world who do not agree with the way we want to shape its future?

Ironies, Oddities, and the American Mission

Does it not seem slightly odd that the most powerful state on earth, whose military strength exceeds that of most of the rest of the world's militaries combined, now feels threatened by an enemy that has no state, no taxing ability, no advanced scientific laboratories or military production facilities, no planes, ships, or standing army?

Does it not seem the least bit ironic that more than two and a half years after the United States responded to the 9/11 assaults with its "war on terrorism" and after swift military victories in Afghanistan and Iraq, the terrorist threat to the United States may be as great or greater than it was on 9/11? That is what CIA director George Tenet told a congressional committee on February 24, 2004. He warned that Al Qaeda "has been transformed from a terrorist organization into a violent, world-wide Muslim movement that will threaten the U.S. and its allies indefinitely, even if its top leaders are captured" (*Wall Street Journal*, February 25, 2004). Does this suggest that at least some of the Bush administration's actions are proving to be counterproductive? Before the same committee of Congress, Lowell E. Jacoby, director of the Defense Intelligence Agency, said that the situation in post-Saddam Iraq, if left unchecked, "has the potential to serve as a training ground for the next generation of terrorists" (*The Washington Post*, February 25, 2004). Yet, the American-led war against Iraq to destroy Saddam's rogue regime was supposed to eliminate one of the sources and supporters of terrorism and thereby put terrorists on notice throughout the world that America will win this "war." Of course, two or three years is a short time, and the huge increase in

American military spending since 9/11 by tens of billions of dollars may en-able the United States to defeat terrorism by military means and bring down or transform every state identified as a "rogue."

However, although the future may indeed become what American leaders now promise, we ought to pause to reflect on the forgotten depths of history. Could it be that America's confidence in its hold on the future actually hin-ders it from recognizing when it has sailed off course? Does forgetfulness of the past keep us from understanding the reasons for some of our most abject failures, thus delaying important course corrections we should be making? For it has not been very long, after all, since one of America's costliest and most extended military campaigns in history failed to produce a promised and certain victory over the relatively powerless Vietnamese.[5] It was not too many years before that when the United States and its allies, following World War II, redefined political borders throughout much of the world and set up the United Nations as a means of encouraging continuous diplomacy, the early resolution of conflict, and other efforts to reduce the risk of war. And not long before that, World War I led to the dismembering of the Ot-toman Empire, which for five hundred years had represented a large per-centage of the world's Muslims. The victorious allies then created a number of artificial states and protectorates (mandates) like Iraq that were expected, under Western tutelage, to eventually catch up with the world of Western progress. What shall we make of the disappointments and failures of those twentieth-century American designs on the future, all of which have an im-portant bearing on the troubling international circumstances in which we now find ourselves?

Muslims do live by memory, inside stories of the past, even if the histori-cal accuracy of what is present to them may at times be questionable. They remember the West's defeat of the Ottoman Empire as if it happened this morning. Consciousness of that devastation is closely bound up with living memories that originated four hundred and even fourteen hundred years ago. Princeton professor Michael S. Doran illustrates how the antagonism be-tween Sunni and Shiite Muslims in and around Iraq today is sustained by liv-ing stories from the past.

> Even before [Saddam] Hussein's regime fell [in 2003], the story of Ibn Alqami was circulating in Saudi religious circles. A Shiite minister to the last Abbasid caliph, Alqami betrayed his ruler by conspiring with Hulagu, the Mongol leader who in 1258 sacked Baghdad and destroyed the Abbasid Empire, the flower of Islamic civilization. Over the past year, Sunni religious conservatives have habitually referred to George Bush as Hulagu II. The moment that U.S.-led forces turned their guns toward Iraq, Sunnis began to ask in reference to

the Iraqi Shiites, "Will the grandchildren of Ibn Alqami follow in their grand-father's footsteps?" When the Iraqi Shiites erupted in joy at the fall of Hussein's regime, their Sunni detractors lamented that once again Baghdad was toppled from within.[6]

There are good reasons, then, for us to ask some probing questions about why the contemporary world has the shape that it does and why it has not yet become the safe haven for democracy that Americans anticipate. Why do so many Americans and so many Muslims think about the past and the future so differently? Current global dynamics, including many oddities and ironies associated with America's dominant role in the world, suggest that, at the very least, we ought to try to understand why Americans possess such future-oriented self-confidence and the assured sense of their destiny as light to the nations and leader of the world.

Clash of Civilizations: America First!

America's sense of a divinely chosen, vanguard mission in the world was born with its Puritan beginnings, gathered strength through the Revolutionary War, and was sealed in the blood of the Civil War. In 1861, Lyman Beecher preached a sermon in his Brooklyn church that was representative of the era, identifying the American cause as "liberty here, and liberty everywhere, the world over. . . . By the memory of the fathers; by the sufferings of the Puritan ancestry; by the teaching of our national history; by our faith and hope of religion; by every line of the Declaration of Independence, and every article of our Constitution; by what we are and what our progenitors were—we have a right to walk foremost in this procession of nations toward the bright future."[7] "By 1914," says Gamble, "the American identity and sense of national mission had accumulated and synthesized a range of doctrines, ideals, and metaphors assembled from Roman antiquity, the Old and New Testaments, Enlightenment rationalism, Romantic nationalism, and evolutionary naturalism."[8] Long before President Reagan denounced the "evil empire" and President Bush called for an end to an "axis of evil" in the world, the pattern had been set. Americans, says Gamble, "have been habitually drawn to language that is redemptive, apocalyptic, and expansive."[9]

Speaking during a trip to China in 2002, President Bush quoted G. K. Chesterton's statement that the United States is "a nation with the soul of a church." This apt phrase remains in circulation and was easily picked up by the president because it discloses a certain truth about the American way of life. Religious faith and vision are not only private matters in America. The

United States as a public entity cannot be understood apart from its founding myth that it is a specially chosen nation, a city on a hill, the exemplar nation of the future. The American polity has been constituted in part by a civil religion, guided by the faith that the nation is in special covenant with God, even if by our day many Americans no longer believe in God.[10] Most still believe in American "exceptionalism." The constantly repeated phrase "God bless America" is certainly political, but it is also obviously religious.

Most Americans feel comfortable with such language because it connects their personal faith and mode of worship with their public way of life even if the personal and public faiths conflict with one other. It is true that in the American way of life the institutions of church and state have been legally separated, but that does not mean that the state and its citizens function nonreligiously. The phrase "God bless America" is not used primarily in private prayers or in worship services. Nor does it usually express a humble plea, begging God to guide, reprove, and correct government leaders so they will do justice rather than injustice. Instead, the phrase is most often heard in public on political occasions as a confident affirmation that God *is* on our side against the enemy. God *will* lead us to victory because we are in the right, and God is for us, not for them. This civil religion is part of what makes America tick.

Today, it is true, Americans do not typically think of their civic faith as religious in the same way they think of church life, worship, theology, and certain kinds of personal experiences as religious. The word "religion" is most often associated with the private realm, not with the political and economic realm, and the relation between private and public religions is often quite ambiguous. Huntington, for example, touches on the public meaning of religion when he offers the following comparative assessment of today's radical Islamism, Marxism, and the Protestant Reformation.

> In its political manifestations, the Islamic Resurgence bears some resemblance to Marxism, with scriptural texts, a vision of the perfect society, commitment to fundamental change, rejection of the powers that be and the nation state, and doctrinal diversity ranging from moderate reformist to violent revolutionary. A more useful analogy, however, is the Protestant Reformation. Both are reactions to the stagnation and corruption of existing institutions; advocate a return to a purer and more demanding form of their religion; preach work, order, and discipline; and appeal to emerging, dynamic, middle-class people.[11]

Contemporary Islamism, earlier Marxism, and Reformation Protestantism are similar, in Huntington's estimation, in that they are ways of life that carry broad public meaning. Yet, when Huntington turns to comment on contemporary America, his talk about religion reverts to the narrower, private meaning of religion as personal "espousal of belief" and use of symbolic language and does not take into account the civil religiosity of the American way of life as a whole.

Like so many Americans, Huntington uncritically accepts the Enlightenment dogma that American public life is secular, not religious. He doesn't recognize that the way of life engendered by Enlightenment rationalism, which tries to relocate traditional religion to a private sphere, is itself an all-encompassing way of life, like Marxism, Islamism, and Reformation Protestantism. The civil-religious character of American life, shaped very significantly by the spirit of the Enlightenment, makes room for many brands of religious piety in private, held together by a common public faith in America's providentially guided leadership of the world on the way toward secular freedom and democracy. As we will see, it is this bifurcating of life into sacred and secular realms under the overarching authority of scientific rationalism that is, from the Islamist point of view, the source of greatest evil in the world today. To fail to understand this is to fail to understand the radical Islamists.

In his original 1993 essay,[12] Huntington raised the question of whether the future, after the collapse of the Soviet Union, would display a different kind of conflict in the world with new fault lines between the antagonists. Violent conflicts, he hypothesized, would no longer come primarily from state fighting state or ideological camp fighting ideological camp, but rather from a "clash of civilizations." The new primary fault line, he said, can, in fact, be found between Muslim and non-Muslim peoples. Although there has been fighting along other fault lines, "between Serbs and Croats in the former Yugoslavia and between Buddhists and Hindus in Sri Lanka," for example, Huntington argued that the "overwhelming majority of fault line conflicts . . . have taken place along the boundary looping across Eurasia and Africa that separates Muslims from non-Muslims."[13] What Huntington missed in his analysis, however, is that the driving motives of earlier state-to-state warfare and ideological crusades were not nonreligious and unrelated to the clash of civilizations. It is just that nineteenth- and twentieth-century warfare among states in the grip of competing nationalisms, socialisms, communism, and liberalism represented clashes within Western civilization, clashes that were as deeply religious as anything we are witnessing today.

Among the many criticisms leveled at Huntington's 1993 essay was one by Saad Eddin Ibrahim, an Egyptian advocate of democracy, not a radical Islamist, who said that "Huntington's article borders on . . . a search for a 'new enemy' for the West in the post–Cold War era. . . . The most damning part of [the essay] is its 'battle cry' conclusion: 'the paramount axis of world politics will be "the West and the Rest."'[14] One can feel the tension here that arises from two different views of the world held by men who both support democracy. Ibrahim wants democracy, but he does not want the American way of life shoved down Muslim throats. This is a religiously deep tension, not a tension between Ibrahim living in a publicly religious civilization and Huntington living in a publicly nonreligious civilization.

Ibrahim is not the only moderate in the Muslim world who is suspicious of American plans for the world's future. It was the United States, after all, that supported Islamist radicals like Osama bin Laden in Afghanistan back in the 1980s when the Islamists were willing to die fighting against Soviet colonialism.[15] Twenty-five years ago, when Americans were more concerned about the dangers of the Islamic revolutionaries in Iran than they were about the rogue state of Iraq (which the United States had already tagged as a sponsor of terrorism), the United States supported Saddam Hussein in his fight against the Iranians.[16] These were hardly manifestations of America's drive to promote democracy and freedom around the world, unless one believes as Americans do that the strategic interests and survival of the United States are the key to the eventual success of democracy and the world's security everywhere. American actions have seldom been confined to narrow political calculations of the realpolitik variety. Back in the 1980s, the righteous West was fighting unrighteous communism in a cosmic drama of good versus evil. America then was the last hope of freedom and the world's future. Protecting God's lead nation in the world is part of the American way of life whether the enemy is Nazism, communism, or terrorism.

Clash of Civilizations: Islam Victorious!

Radical Islamists know that their divine mission requires outright opposition to Americanism. Their main objective is not conquest, says Jason Burke, "but to beat back what they perceive as an aggressive West that is supposedly trying to complete the project begun during the Crusades and colonial periods of denigrating, dividing, and humiliating Islam."[17] Their losses and humiliations of recent centuries have left them deeply troubled and at odds with themselves and with the West (as well as with other parts of the world). Allah's revelations to Muhammad beginning late in the sixth century after Christ are, for Muslims, the final truth about the whole of life and the meaning of history. Living in obedience to those revelations, recorded in the Qur'an, is supposed to lead the faithful to a proper reordering of life in the territory they occupy, the *dar al-islam*—that part of the world where submission to God is practiced. The expansion of Islam will eventually overcome the *dar al-harb*—the territory of conflict where submission to God is not observed—and ultimately the whole earth will become *dar al-islam* and live in peace. A central moral requirement for Muslims, who pray five times every day and confess the basic truths of Islam, is to practice jihad. Jihad does not mean only, or even in the first place, warfare. It means "struggle on behalf of God" or "striving on the path of God" to bring one's own heart and life into conformity to God's will. Every Muslim bears this responsibility. But jihad can, under certain circumstances, also entail warfare, both offensive (*ghaza*) and defensive, to advance or protect the *dar al-islam*.[18]

Although there were many Muslim gains and losses after Muhammad died in 632 A.D., including many intra-Muslim conflicts and divisions, Islam expanded rapidly both by use of force and by other means. By the time the Ottoman ruler Mehmed II conquered Constantinople, the capital of eastern Christianity, in 1453, he believed he had become the rightful ruler of the Christian world, thus drawing it into the *dar al-islam*. He believed that "there should be one empire, one faith, and only one sovereign in the entire world."[19] Over the next two hundred years, the Muslim world expanded to reach from West Africa to what are now the eastern parts of Indonesia. In 1683, however, European forces withstood the second Ottoman siege of Vienna, and from that point forward the Muslim world suffered setbacks, loss of territory, and colonializing humiliations until the Ottoman Empire was finally dissolved as an outcome of World War I.[20]

Part of the severe crisis for Islam in all of this is that there is nothing in the Qur'an that prepares Muslims for the shrinking of the *dar al-islam*. Islam has no theology of defeat and suffering. A further dilemma for Muslims is that in the normative vision of Islam there is only a single community of the faithful, undivided institutionally, disciplining itself and subduing the world. Not only is there no basis in Muslim law—the *shari'a*—for a clear differentiation of institutions such as state, mosque, school, and enterprise, but there is no way to conceive of the political order as a civic bond joining people submitted to Allah and people not submitted to Allah on an equal basis under the same government.[21] Under Islamic authority there can be a toleration of Christians and Jews, but there cannot be a public realm of religious freedom and equal treatment of all.

In the early years of Muhammad's leadership and that of his immediate successors, the caliphs, the highest authority in the community was passed down from Muhammad and represented by the guided caliphs. But disagreement emerged over who should rightfully hold that authority, giving rise to the divide between the Sunni and Shiite branches within Islam. As a consequence, authority in the Muslim world was dispersed. The authority claimed by the Ottoman Turks, in fact, came not through a bloodline of succession from Muhammad or from a claim to high teaching authority, but from conquest. "As the supreme rulers of the Muslim world, the Ottomans saw themselves as the protectors of Islam; they were the new caliphs. They based their claim to succeed the Prophet and the earlier caliphs on their achievements as the greatest fighters in the Holy War of Islam."[22] While different schools of legal or teaching authority emerged and continued in the Muslim world, the Ottoman caliphate established what might be called pragmatic proof of its authority, namely, power. A ruler who could protect and expand the *dar al-islam* could prove himself to be a worthy and recognized caliph. Yet, as the Ottoman Empire declined and especially when it was defeated, it left Muslims not only with a sense of setback and humiliation but also without a major center of power to symbolize the unity of Islam.[23]

Part of what explains the rise of radical Islamism in the late twentieth century is the crisis caused by the growing gap between the weakened, splintered reality of Islam and the normative vision of what Islam once was and ought to become. This is what Huntington describes as the problem of "consciousness without cohesion"[24] and what James Turner Johnson describes as the tension between the ideal and reality.[25] In trying to deal with this crisis, Muslims have taken a variety of approaches, ranging from accommodation to secular governments, as in Turkey, to attempts to recover Muslim faithfulness and consistent public practice. In the case of the radical Islamists, who arose in the 1950s and 1960s, Johnson notes, they have drawn on an earlier version of the rationale for defensive jihad. This idea, which developed at the time of the Crusades, was that "lands once Islamic are always properly part of the *dar al-islam* and Muslims are justified in retaking them as part of the individual duty of defense [*fard 'ayn*]. Specific authorization by the supreme religious leader, the *imam* of the *dar al-islam*, is not needed for such jihad, for the authority to wage this war lies in the personal obligation of each and every Muslim to defend against invaders."[26] Today, radicals like Osama bin Laden lay claim to this justification, asserting that "wars are justified in Islamic law when they are conducted to end exploitation and oppression by the superpowers or to achieve liberation from the forces of imperialism."[27]

Mention of opposition to exploitation and imperialism indicates that bin Laden and other radical Islamists have also incorporated elements from modern Western ideologies into their thinking. Paul Berman emphasizes this to the point of overemphasis in his book *Terror and Liberalism*. Ian Buruma and Avishai Margalit explain the development in detail in *Occidentalism*. Gilles Kepel follows the historical trail of Islamist development over the past fifty

years in his book *Jihad*. The point must be made because modern ideological
movements aiming to put an end to evil by radically cleansing the world represent a kind of secularization of Islam and Christianity, along with the
sacralizing of new carriers of "redemption" and final judgment. The difference between Christianity or Islam and the modern ideologization of either
one is not necessarily clear in the minds and hearts of those who long for release from oppression and humiliation and for victory over their foes. Moreover, ideologies like Marxism and National Socialism, as well as contemporary Islamism, are not nonreligious. They generate this-worldly visions of a
cleansed earth, the end of evil, or the redemption of humanity.

Sayyid Qutb, the mid-twentieth-century Muslim philosopher who inspired the Muslim Brotherhood in Egypt and Osama bin Laden, incorporated
a number of Western ideological influences in his radicalization of Islam.
Qutb's fundamental criticism of the West was that Christianity was at fault
for separating the secular from the sacred, thus dividing the world and allowing a rationalizing, secular materialism to take control of life in the West.
"God cannot be shunted into a corner," Qutb argued. "God must rule over
everything."[28] The revival and expansion of Islam, therefore, according to
Qutb, must begin in the heart with the recovery of total commitment to God
in all things and a cleansing of the world from its corruption. For this, the re-
vitalization of jihad both personal and public is necessary. For Qutb, according to Buruma and Margalit, "the whole world, from decadent Cairo to bar-
barous New York, was in a state of *jahiliyya* [barbarian, idolatrous ignorance].
He saw the West as a gigantic brothel, steeped in animal lust, greed, and selfishness. Human thought, in the West, was 'given the status of God.' Material greed, immoral behavior, inequality, and political oppression would end
only once the world was ruled by God, and by His laws alone."[29]

According to Roger Scruton, Qutb gave Islam "a decidedly modernist,
even 'existentialist' character. The faith of the true Muslim was, for Qutb, an
expression of his innermost being against the inauthentic otherness of the
surrounding world. Islam was therefore the answer to the rootlessness and
comfortlessness of modernity, and Qutb did not stop short of endorsing both
suicide and terrorism as instruments in the self-affirmation of the believer
against the jahiliyya."[30] Islam is not a "death cult," according to Buruma and
Margalit, but bin Laden's language, influenced by Qutb, does have "historical roots." It goes back to the Assassins, a millenarian Shiite sect of the
eleventh and twelfth centuries, who "took it upon themselves to kill unrighteous rulers and their followers" and who committed ritual suicide.[31]

Without doubt, contemporary Islamists who are willing to commit suicide
to try to thwart Western civilization and American-led progress into the

future present a threatening face. Movements inspired by such a vision and commitment are not to be taken lightly. But to fear Islamist radicalism as the rising wave of a mighty military threat to America and the West would be a mistake, according to Kepel. "In spite of what many hasty commentators contended in [9/11's] immediate aftermath, the attack on the United States was a desperate symbol of the isolation, fragmentation, and decline of the Islamist movement, not a sign of its strength and irrepressible might."[32]

What is clear is that Americans and their leaders should not have marched off boldly into a "war" on terrorism in the Muslim world, ignorant of the deep religious roots out of which both they and their attackers spring. The forgotten depths of history and religion, modern as well as traditional, go very deep indeed.

CHAPTER THREE

⌒

Earliest Sources of the
West's Design on the World

Three main cultural streams combined to create the European experience
that laid the foundations for modern international politics. The first is the
biblical tradition of Israel and Christianity. The second is the combined
Greco-Roman tradition. The third is the synthesis of the first two in the
Christian-classical or Christian-imperial tradition, which emerged with the
collapse of the Roman Empire and constituted Europe for more than a thousand years. The modern era of government began during the time when the
Roman Catholic Church was losing its spiritual, moral, and legal hegemony
in western Europe due to the Reformation and other cultural, economic, and
political developments of the fifteenth and sixteenth centuries. The gradual
decline of Christendom made way for the emergence of the Western state,
which is now the dominant unit of government throughout the world. Today, nearly two hundred states worldwide share in the strengths and the
weaknesses of the modern state system. To understand the state's triumph
throughout the world, we need to reach back into history.

The Biblical Tradition

Ancient Israel and the early Christian communities followed a way of life governed by faith in the one God, creator, and ruler of all things.[1] From the biblical point of view, human creatures, male and female, have their identity as
the image of God, created to worship and serve God above all as they work to
fulfill their divine calling of history-making dominion over the earth. Because

of their disobedience against God (the fall into sin), the human generations have produced every kind of inhuman deformity: hatred, greed, theft, oppression, and murder, distorting all of life on earth. In the face of these degradations, God not only brought judgment on the human generations but also acted mercifully to provide divine deliverance.

The story of Israel begins with God's unique covenants with Abraham, Isaac, and Jacob (Israel), promising that through Abraham's offspring all the nations of the earth would be blessed. In fulfillment of that promise, God saved Egypt from famine through Jacob's son Joseph and then liberated the children of Israel from bondage in Egypt. Through Moses, God made a creation-renewal covenant to establish Israel as an independent people and gave them the law and the promised land. In subsequent promises, particularly to Israel's kings David and Solomon, God again assured worldwide blessing through the coming messianic kingdom of righteousness. In the great crises of Israel's and Judah's demises at the hands of the Assyrians and Babylonians, God's prophets explained both the meaning of the divine judgment on Israel and the nations and prophesied that God would in the end fulfill the covenant promises to Israel.

According to the disciples of Jesus, Jesus is the Messiah promised to Israel, the Christ, who will, indeed, fulfill all covenant promises and establish God's all-embracing, everlasting kingdom. The writer of the Letter to the Hebrews looks back over the history of God's covenants, beginning with the creation of the world, and explains that Abraham "by faith made his home in the promised land like a stranger in a foreign country; he lived in tents, as did Isaac and Jacob, who were heirs with him of the same promise. For he was looking forward to the city with foundations, whose architect and builder is God" (Heb. 11:9–10). Israel, in other words, as God's chosen people, is an earthly exemplar pointing ahead in faith to the city that God is building, a city into which people of all nations may now enter through faith in Israel's Messiah, Jesus Christ. In fact, says the author, none of the great exemplar's of faith "received [in their own day] what had been promised. God had planned something better for us so that only together with us would they be made perfect" (11:39–40). The city of God will be revealed only when the faithful from all nations of all ages receive it together as God's gift. From a biblical point of view, then, the earth is a single world, made so both by God's act of creation and by means of the Messiah's culminating judgment and redemption of the whole world. Consequently, all nations, authorities, kings, and kingdoms exist by God's grace and are ultimately accountable to the one God who will bring each one to account on the day of judgment.

According to the book of Daniel, Darius the Mede, who took over the kingdom of Babylon after the Babylonians had defeated the remaining tribes of Israel about six centuries before Christ, was led to just this confession. After witnessing the actions of the God of Daniel, an exiled Jewish scholar-prophet, Darius declared,

> I issue a decree that in every part of my kingdom
>   people must fear and reverence the God of Daniel.
> For he is the living God
> and he endures forever;
> his kingdom will not be destroyed,
> his dominion will never end.
> He rescues and he saves;
> he performs signs and wonders
> in the heavens and on the earth.
> he has rescued Daniel
> from the power of the lions (Dan. 6:26–27).

The prophet Isaiah made clear that God's rule over the earth places all rulers and kingdoms at God's disposal. "Before him all the nations are as nothing; they are regarded by him as worthless and less than nothing" (Is. 40:17). "Heaven is my throne and the earth is my footstool," God declares (Is. 66:1).

However, the mighty God of Israel, unlike other gods, is concerned above all with the poor and the oppressed. Job recollects his glory days as a public official and servant of God when both young and old stood in awe of him. Why did they revere Job?

> [B]ecause I rescued the poor who cried for help,
> and the fatherless who had none to assist him.
> The man who was dying blessed me;
> I made the widow's heart sing.
> I put on righteousness as my clothing;
> justice was my robe and my turban.
> I was eyes to the blind
> and feet to the lame.
> I was a father to the needy;
> I took up the case of the stranger.
> I broke the fangs of the wicked
> and snatched the victims from their teeth (Job 29:12–17).

Part of the human calling to serve God, in other words, is to exercise a governing responsibility on earth to uphold justice. Public officials of Israel bear responsibility before God, the ultimate king and judge of the earth. In fact, when God condemned the chosen people for their faithlessness, it was for their callous disregard of justice. Isaiah, conveying God's word, says,

> When you spread out your hands in prayer,
> I will hide my eyes from you;
> even if you offer many prayers,
> I will not listen.
> Your hands are full of blood;
> wash and make yourselves clean.
> Take your evil deeds
> out of my sight!
> Stop doing wrong,
> learn to do right!
> Seek justice,
> encourage the oppressed.
> Defend the cause of the fatherless,
> plead the case of the widow (Is. 1:15–17).

For those willing to seek God and to do justice, God promised wisdom of the kind epitomized by Solomon's deeds and proverbs. Solomon learned that

> The horse is made ready for the day of battle,
> but victory rests with God (Prov. 21:31),

and that

> Rich and poor have this in common:
> The Lord is the Maker of them all (Prov. 22:2).

A wise ruler in Israel knows that

> All a man's ways seem right to him,
> but the Lord weighs the heart (Prov. 21:2);
>
> The Lord detests differing weights,
> and dishonest scales do not please him (Prov. 20:23).

Wisdom of this kind, garnered within Israel by those who loved God, who sought the ways of life, and who pursued justice, was generated by practical faithfulness to God in doing the work that God gave them to do.

Not many generations after the Jewish exiles in Babylon were allowed to return to Jerusalem to rebuild the temple, the region fell under the control of new conquerors and finally the Romans. It was when Rome had ultimate control over the promised land that the young rabbi Jesus announced that the kingdom of God was at hand and called disciples to join him and his cause. Yet, neither before nor after his crucifixion and resurrection from the dead did Jesus call for the reconstitution of Israel's separate territorial existence and the overthrow of the Roman authorities. Nor did he ask his followers to take up swords to establish a new form of government for themselves or to try to conquer the world to achieve God's promised kingdom. Instead, Jesus commissioned his disciples to go to the far corners of the earth to proclaim his lordship (Acts 1:1–8; Matt. 28:16–20). For in proclaiming the inauguration of God's kingdom they would be bearing witness to the good news that the Messiah had come and would come again to fulfill all of God's promises to Israel and the nations. The governing authorities, of whatever kind, even in Rome, were acknowledged by Jesus and his apostles as having responsibility, under God, to do justice (cf. I. Pet. 2:13–17; Jn. 19:10–11; Acts 25:1–12). As Paul put it, they serve as God's ministers to commend the good and to punish the one who does wrong (Rom. 13:1–4).

According to Gospel writer Matthew, when Jesus had been raised from the dead, he stood with his disciples and explained that "all authority in heaven and on earth has been given to me" (Matt. 28:18). Not only does the biblical witness refer to God's authority above all earthly dominions; it points ahead through history to the eschatological completion and fulfillment of God's reign when the messianic King of kings will unveil the city of God. Thus, kings and rulers hold limited sway in this age, and only by God's allowance. They are accountable in their offices to do justice lest God depose them and bring them to judgment in the end. Only the city of God will stand forever.

In biblical terms, therefore, no tribal, feudal, imperial, or state authority may claim to be sovereign in an ultimate sense. Only God is sovereign. Living in awe before God, humans must do two things at the same time. First, they must heed God's condemnation of idolatry by turning from, and calling into question, every absolutization of nation, state, or empire. This means that neither the Roman imperium nor any other form of human governance (whether Israel's monarchy or a modern state) may serve as the goal, the highest authority, or the widest community of human meaning and responsibility. Second, with respect to the governing responsibility that God has given humans, they must exercise it by doing justice in tune with God's two great commandments: to love God above all and to love one's neighbors as oneself.

A biblical view of government thus requires a creationwide perspective grounded in the recognition that this is God's one world in which all peoples and governing authorities are subordinate to God's demands for justice. Justice is not an abstract principle or a standard arrived at by human reasoning. It is not an ideal. Its way will be discerned by tracing out the paths of wisdom and doing God's will for life in this world. Justice is God's commandment, and wisdom is God's gift to the image of God, who has been called to make history in the ongoing development of the human generations until God's kingdom comes in its fullness.

The Greco-Roman Tradition

In ancient Greek experience, the highest and widest human community was the polis—the city-state. This was the context in which the philosophical work of Socrates (470–399 B.C.), Plato (427?–347 B.C.), and Aristotle (384–322 B.C.) emerged. When Alexander the Great later subdued the Greek city-states in the course of building his empire, the structure of the polis as a form of self-contained governance was destroyed or subordinated to imperial governance. Nevertheless, much of our vocabulary about government today—politics, polities, monarchy, aristocracy, democracy—is Greek, a language and an experience that were taken up, in part, by the Roman imperial order that subdued Alexander's empire.[2]

The primary political influence on Western history from classical Greece comes from what are sometimes called the realist and the idealist directions taken by its most influential interpreters and thinkers. Human life in the polis was believed to be determined in part by the cosmic rhythms of birth, growth, decay, and death. *Realism* dictated that in governing society, leaders must come to grips with the realities and limits of nature, including human nature with its needs, passions, and conflicts. However, Plato and Aristotle, who were inspired by Socrates, sought a wisdom that could reach above and beyond the cycles that governed transient life to grasp what endures, even if the enduring truth of what is good could be grasped only in theory as a normative *ideal*.

The challenge of governing a Greek polis and conducting war against others exposed different kinds of successful and unsuccessful leadership, military strategies, and means of control. Those who governed realistically had to make judgments about how best to gain advantage, increase power, and achieve various ends. Justice was not the preeminent concern or standard of such action. Robert D. Kaplan presents this view in his brief sketch of Greek historian Thucydides (c. 471–400 B.C.), a contemporary of Socrates. Thucydides' classic history of the Peloponnesian wars, says Kaplan, "may be the seminal work of international relations theory of all time. It is the first work to introduce a comprehensive pragmatism into political discourse."[3] Kaplan summarizes Thucydides' outlook this way:

> Whatever we may think or profess, human behavior is guided by fear (*phobos*), self-interest (*kerdos*), and honor (*doxa*). These aspects of human nature cause war and instability, accounting for *anthropinon*, the "human condition." The human condition, in turn, leads to political crises: when *physis* (pure instinct) triumphs over *nomoi* (laws), politics fails and is replaced by anarchy. The solution to anarchy is not to deny fear, self-interest, and honor but to manage them for the sake of a moral outcome.[4]

Thomas Pangle and Peter Ahrensdorf argue, however, that behind Thucydides' descriptive realism lies the judgment that "justice is a concern that no state or statesman can escape. . . . Thucydidean realism sees through the moralism of states that claim to fight for justice, but that realism simultaneously discerns the benefits of, and the truth hidden in, such moralism."[5] The demands of justice are thus inescapable.

The second direction of Greek political thought is exemplified by Plato and Aristotle, who did not think of themselves as unrealistic but as citizens who wanted to realize the highest and best of what it means to be human. And that achievement requires knowledge of how to shape the best polis— the polis that is able to realize human potential at its best, richest, most truthful, and most mature. Their philosophical (love-of-wisdom) quest for what is enduringly best opened their minds to a vision of a transpolis order of justice. Yet, what they envisioned could probably be realized only in thought and dialogue, not fully in practice. What was most significant about classical philosophy for the future of Western political experience was the weight these thinkers placed on disciplined reason as the means of discerning and clarifying the standards for shaping the best life in society. Even though the polis itself did not endure, the kind of "academic" institution that Plato inaugurated with his Academy and that Aristotle initiated in his Lyceum is still with us.

Reason for Plato and Aristotle was not an autonomous, self-authorizing human function; rational inquiry in pursuit of wisdom opened the inquirer to the "beyond"—to the ultimate ground of existence. Nevertheless, that which lies beyond is the highest qualifying standard, or paradigm, of what it means to be human. According to Eric Voegelin, the great theme of Plato's late work, the *Laws*, revolves around the question of "whether paradigmatic order will be created by 'god or some man' (624a). Plato answers: 'God is the measure of all things' rather than man (716c); paradigmatic order can be created only by 'the God who is the true ruler of the men who have *nous* [reason]' (713a); the order created by men who anthropomorphically conceive themselves as the measure of all things will be a *stasioteia* rather than a *politeia*, a state of feuding rather than a state of order (715b)."[6] In this Platonic vision we see that the god who transcends humans is the one who rules those "men who have reason." The quest for the good life and thus for the best polis is a rational quest through which humans seek to attune themselves to the order of the god who is the standard of rational attunement.

The closest that Plato came to a vision of human fulfillment through the establishment of an ultimately just order, according to Voegelin, was in his reinterpretation of the eras of Cronos and Zeus. During the age of Cronos, according to Plato, people lived "under the direct guidance of the gods," and later in the age of Zeus, they lived in man-made city-states (*poleis*). A new age is now necessary, says Plato.

> After the unhappy experience with human government in the age of Zeus, the time has now come to imitate by all means life as it was under Cronos; and as we cannot return to the rule of daimons [gods], we must order our homes and poleis [cities] in obedience to the *diamonion*, to the immortal element within us. This something, "what of immortality is in us," is the *nous* [intelligent mind] and its ordering is the *nomos* [law]. The new age, following the ages of Cronos and Zeus, will be the age of Nous.[7]

For Plato and Aristotle the highest end of life is to be found through ordered intelligence in an intelligently ordered polis. Yet, every polis needs to defend itself, and that requires the devotion of its citizens to militia service and administrative management. This fact exposes a tension between the training of wise leaders and the practical ordering of the polis. The life of theoretical inquiry in pursuit of wisdom requires leisure; the life of governing and defending a polis requires spirited action. A just city must be ruled by those who love wisdom, parallel to the way that a truly mature person must be ruled by *nous*. Yet, not everyone in the city can be a philosopher, for then there would be no one to administer and serve in the militia or to perform the daily labor. Consequently, the polis depends on the work of many who are not wise and who will, as individuals, be ruled by their passions or worse. How, then, can a polis be well ordered if not all of its citizens are rationally well-ordered persons? Aristotle's attempt to resolve this tension, according to Pangle and Ahrensdorf, is to hypothesize that "the active civic virtues" must be seen as "parallel to the leisured and self-sufficient theoretical life, both of which take as their model the purely theoretical activity, life, and virtue of the god who heads the entire cosmos conceived as a quasi-organic unity."[8] We may, of course, ask whether such a resolution carries anything more than theoretical or ideal weight.

The limits of classical Greek philosophy for international relations arise from philosophy's polis-confinement. Theoretical thought sought a transcendence that is spiritual and intellectual, but it could not escape the limits of the experience of the polis. "The city, even or especially the best city, remains more a closed than an open society," according to Pangle and Ahrensdorf. "For even a city ruled by the most rational conceivable rulers—philosopher-kings or their moral reflection—would have to maintain the austerity, the exclusivity, the rootedness, the intimacy, the military spirit, that we have seen to be essential or inescapable attributes of a healthy civic order."[9]

The implications of this confinement are enormous for the future of international relations because those who are under the influence of Greek thought will tend to emphasize either the priority of the practical internal ordering and preservation of their polis, empire, or state, on the one hand, or the priority of transpolitical rational standards that are theoretical in nature, on the other hand. There appears to be no framework here for thinking practically and institutionally about "inter-political" or "cosmo-politan" governance of all peoples, nations, and states together.[10] So-called realism is likely to dominate, therefore, when any polis or state goes to war or seeks to promote its best interests in the anarchic international arena. The so-called idealist approach, on the other hand, is likely to be adopted by those who, because of guilt or a longing for peace and justice, are driven to the intellectual quest for what ought to be, a quest that produces only *theoretical* judgments about how to transcend the degradations of war and conflict.

Soon after Aristotle died, a school of thought called Stoicism arose in Greece, reaching maturity in the Roman Republic. Because of the Stoic contribution to the shaping of the Roman Empire's *ius gentium* (law of nations), its influence extended into medieval Christendom and on into modern political life, including the early American republic. "To the Stoics," F. Parkinson explains, "the world was a unit, irrespective of the manifold [political] particularisms which it displayed, and an object from which to extract a set of laws."[11] Stoicism continued the rational quest initiated by Plato and Aristotle, the quest for enduring principles of the cosmos and human social life. However, Stoicism matured after the city-state had declined and the Roman order had begun to take control of the wider Mediterranean world.

Chrysippus (280–207 B.C.), one of the greatest Athenian teachers, developed the idea of an order of world law that stood above the social and political distinctions apparent all around us. This law, Parkinson explains, "applied to all states as much as to individuals. Harmony among states was a Stoic ideal and could conceivably be attained if all states were linked together in a system of universal values based on principles of equality. In the Stoic mind, customs varied, but the element of reason which underpinned natural justice was uniform."[12] Stoicism had a great influence on Roman law because of its emphasis on the universality of reason and law above particular cities and nations. This guided the application and extension of Roman law to new peoples who were conquered and incorporated into the empire. The resulting body of legal interpretation was called *ius gentium*—"the law common to all people making up the Roman Empire."[13]

Marcus Tullius Cicero (106–43 B.C.) summarized the Stoic philosophy of law, reason, nature, and God in a way that became its classic statement:

> There is in fact a true law—namely, right reason—which is in accordance with nature, applies to all men, and is unchangeable and eternal. By its commands this law summons men to the performance of their duties; by its prohibitions it restrains them from doing wrong. Its commands and prohibitions influence good men, but are without effect upon the bad. To invalidate this law by human legislation is never morally right, nor is it permissible ever to restrict its operation, and to annul it wholly is impossible. . . . It will not lay down one rule at Rome and another at Athens, nor will it be one rule today and another tomorrow. But there will be one law, eternal and unchangeable, binding at all times upon all peoples; and there will be, as it were, one common master and ruler of men, namely God, who is the author of this law, its interpreter, and its sponsor.[14]

Voegelin points out that the Ciceronian formulation has remained a constant in history "because it is the only elaborate doctrine of law produced by the ecumenic-imperial society."[15] It became the formative force in Roman law and was adapted by the early Latin church fathers who did not independently develop a philosophy of law grounded in the biblical, covenant-wisdom tradition. "The background of Roman law in the formation of the European lawyers' guilds, and the neo-Stoic movements since the Renaissance, have left us the heritage of a 'higher law' and of 'natural law.'"[16] In fact, we could go so far as to say that the Stoic emphasis on rationality and legality as the primary ways of understanding God's timeless relation to this world came to dominate Christian political thinking from the early medieval period through modern times. This mode of thought gained dominance over the biblical understanding of life as the covenantal unfolding of God's revelation through creation—including human history—toward the eschatological fulfillment of God's messianic kingdom in the city of God. There are divine commandments and an ordering of creation in the biblical frame of reference, but God's relation to humans and the world is not channeled and qualified primarily by rational legality or legal rationality as it is in Stoicism.[17]

In a work titled *On Duties* (*De Officiis*), apparently written "as a manual for young Romans who are about to begin their careers as administrators and policemen of the imperial system,"[18] Cicero argues that nature has prescribed that humans should want to take care of other humans. If we are all "embraced by one and the same law of nature," then "we are certainly prohibited by the law of nature from doing wrong to another. . . . Moreover, those who say that citizens must be respected, but not outsiders, sunder the common association of the human race; once this is gone, kindness, generosity, goodness, and justice are utterly destroyed."[19] However, when Cicero turns to the "laws of war" (*iura belli*) and argues that human beings should always try to decide matters "through discussion," he admits, nonetheless, that there will be times when they must have recourse to the inferior method, more appropriate to beasts, of undertaking war so that "life may go on in peace without injustice."[20] In fact, according to Cicero, preserving peace and upholding the common good in Rome may even require commitment to the tradition of expansion, which means that some warfare may be necessary to enlarge the territory of the republic. For despite our close bond with people of every city and nation, Cicero goes on, our bond to fellow citizens and especially to our family comes first.[21] "Cicero implicitly reaffirms the fundamental classical contention about the principle of natural right that ought to guide political life: the strongest natural human attachment, and therefore obligation, is to one's city and to one's true kin. From this it follows," say Pangle and Ahrensdorf, "that whatever we owe to all other human beings, simply on account of our common humanity, is dwarfed in significance and substance by what we owe to our fellow citizens and true kin, given the richer common good and hence far closer ties that bind us to them."[22] So, in the end Cicero was not able to go beyond Aristotle or Plato in articulating the basis for a truly universal political order of all peoples on earth.

In reference to Marcus Aurelius (121–180 A.D.), Parkinson illuminates the same tension between Cicero's ideal of legal universalism and the particular reality of the Roman Empire. Emperor and Stoic philosopher Marcus Aurelius made the famous remark, "My city and country is Rome—as a man it is the world." But what happens when the "Roman citizen" and the "man of the world" come into conflict? "Here was the philosophical frame," says Parkinson, "within which the tragic dilemma of international relations was to pose itself time and again, with the freedom of individual states pitted against the ideal of a preordained universe."[23]

The rational, moral, and legal universalism of Stoic philosophy could not corral the diversity of nations and political powers into a universal community of peoples, a community of nations. The *ius gentium* may have been able to overcome the confines of the Greek city-state and, to some degree, integrate diverse peoples into the Roman Empire. But the "higher law" behind the *ius gentium* appears to be the kind of ideal that could only be called "universal" after the Roman Empire had brought the "whole earth" under the rule of its law. Thus, the higher law of Cicero and Marcus Aurelius transcended Roman imperial reality only in theory, much the same as Aristotle's philosophy transcended the polis only in theory.

Looking Ahead

Anticipating what will follow, let us summarize briefly some of the key elements of the ancient traditions that have had a formative influence on western Christendom and on modern government and international relations. Because of biblical Judaism and Christianity, the recognition of human accountability to a living, judging, redeeming God above all law and human governance will not easily disappear. No particular form of government or polity is held up as an unchanging ideal in the biblical frame of reference. All human authorities stand under God's authority and standards. The idea of limited government and opposition to tyranny, arbitrariness, and totalitarianism derive in large measure from this tradition. The denunciation of unjust laws and governments by appeal to God's demand for justice reflects the prophetic tradition, which takes sin seriously, even the sin of God's chosen people. The belief that this is one world in which all human beings— the image of God—share the same high dignity and deserve equal treatment is also rooted in the biblical tradition—in the story of creation. Perhaps most important is the biblical-covenantal sense of dynamic history—the unfolding of the generations toward an ultimate destiny, toward the final revelation of the kingdom of God—the city of God. This is a multigenerational, creationwide movement, encompassing all of humanity. Therefore, the Christian gospel must go out to the farthest corners of the earth. Nothing in human history and experience stands outside this drama of God dealing with humanity through creation mandates and covenant promises of judgment and redemption, a drama that will culminate in the eschatological city of God. While this sense of history, oriented toward God's coming kingdom, remains strong among many Christians and Jews even today, it has been overtaken in the modern era by various secularized ideals of this-worldly progress and earthly fulfillment. Diverse nationalisms, democratism, communism, freedom-idealism, radical Islamism, and other ideological movements hold out different hopes for a human-made "heaven" on earth or of an earth finally cleansed of ignorance or evil. Each ideology supplies its own substitutes for the chosen people, the forces of darkness, the final judge, the messianic savior, and the city of the new humanity.

Because of the Greeks and the Roman Stoics we experience the continuing influence of the idea—later incorporated by the modern state—that the political order represents the most encompassing community of human life. Even religions and religious authorities are thought to function as dimensions or aspects of the political community, whether polis or empire. Various forms of imperialism, statism, and nationalism feed on this, particularly when the state becomes the primary carrier of nationalist and other ideological missions. We also continue to experience the strong influence of rationalism and appeals to reason and science as the primary means by which to rise above passions, interests, and religious fanaticism in order to build well-ordered polities and a well-ordered world. Yet, the high standards of justice in Platonic, Aristotelian, and Stoic thought could not be universalized practically beyond the confines of the polis or the Roman Empire. So one of the great tensions of modern international relations remains irresolvable on that basis. This is to say that various calls for human rights, international law, global peacekeeping, and transnational governance typically appeal to a universal rationality or legal ideals that are unable to gain practical dominance over separate states. Consequently, realists concentrate on the control and use of state power to maintain and enhance state interests, skeptical about idealist appeals to transnational standards of justice.

CHAPTER FOUR

⤴

Western Christendom

The Formation of European Christendom

As the Christian gospel spread through Roman-controlled territories around the Mediterranean Sea, many gentiles without much or any knowledge of Judaism and its scriptures became Christians. Learning to live as Christians meant contending with the legitimacy or illegitimacy of their local and Greco-Roman cultural habits and their local and Roman-imperial governments. Within three centuries, despite frequent political persecutions at the hands of Roman authorities, Christians had nurtured and communicated a way of life that became so influential that soon after Constantine laid claim to imperial authority in 306, he began to legitimize Christianity as a religion of the realm.[1] By this time, political life and thought had changed considerably from that of the early Roman republic, the Greek polis, and God's covenanted order with Israel. Harold Berman, writing to explain subsequent developments in the Western legal tradition, explains, "The West . . . is not Greece and Rome and Israel but the peoples of Western Europe turning to the Greek and Roman and Hebrew texts for inspiration, and transforming those texts in ways that would have astonished their authors."[2]

Governmentally and legally speaking, Roman imperial ideology, which incorporated Stoic legal thought, was shaping the empire's codes, practices, and institutions within which Christians had to find their way, whether in opposition to, or in support of, that order. At the same time, Roman authorities were being forced to decide how to fight or give support to Christianity. When the official "Christianization" of the empire began with Constantine, Christianity was merely granted the "privileges of a 'licensed cult' (*religio licita*)."[3] With that privilege, however, Constantine intended two outcomes, according to Charles Cochrane. The first was "to create a world fit for Christians to live in," and the second was "to make the world safe for Christianity."[4]

Importing Christian language into the imperial frame of reference led eventually to the dogma that "Christ's fullness of power in heaven" was now "embodied in his vicegerent on earth,"[5] that vicegerent being the emperor of the whole realm. As Walter Ullmann explains,

> Pagan imperial cult was simply continued in the Christian empire. Whilst the emperor himself had become Christian, his government carried on the pagan idea of the empire. . . . This system of government, called perhaps inelegantly, Caesaropapism, culminated in what for all practical purposes was the exercise of power and authority by divinity through the emperor: indeed, he was Autokrator and Kosmokrator, ruling the "world" identified with the Roman empire, as if he had been God himself. Hence he was in every respect above the law, since there was no body, no authority, no tribunal that could sit in judgment on him. . . . Ecclesiastical organs, such as councils, had no standing, unless summoned and approved by the emperor.[6]

In other words, the church was recognized and authorized by the emperor as a subordinate witness to God's governance of the world through Christ's only earthly vicar, the emperor. Along with the Roman imperial structure there also came "Stoic notions of universality," as F. Parkinson explains, leading to "the transformation of Seneca's conception of a universal mankind held together by universally valid moral ties" into the idea of a universal Christian "theocracy imposing a universal dogma binding on rulers and their subjects alike."[7]

Constantine eventually moved his imperial headquarters to the ancient town of Byzantium, which he rebuilt and renamed Constantinople, referring to it as the new, or second, Rome (*altera Roma*).[8] Centuries later, when eastern and western parts of the empire and the church would split, the caesaropapist arrangement would be continued in the Byzantine Empire of the East and upheld by the Orthodox Church. Then, in the sixteenth century Ivan III of Muscovy would "put forward the claim that Moscow, as the true successor in religious orthodoxy to Rome and Byzantium, was the Third Rome, and he assumed the title of *tsar* (Caesar)," and Ivan IV would declare himself "Tsar of All the Russias" in 1547.[9] With regard to the wider concern of this book, it is worth noting O. Edmund Clubb's comment about Russia and China. With the expansion of tsarist Russia from Muscovy out to "all the

Russias," says Clubb, "there had begun to take form a nation which, in its claim to divine legitimacy and orthodoxy, bore a certain resemblance to that Oriental Middle Kingdom which assumed that the occupant of the Dragon Throne at Peking was the legitimate ruler of all mankind."[10] However, the Son of Heaven on the Dragon Throne, empowered by the Mandate of Heaven, had no obligation similar to that binding on Christian emperors and popes, to evangelize or conquer uncivilized peoples. From the Middle Kingdom's point of view, foreigners would eventually recognize the true center of the world and would come to kowtow to the Son of Heaven.

In the western part of the Roman Empire, in reaction to the emperor's claim that he held authority over the church, a contrary argument was generated from within the church, beginning most notably with Pope Gelasius I (492–496) and reaching legal solidification under Pope Gregory VII between 1075 and 1122. This was an *ecclesiastical* argument contending that the responsibility of earthly governors to eradicate evil by the power of the sword is not primary but rather "an auxiliary function in the divine scheme of things."[11] Earthly rulers who are Christians are members of the body of Christ and thus, as lay churchmen, cannot stand outside the church; in fact, they are subordinate to ecclesiastical authority and church law. The proper hierarchical order on earth, then, should begin with the pope as the ultimate *auctoritas* (authority) in human affairs and the one who holds the superior spiritual sword. Below papal authority stands the emperor and other earthly rulers, who bear *regia potestas* (power to govern) and may rightfully hold the secular sword if approved by the church. These Gelasian statements, according to Ullmann, were "the first clear enunciation of the concept of sovereignty within a Christian corporate body. . . . The pontifical 'authority' in a Christian world was all the greater as it had to render an account of the doings of the kings on the day of judgment."[12]

In sum, the difference between the imperial and the papal views was this: "To the emperor it was the Roman empire, pure and simple, which had become Christian; to the pope this same body was the Church (comprising clergy and laity) which happened to be the Roman empire."[13] The same Roman, hierarchical conception of divinely authorized government over a single human body (corpus) held sway. The dispute was over how the hierarchy from God through Christ to humans was to be identified and ordered. In the West, the bishop of Rome—the divinely delegated vicar of St. Peter, ordained by Christ—laid claim to sovereignty over the whole Christian body, including its "secular rulers." In the East, as emperor Justinian (527–565) argued, the emperor was the sovereign who directed and ruled all subordinates in the empire, including the church, "in accordance with

Christian principles emanating from the fount of all Christianity, the divine majesty of the emperor himself."[14]

As the Roman Catholic Church worked to consolidate its authority in the face of church conflicts and disputes within the fractured empire, Emperor Justinian, in Constantinople, worked to achieve his goal of unifying and revitalizing the empire. Toward that end, his great ambition was to codify all of Roman law. Consequently, upon his ascension to power in 527, he appointed a commission to carry out the task. Within six years, his jurists had gathered and composed the *Corpus Juris Civilis*, the two main parts of which were the *Digest* of general principles and private law and the *Code* of public laws—the laws of the emperors. Ullmann remarks that "the *Digest* created something completely new," and the *Code* and the *Digest* together made available "for the first time in medieval Europe books which contained all Rome had ever stood for—the law."[15] Among other things, the *Code* "set forth an unadulterated monarchic form of government in the guise of the law," reversing the Gelasian thesis and making clear that "there was no room for a jurisdictional primacy of the pope."[16] The church council called by Justinian in 536—the Council of Constantinople—"entirely supported the imperial scheme when they declared that 'nothing must be done in the church against the command and will of the emperor.'"[17]

Judith Herrin's thesis is important for our consideration at this point. In her book *The Formation of Christendom*, she argues that in order to account for the rise of the West, it is essential to understand the three-way competition for control over the declining Roman Empire by eastern Christianity, western Christianity, and Islam between the fifth and the ninth centuries. The eastern Mediterranean region was the center of gravity around which these three heirs of the old empire mutually influenced one another. As the ancient world collapsed, says Herrin, "faith rather than imperial rule" became the qualifying feature of the rightly ordered world—"what Christians called the *oikoumene*, and Muslims, *Dar al Islam*."[18] Byzantium (eastern Christendom), for example, was "an essential factor in the development of both the West and Islam, for it was at one and the same time the power that frustrated the Muslim challenge to Christianity, even while it failed to confine Islam to Arabia. This combination resulted in deadlock in the East."[19] Neither the emperors in Constantinople nor the califs who succeeded the prophet Muhammad, says Herrin, "were able to lay claim to the Mediterranean area as a whole. It was this check that allowed a separate medieval Christendom to exist in the West, where spiritual loyalty to Rome became transformed into a supranational authority independent of any secular power."[20]

In the West, a greater diversity of institutions and fractious cultural sources led eventually to a more dynamic development of society than occurred in either Byzantium or the Muslim lands. The West's social and cultural potential was shepherded by church authorities, but its expansive potential, says Herrin, developed because of "the existence of separate, independent authorities, civil as well as ecclesiastical. The mutual antagonism and rivalry of these authorities, which rarely led to the passive subordination of 'church' by 'state' or vice versa, created a tension and a competitive focus in society that had no parallel in the East."[21] At the same time, says Herrin, "Christendom was also a polity in the West, not just a religious order. The intellectual, institutional, and artistic tenacity and influence of its faith played a decisive role in the emergence of the modern world."[22]

Augustine, Aquinas, and Just War Doctrine

The two most influential and representative teachers of the Christian church between Constantine's ascension to imperial office and the height of western Christendom a thousand years later, were Augustine (354–430) and Thomas Aquinas (1225–1274). Augustine is recognized as the most important father of both the eastern and western branches of Christianity. Aquinas is the preeminent philosopher-theologian of the Roman Catholic Church. They are the chief intellectual architects of the Christian-Roman synthesis that reached its height in the twelfth and thirteenth centuries. The central element of this architecture as concerns international relations is the just war doctrine, whose contemporary relevance we will assess in a later chapter. But concern about warfare arose from a larger concern about the very identity and responsibility of the people of God—the church of Christ—in history and how this people should relate itself to the religiously pagan cities, peoples, and empires of this world.

Augustine
Augustine's contribution to Western political life comes largely from his argument that all human governance and political community in this age (*saeculum*) is subordinate to the transcendent kingdom of God in Christ. This is the distinctively Christian theme running through his writing and preaching. The "city of God" (*civitas dei*)—the community of those whose lives are shaped and organized by the love of God in Christ—will be fully realized not on earth and not by political means but in the eschatological culmination of human history when Christ returns. The "earthly city" (*civitas terrenae*), by contrast, is organized (or disorganized) around the spirit of self-love and a

preoccupation with life in this age. Consequently, Christians must pursue their pilgrimage in this world very carefully, often in opposition to, but sometimes by making use of, the social arrangements organized by those who are motivated by self-love. For both Christians and non-Christians live together in this age, and all are sinners.[23]

From Augustine's point of view, say Thomas Pangle and Peter Ahrensdorf, no earthly nation "possesses more than a faint awareness of true justice and of the true object of love. Every city is 'Babylon,' and the predominant goal of its way of life is a more or less corrupt attachment to earthly prosperity. Coercive rule, private property, and slavery characterize the actual regimes on earth."[24] Nevertheless, Christians cannot live elsewhere, and even though the actual regimes in this world are not noble, "they are necessary, just as a modicum of material welfare is necessary. 'For, as long as the two cities are mingled together, we [Christians] can make use of the peace of Babylon; from Babylon the people of God are so liberated by faith as meanwhile to be but pilgrims.'"[25] The "peace of Babylon," as George Weigel explains, is defined by Augustine as *tranquillitas ordinis*, the tranquillity of a public order, which is not yet the just order of the city of God but an order in this age that keeps sinful creatures from anarchy and makes room for Christians to develop virtues appropriate to the Christian way of life.[26]

The ambiguities inherent in Augustine's thinking about the relation of the city of God to the earthly city in this age (*saeculum*) have both benefited and plagued Christians—and the West more generally—to this very day. On the one hand, the benefit has come from recognizing the need to be cautious, even skeptical, and often critical, of the claims made by earthly governments (and political parties and ideological movements), particularly when they claim to be inaugurating peace and justice on earth. Human government, whether by emperors or democratic parliaments, is limited both because it is human rather than divine and because it is deformed by human sinfulness.[27]

The benefit, from a Christian point of view, also comes from Augustine's insistence that hope must be oriented toward that which God will accomplish ultimately in Christ. Our present hope for a more just future need not suffer constant disappointment or be dashed altogether as a result of the failed efforts of mere mortals using political means on earth. The course of history will not be progressive in the sense of showing a constant human improvement because sin will always lead to depravity and destruction. But true justice and the realization of a loving human community will come about by means of God's grace through Christ's judging and redeeming work. This is the faith and vision by which the church must live.

Christopher Dawson argues that this Augustinian view of the church, oriented toward the city of God, was one of the primary inspirations of the monastic tradition, which, in turn, was the major dynamism of the reform movements in the church throughout the Middle Ages, including the reforms made by Pope Gregory VII in the eleventh century.[28] Monasticism carried with it the prophetic tradition of the Bible, bringing criticism from above to the powers of this age. Gregory VII, in other words, was inspired to free the church from its dependence on secular power because that dependency "consecrated the status quo and surrounded vested interests with the halo of sacred tradition," all of which kept the church from being what it ought to be.[29] The church should not accommodate itself to the patterns and political institutions of this age but should be a faithful witness to the city of God. Efforts to reform and purify the church from any tendency to accommodate itself to the spirit of the earthly city were inspired by the monastic movements. When, according to Dawson, the dynamism of this "prophetic and evangelical vocation of the early Friars became subordinated to the demands of ecclesiastical power politics" in the thirteenth century, it produced "a rift in the reforming movement from which medieval Christendom never recovered."[30] As we will see, the monastic reform movements spawned the Reformation and help to explain the character of the Puritan experiment in New England.

In Augustine's writings, the question of how Christians, who are motivated by Christ's love, should fulfill their earthly civic responsibility is not answered clearly and unambiguously, however, and that helps to explain part of the tension Dawson is struggling with. If the city of God is truly eschatological, then shouldn't the Christian pilgrimage, motivated by love for God, move in a direction quite counter to that of the "Babylonian" way of life (death), which is pursued by those who are predominantly and corruptly attached to earthly prosperity and oriented by self-love? How can those who love Christ cooperate in or make use of "coercive rule, private property, and slavery"? This does not appear to be possible, and that conviction charted the course for many of the monastic orders. Yet, this is not Augustine's unambiguous conclusion. The use of force is needed, he says, to maintain the minimal peace of the earthly city.

What does Augustine mean when he says that Christians "can make use of the peace of Babylon" and that they, too, need a modicum of material welfare? Is he suggesting that this relative peace and modest welfare on earth actually derive from the Babylonian way of life? Or does he mean that the social benefits derive from God's grace and mercy in upholding the good creation, despite sin? If the latter is true, then it would seem that Christians should indeed cooperate in helping to sustain the earthly city to the extent that they can do so by living in accord with God's high principles of love and justice. Even though they would be aware that justice and love can never be fully realized in this age, due to sinful selfishness and disregard of God, Christians would understand nonetheless that the principles to which they appeal in trying to cooperate with Babylonians are the standards of the city of God not yet realized, rather than the corrupt purposes of Babylon. Thus, Christians could live in and contribute to, but not compromise with, the ethos of the earthly city.

If, however, Augustine means that the modicum of order and material welfare in the earthly city is actually made possible by the Babylonian way of life, then it would appear that Christians, in order to cooperate in it, would have to stoop to lower or even anti-Christian standards in order to try to get along with the Babylonians in this age. Christians would have to act somewhat dualistically: expressing full Christian love in some aspects of their lives while acting in accord with the principles of the earthly city in activities such as governing, buying and selling property, and going to war. In that case, they would become part of the earthly city while at the same time trying to live in the spirit of Christian love, oriented toward the city of God. Various types of dualistic response are precisely what developed in subsequent history. For some Christians, the higher way of love is the path that the clergy, monks, and very pious Christians should follow, while ordinary Christians may follow the lower path of cooperating in the affairs of the earthly city as long as they participate in the church's sacraments for the forgiveness of their sins and the nurturing of their faith, hope, and love in anticipation of eternal life. For other Christians, the way of love is personalized and internalized, while the business of getting along with Babylonians in this world is delegated to the political and economic institutions of the public world. Seeking earthly peace by means of these and other dualistic adaptations has not been considered to be fully compatible with the highest expression of Christian love, but rather has been accepted as an accommodation to lower standards for the purpose of surviving and getting along in this fallen world where society can never reflect true love and justice.[31]

Robert D. Kaplan judges that Christians have never had a public ethic because Christian love either keeps them out of the political arena or allows them to enter it on terms other than those of Christian love.[32] Although I believe Kaplan is mistaken in his historical judgment, perhaps there is some evidence for his thesis in the Augustinian idea that the relative peace and order of life in this age is possible because of the faint awareness that even Babylonians can have of the semblances or vestiges of justice that are left over in human conscience after the fall into sin. Augustine's argument in this regard depends largely on Stoic and neo-Platonic philosophies and thus can be seen as pagan rather than Christian.[33]

Later in his life, when Augustine was struggling with the Donatists, a group he saw as heretical, he argued that Christian rulers in this world should want their mother, the church, to have peace in their time, and he urged them to serve Christ "by making laws for Him and for His cause."[34] In other words, Augustine later found reason to argue that earthly rulers, if they are Christians, can use governmental power and authority to serve the cause of Christ and not merely to try to maintain a tranquillity of order in this age. This language could be used by either Constantinian imperialists or by those who acknowledged papal preeminence. In both cases, the argument found resonance within an empire that was beginning to change from a declining pagan Roman body to a rising *Christian* Roman body—a *corpus christianum* whose laws would be systematized, codified, pluralized, and transformed by emperors and popes, beginning with Justinian and climaxing with Pope Gregory VII. In both wings of the church, Augustine's later teaching was also used as a basis for ecclesiastical support of holy war and the principle of "vindicative justice," both of which justified the Crusades against Islam.[35]

In the early stages of Christian accommodation to the Roman Empire, Augustine reflected critically on the use of force, encompassing what we today would categorize as police actions, as well as actions of the military. Because of sin, humans are divided against themselves, and warfare expresses that sinfulness. To restrain violence and to preserve a modicum of earthly peace, God has given rulers authority to use force, and Christian soldiers should, in good conscience, follow the commands of their superiors. Nevertheless, Augustine asks, what kind of responsibility do *Christian* commanders and kings have when they serve in these offices? He answers, as Pangle and Ahrensdorf explain, that "the wise man wages just wars."[36] This means, among other things, that there must be a just cause that requires a Christian ruler to take up arms. Moreover, he should do this reluctantly and only after other means of overcoming the injustice have failed. In addition, the ruler's use of force must be motivated by the love of others, even the enemy, and not by self-love, hatred, or a desire to kill. Then, in the midst of battle, the Christian soldier must conduct himself with benevolence toward the enemy so that after the war it will be easier to establish peace.

It is clear from Augustine and from the history of Christendom, however, that the public responsibility of government to uphold peace and justice included protecting and advancing true religion. Thus, "warfare in defense of religion was an inclusive and pervasive concept" in the development of the just war doctrine, as James Turner Johnson explains.[37] By the time Augustine's defense of just war had been worked out and implemented in western Christendom, justifiable war in defense of religion included the punishment of heresy and the "retaking of things wrongly taken." The latter eventually came to include the Holy Land, leading to papal authorization of the Crusades to take back the Holy Land. The Crusades, conducted with relatively little success, took place between 1095 and 1270.[38] "This line of reasoning," says Johnson, "blurred the distinction between offensive and defensive use of force more thoroughly than that between preemptive and reactive resort to force."[39]

In the twelfth century, when regional Muslim leaders Nur al-Din and Saladin were fighting the Christian crusaders, they developed an argument for "defensive jihad" that was very similar to the Catholic Church's argument for defensive holy war, with the exception that it did not require authorization by a legitimate ruler as it did in western Christendom. The Nur al-Din and Saladin argument was also different from that of classical Islam. The earlier classical view was that jihad is expansionist—"always to extend the boundaries of the *dar al-islam* to new territory with the ultimate end of occupying all the earth," whereas the later view was one of "collective defensive war for the faith under the command of a local ruler but authorized by the individual duty of all Muslims."[40] This view assumed that "lands once Islamic are always properly part of the *dar al-islam* and Muslims are justified in retaking them as part of the individual duty of defense. Specific authorization by the supreme religious leader, the *imam* of the *dar al-islam*, is not needed for such jihad, for the authority to wage this war lies in the personal obligation of each and every Muslim to defend Islam against invaders."[41]

William Stevenson emphasizes the paradoxes in Augustine's reasoning about war precisely because of Augustine's somewhat ambiguous view of the relation between the city of God and the Babylonian city of self-love.[42] Stevenson concludes that

> Augustine did not intend to detail a doctrine; rather, he sought to resolve a tension. As bishop of a firmly established church he found himself confronted both by the essential otherworldliness of his religion and by the necessity of maintaining the church's position *in the world*. In order to reconcile these two, in a sense opposing, necessities, Augustine conceived of "just war." However, one fights not for "justice" but for "peace." More important, one fights not with confidence and enthusiasm but with resignation and humility. One listens for God's will in the particular circumstances and attempts to follow God's lead humbly, remembering all the while that one is ultimately blind both to one's own true motivation and to the historical consequences of one's action.[43]

By the end of the Gregorian revolution in the West,[44] which began late in the eleventh century, "the law," including a rationale for justifiable warfare, had become a hierarchical manifold ranging from the top with the church's canon law down through monarchical public law to a variety of feudal, urban, manorial, and commercial legal systems. "In the late eleventh and early twelfth centuries the church in the West achieved for the first time a legal identity independent of emperors, kings, and feudal lords. There was a separation of the church from the secular authorities and a separation of ecclesiastical law from other modes of ecclesiastical control," as Berman explains. "Yet all this would have been impossible if a preexisting community, the *populus christianus*, had not been formed in Europe between the fifth and eleventh centuries."[45] In other words, the variety of separations among realms and institutions all took place within a body or community thought of as a single Christian people.

Aquinas

Thomas Aquinas is the one who brought to clearest philosophical and theological articulation the place of law and government in western Christendom following the Gregorian revolution. The new ingredient in Aquinas's thinking was the work of Aristotle, which had recently been recovered by Muslim philosophers.[46] While building on Augustine and later Christian fathers, Aquinas used Aristotle to develop a rationally normative view of earthly political life that could overcome the ambiguities inherent in Augustine's understanding of the relation between the two cities. Aquinas went beyond Augustine's acknowledgment of leftover vestiges of the natural law in human consciousness and argued that institutional political life as a whole is natural to humans. Moreover, the requirements of justice for political life can be known and enacted by rational creatures because "law is the directive of reason promulgated by a competent authority for the common good."[47] The church's sovereignty over earthly rulers thus represented a kind of spiritual and moral supremacy that did not necessarily put it in tension or competition with political authority but rather complemented it.[48]

Aquinas in this way rejuvenated the ancient Greek and Roman idea of citizenship as a natural human responsibility. The citizen is more than just a *subject* who must obey superior authority. The citizen participates in political society and helps shape government for the common good. Drawing Aristotle into the western church's understanding of a hierarchically unified *corpus christianum* opened the way to a new conception of "political government" (*regimen politicum*), a form of government "which for Thomas existed when the Ruler had his powers circumscribed according to the laws of the State."[49]

This stood in contrast to "regal government" (*regimen regale*), in which the full powers of government are vested in the person of the king or emperor.

If, therefore, political life is natural to human beings and they participate in it as citizens and not merely as subjects, then, according to Ullmann, a knowledge of politics is possible that focuses on the realization of the political nature of human beings.

> Political science was to [Aquinas] the science of government as far as it related to the natural product, the State. As such it was primarily concerned with practical matters, and not with speculation. It was what he called *operativa*. . . . And the basis of this "operative science" was natural-human reason with which man was endowed by nature. This became the pivotal point in his system. This human reason received its direction and orientation from concrete experience which, he said, was especially noticeable "in the natural things" as well as "in moral matters." Still more important, political science had its working principles within itself—it needed no outside agency to make it work—and hence he called political science the most practical as well as the most fundamental and "architectonic" of all the sciences, "aiming as it did at the perfect good in human affairs."[50]

This idea of the state was new, according to Ullmann, the result of Aquinas's synthesis of Aristotelian and earlier medieval ingredients, building upon the pluralizing legal revolution of Pope Gregory VII. "State" and "church" could be distinguished within the same *corpus christianum*. Ullmann emphasizes the radicalness of the distinction rather than the unity of the community in which both function: "the State was a matter for man or the citizen only: it had neither in its origin nor in its working anything to do with any ecclesiastical authority. . . . To Thomas the State was a *corpus politicum et morale*, a body politic with moral ends which took into account the social habits and customs of its citizens. The church on the other hand was a mystical body (*corpus mysticum*)."[51]

As a natural body, the political community needed to be developed in accord with the natural law, which, as Pangle and Ahrensdorf explain, is Christendom's inheritance from the Stoics and Cicero rather than from Aristotle. Oliver and Joan O'Donovan emphasize the unique synthesis that Aquinas achieved in expressing the meaning of law. His treatment of law in the *Summa Theologiae*, they write, "offers an unprecedented integration of juristic, theological, and philosophical contributions that transcends his debts to Aristotle, Augustine, his immediate Franciscan and Dominican predecessors, and to the Roman legal scholarship in full flowering at both the papal and imperial courts."[52] The natural law, for Aquinas, is a moral law that manifests the eternal law of God and holds for everyone, regardless of their faith. According to this rationally accessible, natural law, "it is always wrong and misguided for an individual, in relations with other individuals, or for a nation, in relations with other nations, to depart from or to make any exceptions to the immutable rules of morality in order to attain what may falsely appear to be a greater good (such as security or even survival)."[53]

This is the framework in which Aquinas's just war reasoning is situated, though it is interesting that he does not treat just war in his discussion of natural law but in his consideration of the theological virtue of love. Aquinas, like Augustine, says that in the light of the New Testament, war appears to be a manifestation of sin. But must it always be so? Following Augustine, Aquinas argues that war can be justified if it is waged by a proper governing authority and carried out for a just cause with the right intention of promoting the common good. Although Aquinas's discussion of justifiable warfare is brief, he considers the requirements of justice in the actual conduct of a war, including the obligation of the government and military authorities to be truthful and not to deceive the enemy.[54] In the final analysis, says Weigel, the contribution of Aquinas comes not so much from his arguments about the morality of war but from "his more developed theory of peace as a human possibility within a rightly ordered political community."[55] Aquinas has a more positive view of government and the political community than did Augustine and sees war as more than primarily punitive and remedial. He "locates the question of peace within the larger context of political community as our natural home in this world. It would not be an exaggeration, then," says Weigel, "to argue that Aquinas transformed *tranquillitas ordinis* from a negative to a positive concept."[56]

Thomistic refinement and enlargement of just war principles depends on the idea of the naturalness and goodness of political life and the fact that the natural law, expressive of the eternal law, holds for all nations and empires. Consequently, Aquinas does not approach government and the ambiguities of war as Augustine did, primarily in the context of the antithetical ways of life exhibited, on the one hand, in the Christian community oriented by the love of God (moving toward the city of God), and, on the other hand, in the community driven by self-love (the earthly city). Christian cooperation in the life of the political community is, in principle, a wholly positive thing, not fraught with the burdens that Augustine saw in it. Aquinas is also in a different position than Augustine relative to the church's position in the world. The significant moral and even legal obligation of political authorities to an authority higher than themselves—the Roman Catholic Church—was institutionally concrete. In other words, the more encompassing authority of the church constituted a kind of international community under a common law, the church's canon law, somewhat like the old Roman Empire constituted the universal community for different subordinate peoples. Dawson nicely summarizes this point, which is crucial for our future consideration of international law and institutions. The reformed papacy of the eleventh century, he says,

> was the real heir of the Roman tradition of universalism and international order. For the Church was not only a much more universal and comprehensive society than the medieval state; it exercised many of the functions that we regard as essentially political. As F. W. Maitland used to insist, it is impossible to frame any acceptable definition of the state which would not include the medieval Church. It was a sovereign power [though without its own military] that imposed its own laws and enforced them in its own courts by its own judges and lawyers. It possessed an elaborate system of appellate jurisdiction, an organized bureaucracy and an efficient system of centralized control carried out by permanent officials and supervised by the visits and reports of the legates who played such a prominent part in the international life of Christendom.[57]

Ullmann, like Berman, underlines the importance of the differentiation of jurisdictions that Christendom represented at that time. "The citizen—political man—answered the description of a being different from mere man. Thereby the spectre of splitting up man's activities begins to be discernible and herewith the subjection of man to different sets of norms and postulates (political, religious, moral, economic, etc.)."[58] The idea of the political community of citizens and government under a higher natural law emerges, then, only in the larger social context of the "one Christian people," which by the time of Aquinas was very much supervised spiritually, morally, and in important respects even legally by the Roman Catholic Church's papal authority and canon law. The distinguishable naturalness of political life is thus, for Aquinas, not a realm of completely autonomous, independent sovereignties, but a particular sphere of institutional life within Christendom. Nevertheless, the ultimate destiny toward which the church reaches on behalf of humankind is not a perfect state or empire on earth but rather the vision of God experienced in communion with all the saints in eternal life.

The question is, what will happen, politically speaking, if the Roman Catholic Church loses its hold on European society through its canon law and its moral and spiritual authority over rulers. Western Christendom represented a synthesis of Roman, biblical, and Greek ingredients. It was diversified institutionally, yet organized hierarchically as a single *corpus chris-*

tianum. This is not the kind of international society we know today. This is not the world in which the United States emerged. What happened in the five hundred years between the death of Aquinas in 1274 and the American Revolution of 1776?

CHAPTER FIVE

⤴

The Rise of the Modern State

The two greatest inventions in history, writes Martin Van Creveld, were the separation of government from ownership, achieved by the Greeks, and the modern state, which was "invented" in western Europe between 1300 and 1648.[1] S. E. Finer says that "the sixteenth century forms the watershed in the political development of Europe and via Europe, of the entire world, for Europe is the birthplace of the modern state."[2] To understand what the state is, says Van Creveld, we must see how monarchs (almost exclusively) triumphed in power struggles with the Roman Catholic Church, the Holy Roman Empire, the nobility, and the towns. Nevertheless, the rise of the state, leading eventually to the end of the Holy Roman Empire and the nobility, did not eliminate the church or the towns, but positioned them differently in relation to the public legal governance of states. Moreover, in most cases the modern state has outlived monarchy.

The diversity of institutions just mentioned underscores the complexity of the social and political structure of Europe between the fourteenth and seventeenth centuries. According to Paul Kennedy, the "political fragmentation" of late medieval Europe is exactly what portended the West's rise to power. The fact that no single authority could monopolize the production, acquisition, and control of all weaponry in Europe, for example, meant constant competition and continuing innovation among different powers, leading eventually to the West's military supremacy in the world.[3] When outward movements of exploration, trade, and evangelization from multiple European centers picked up steam, the new states were on their way to becoming the chief organizing forces of the world. The primary reason why Europe's dynamism kept building, says Kennedy, was that

> the manifold rivalries of the European states, already acute, were spilling over into transoceanic spheres. Try as they might, Spain and Portugal simply could not keep their papally assigned monopoly of the outside world to themselves, the more especially when men realized that there was no northeast or northwest passage from Europe to Cathay. Already by the 1560s, Dutch, French, and English vessels were venturing across the Atlantic. . . . With royal and aristocratic patrons, with funding from the great merchants of Amsterdam and London, and with all the religious and nationalist zeal which the Reformation and Counter-reformation had produced, new trading and plundering expeditions set out from northwest Europe to secure a share of the spoils.[4]

From these comments alone we can see that states were not simply new means of organizing power and relocating sovereignty. The new states reconfigured the way that a wide range of human aspirations and socioeconomic ambitions would be related to one another and to the law.

The Formation of the State

Let us consider briefly each of the struggles Van Creveld mentions as crucial to the formation of the modern state.

The Roman Catholic Church at the height of its authority and influence in Europe was not a political empire, but it did hold predominant spiritual, moral, and even degrees of legal authority throughout most of politically fragmented Europe.[5] However, as trade and concomitant economic activities expanded and diversified, and as scholarship and other social practices changed, the church's relations to the estates, towns, nobility, small kingdoms, and the Holy Roman Empire became ever more difficult. However flexible the church-supervised system was in holding together the social, political, and economic life of Europe, that order increasingly became a disorder as conflicts multiplied. In the late fourteenth century, the church experienced the Great Schism, when two and even three popes contended for the highest position of authority. Ongoing struggles to reform the church would soon lead to an unstoppable Reformation, producing new ecclesiastical bodies separated from Rome. Not only did the Catholic Church's authority suffer diminishment, but its properties were being seized by local and regional rulers who supported the Reformation or otherwise saw openings for takeover. Moreover, given the church's own recognition of the relative autonomy of political authority, some of the new humanists, like Machiavelli, began to argue publicly that wise government did not depend on ecclesiastical sanction.

All of these developments undermined the Roman Catholic Church's pre-eminence and therewith made room for conflict, confusion, and a struggle for political control in different regions of Europe. The situation cried out for a means of ordering the disorder, yet the struggle among those who tried to fill the vacuum led to wars among rulers as well as to revolts of people such as those in the Low Countries (today's Netherlands and Belgium) against the claims of their imperial overlords. In all of this, papal authority was under attack. All the "national revolutions from the sixteenth century on—except the American—were directed in part against the Roman Catholic (or in Russia, the Orthodox) Church," says Harold Berman, "and all of them transferred large portions of the canon law from the church to the national state, thus secularizing them."[6]

The decline of Christendom cried out for more than simply a means of stopping conflict. The crisis was spiritual and not narrowly political or legal. If Christendom no longer convincingly represented the truth of humanity moving toward its fulfillment in the city of God, then what was—what would prove to be—the truth about human life? Reformers sought to purify the church so it could again become the true representative of humanity redeemed by God. Rising humanists sought rebirth and the redirection of society through new sciences, as well as the recovery of ancient learning. The monarchs did not stand above this fray but had to use the power and money at their disposal to seek certain ends—to decide, for example, whether to support one of the Reformers or to back the Counter-Reformation, whether to seek new sources of wealth or to be satisfied with what they had, whether to make room for new sciences and free thought or to clamp down on heretics and disturbers of the peace.

The modern state also took center stage, says Van Creveld, as a result of a struggle with the Holy Roman Empire, which did not gain that name until 1254.[7] This was the empire that grew from Charlemagne's Frankish kingship in the eighth and ninth centuries when feudalism was filling the power vacuum left by the collapse of the old Roman Empire. Once Charles became a king (*rex*) rather than a mere tribal chief (*dux*), he assumed a position of authority with some of the characteristics of eastern caesaropapism. He called church councils and made church law even before he agreed to be crowned emperor by the bishop of Rome in 800.[8] However, the regime that took the title of Holy Roman Empire in 1254 was not like the empire of Constantine or Caesar Augustus. It was not really a geographical entity at all but a military and spiritual authority attached to a king who traveled from city to city to fight battles and hold court.[9]

The fact that the empire did not officially disappear until 1806, when Francis II gave up the title of Holy Roman Emperor to become emperor of Austria, shows the power of the memory of the old Roman Empire and the strength of the spiritual and emotional desire for a universal order of law and peace. Dante's *De monarchia* and Marsilius of Padua's *Defensor Pacis*, late in the thirteenth century, both argued for the primacy of the emperor, not the pope, in ordering society and keeping the earthly peace. By the time Charles V was installed as emperor in 1519, however, subordinate princes of the realm had already secured a voice in imperial affairs. And the same Reformation that undermined the universal authority of the pope also empowered Protestant rulers to assert their independence from the emperor. In the early 1600s, the Hapsburgs tried to restore imperial power and launched what became the Thirty Years' War. They did not succeed, however, and in 1648 the Peace of Westphalia "marked the monarch's triumph over both the [Holy Roman] Empire and the church."[10]

"As a sharp line was drawn between the territories that belonged to the Empire and those that did not, the Emperor [also] lost whatever pretension over other rulers that he still retained," says Van Creveld.[11] The territories that remained within the empire "were given practically all the privileges of sovereignty, including the right to maintain their own armed forces and . . . the right to make alliances both among themselves and with foreign powers 'so long as they were not directed against the Emperor.'" The Holy Roman Empire had reached the point where "instead of protecting the peace of others, [it] needed protection itself."[12]

Both the Roman Catholic Church and the Holy Roman Empire were bound up together with local authorities in an intricate social, legal, economic, and spiritual network. Central to that network were the nobles, who eventually experienced the same diminishment that church and empire experienced. Beginning in England, where the nobles at first gained greater say in affairs of governance at the expense of the church, they were eventually subordinated to the centralizing monarchical power. Countless fratricidal wars and the Reformation were major factors in this process throughout Europe, Van Creveld explains. "From being the crown's competitors, the nobility was turned into its associates. From wearing armor, rallying to the royal cause, and carrying their own banners while fighting for it they were, shortly after 1648, made to don uniforms and thus literally turned into 'the king's men.'"[13]

Van Creveld also calls attention to the struggle against Europe's towns. These were independent, corporate bodies, many of which had endured since Roman times. "Just as each nobleman was, to some extent, his own lord and exercised power inferior to, but not essentially different from that of the king, so towns had their own organs of government."[14] As monarchical power grew, however, the cities were subordinated to central authority either by losing their charters and self-government altogether or by becoming subject to the higher political authority and laws of the new territorial states.

There were two important exceptions to the process of monarchical triumph over towns, namely, Switzerland and the Netherlands, where geography and Calvinism played important roles in making them exceptions. Far from surrendering to royal government in those countries, says Van Creveld, the towns themselves took over. "The greatest achievement of the Swiss towns consisted in that, unlike their Italian counterparts, they never lost the loyalty of the countryside—the cantons—over which they ruled."[15] In the Netherlands, by contrast, the House of Burgundy had all but taken over the towns from late in the fourteenth until the middle of the sixteenth century. But when Charles V's son Philip tried to suppress the Reformation in the Low Countries, he met with a powerful revolt. The towns of the region formed an alliance and fought Philip from 1568 to 1648, finally achieving their independence and, like the Swiss, forming a decentralized federation. The Dutch war for independence, it is important to remember, "was paid for almost entirely by the now highly prosperous, and prospering, cities of Holland and Zealand,"[16] whose wealth was being amassed through trade. These were the commercial venturers who founded New Amsterdam, which would become the city above all cities of the world to represent Western modernism—symbolized so significantly in its twentieth-century twin trade towers.

All of these struggles unfolded in such a way that the locus of political and legal power shifted to the monarchs across Europe and to confederal Switzerland and the Netherlands. The single most important factor in this process, says Van Creveld, was the prolonged "conflict between pope and Emperor which enabled the monarchs to play one off against the other. . . . As it was, religious reform and the fragmentation of Imperial political power marched hand in hand, culminating in the Reformation."[17] As the power of the monarchs grew, they "began to change the way they did business and presented themselves to the world."[18] With respect to military affairs, they shifted from direct involvement to commanding from a distance through field officers. They changed from governing as itinerants to settling down in one place and building the necessary infrastructure and bureaucracy needed to govern. And once they chose to stay put, the size and splendor of their courts grew.

Defining State Sovereignty

Part of what was generated by the Peace of Westphalia was the marking off of territorial boundaries within which each monarch was sovereign. Within those boundaries, in other words, the government, whether monarchical or otherwise, claimed sole governing authority, meaning that no other government was allowed to compete with it. Sovereignty also meant that no other authority within each territory had a right to use force to achieve its purposes. The new governments monopolized the use of force within the territory of their jurisdiction. Nobles could no longer raise independent armies; towns could not independently form their own defense forces. Feudalism gradually came to an end; towns and cities became lower levels of government within the single territorial jurisdiction of the sovereign state. Even the most decentralized federations of the Netherlands and Switzerland had to determine the kind of authority their central or confederal governments would hold within, and on behalf of, their states, over which no outside government could have a say.

The newly sovereign states did not arise, however, by self-authorization. They required legitimation. Throughout human history, governments had depended on some form of divine legitimation. It was impossible to think of government as self-legitimating. Even the new humanists, such as Machiavelli, appealed to older pagan traditions of legitimation or were redefining human beings as "terrestrial gods," thus making it possible to understand political authority as "divinely" self-authorized.[19] Many of the monarchs in Protestant lands claimed the right to rule by direct delegation from God and positioned themselves in authority over new "state churches" in a revised version of caesaropapism called Erastianism. In Catholic lands the church's ordination of the monarch, or the upholding of Catholic doctrine by the monarch, remained crucial for legitimation. Finer argues that Erastianism even extended into Catholic countries. "Francis I of France and Ferdinand and Isabella in Spain contrived to establish such a control over their states' Church establishment that, though remaining thoroughly Catholic in doctrine, they were quasi-national in character."[20] In all cases, it remained inconceivable that a political order could hold together without the recognition or establishment of one religion. The consequence of the Peace of Westphalia, which confirmed and extended the principle of the Peace of Augsburg (1555), was that the religion of the ruler would be established as the religion of the territory.

Along with direct or indirect divine legitimation of government, certain other features of ancient vintage also shaped the identity of the emerging states. Part of what made the new state conceivable as sovereign was the ancient Greek experience of the polis and the Roman experience of the republic. The ancient polis and republic were, of course, cities, not wide territorial domains that contained many towns and cities. But the idea of a political *whole* that serves as the most complete human community was strongly in play. Yet, whereas for Aquinas the political community had its proper place within a larger *corpus christianum*, the new states did not have that as their milieu. What, then, would constitute the larger community of peoples now being organized into separate states? Or would there henceforth be no larger trans-state community?

Perhaps most important in qualifying the state as sovereign was its authority to enforce law within and throughout its territory. In this respect, the state as chief lawmaker and adjudicator exhibited roots in the Roman Empire going back through Cicero and the early republic to the Stoics. The Roman Empire was all about extending law as the means of establishing order, but to do that it had to be in the position to enforce law. Law and force, right and might—these are the defining qualifications of political order, and this would also prove to be true for the sovereign state. Yet, we may ask, if each state, alongside other states, is a miniature empire of enforced law, how is order among the states to be kept? Who enforces law on them? If there is a universal divine law or natural law above the monarchs, how is that law implemented and enforced on all of them together in order to make manifest the universal applicability of the law to all of humanity? Or does the rise of state sovereignty and the collapse of Christendom mean the eclipse of all universality, the end to every ordering principle transcending the state, making of each state a law unto itself? The governments of the new states would hold sovereign *power* within their territories, but were they truly sovereign over and above all *law*?

Taking into account everything just said about "sovereignty," we must be careful not to read a later and narrower meaning of the term into the situation that existed during the early phases of the new political era. The states that emerged from the Peace of Westphalia did not drop from the sky fully formed, mature in their autonomous sovereignty, and unrelated to the others. Rather, each one came into existence from out of the same Greco-Roman-Christian history, the same breakdown of western Christendom. The Treaty of Westphalia was an *agreement*, a treaty, entailing mutual recognition among states and even a basis for common rules of diplomacy and war. In other words, partly because the Roman Catholic Church's canon law had functioned as a form of international law, incorporating many aspects of older Roman *ius gentium*, the new European arrangement of separate governing units contained many common legal and moral components, including agreed-upon criteria for judging justifiable warfare. The fact that sovereignty later came to mean each state's right of immunity from any outside intervention represents a considerable reduction of the original meaning of state sovereignty.[21] Yet, it is also true that while the new mode of sovereignty depended on and fed off of ancient and medieval experiences of an extended, international community, the modern state did something new with the inheritance. In many respects, the belief in universality was transfigured into an endorsement of particularism—the *universal* right of each state to be sovereign. Every people or nation, universally, should be allowed to govern itself in its own particular, sovereign way.

Renaissance, Reformation, and Citizenship

European society in the fifteenth through the seventeenth centuries was radically reconstituted by the Renaissance and the Reformation. Both movements challenged the meaning of Christendom, but they were inspired by different visions and missions.

The Renaissance

The Renaissance engendered enthusiasm for the culture of pre-Christian Greece and Rome. Its leaders longed for a rebirth of humanism and the release of humanity from the dark prison of Christendom. The movement took both a secularizing and a sacralizing direction. Secularization meant gaining cultural and political freedom from ecclesiastical control. The aim was to release the *saeculum* (secular world) from the church's oppressive manipulation. Yet, the secularizing mission did not aim for the reinstatement of old Greek and Roman cultures pure and simple. Instead, the ancients served as the point of departure for a new spiritual movement that also represented a transmutation of Christianity. If the pope and the church were no longer taken to be authoritative for life in this world, then humans were free to establish a new authority by which to make history. If the *saeculum* is not necessarily bound to a transcendent realm, then humans are free to shape it as their creative ingenuity directs. And if humans themselves are sovereign over what is secular, then they must be the gods of this world. Secularization, in other words, led to the sacralizing of humanity in the here and now. Human rebirth, achieved particularly by the release of reason from superstition and church-imposed dogma, meant gaining rational control over secular life.

In a very short time the new humanists gravitated to science as the light that would be trusted to dispel the darkness of the past centuries.

We now recognize the Renaissance as the era in which a new faith was born, inspiring the search for a new way of life. Disciplined rationality—exhibited at is best in the new sciences—showed that humans could trust reason as their guide to world mastery and human autonomy. At least with regard to life in this world, humans could become the creators and redeemers of themselves. It was not sin that held them back but ignorance—and the way out of ignorance was to be found through the disciplined use of reason. If the world, formerly conceived as God's creation, were reconceived as Nature, subject to human mastery, then humans themselves would be the gods of this world. Thus, the sacralizing of secular humanity: humans were to be seen no longer as God's servants journeying toward an otherworldly destiny but as the gods of this world, the masters (or at least, potential masters) of the universe.[22]

The Reformation

The Reformers, in contrast to the new humanists, were praying and working for a different kind of rebirth and renewal of life.[23] They wanted the purification of the church through a recovery of biblical illumination and the power of God's Spirit. The renewal that was needed would come not from a supposedly autonomous rationality that overcomes ignorance but from the forgiveness of sins and the reinstatement of humans, with all their capabilities, in the service of God. The Reformers urged believers to accept all human labors and stations in life as Christian vocations—callings from God. The gospel calls for the renewal of all of life. Humans bear real responsibility to develop this world—its family life, agriculture, arts, sciences, commerce, and government. Life may need to be liberated from the Roman Catholic Church hierarchy, but it must not be disconnected from God.

With regard to government, however, the Reformation did not go very far. The Reformation contributed to the rise of the state but not by way of developing a distinctively reformed view of the political community or of international relations in a post-Christendom world.[24] What did come to the fore was the tension between the more Augustinian and the more Thomistic ideas of the purpose and limits of government. Does government represent a mere dike against sin, a means primarily of keeping order in a world always tending toward disorder as humans pursue their earthly pilgrimage toward the final judgment and the eschatological city of God? If so, then government's purpose is very limited, and those who govern should do so very cautiously. If, on the other hand, government should be trying to perfect a natural political art with the aim of realizing the common good of particular political communities or nations, then a somewhat different motivation becomes operative. Monarchs, and even democratically elected governments, might feel compelled to accomplish any number of goals for the strengthening of their states, depending on the primary spirit or interest that inspires them. Perhaps the chief aim will be to fulfill nationalist aspirations, or to extend the state's borders, or to expand its wealth and productivity. Perhaps the aim will be to try to help one's own subjects or citizens realize more of their intellectual, cultural, and economic potential. The Reformers reached no consensus on these matters and generated no new philosophy of government and law. Anabaptists wanted a church free from state control. Calvinists and Lutherans tended to stress the more limited, retributive functions of government in what they hoped would remain Christian societies, though Calvin and many of his followers were duly concerned with dimensions of distributive justice and equity.[25]

Citizenship

Also crucial to the transformation that occurred with the rise of the modern state was the maturation of the meaning of citizenship and the exercise of civic responsibility. The triumph of the monarchs positioned them, they hoped, to be the mediators (or in some cases, the dictators) of the law to their *subjects*. Most monarchs, says Finer, "strenuously and ceaselessly aspired to become *absolute*. By 1660 most of them were."[26] But just at the time when the monarchs were coming into their own, the revival of the idea and practice of citizenship was already well under way. What actually developed throughout much of Europe in the centuries ahead, therefore, was the codification and eventually the constitutionalizing of the "rule of law." On the one hand, this meant that nobles, land owners, and church authorities succeeded in forcing monarchs to acknowledge their rights, in some cases including their property-holding rights, as something prior to and not dependent on the person of the monarch. Limiting government in its relation to citizens, says Finer, depended on the distinction "between public law and private law, between private ownership and state power, and the distinction resurfaced [sic] between the private person of the monarch and the *res publica*, which came to be conceived as an abstract and faceless nomocracy [rule of law]."[27] The "rights of Englishmen," which began to be articulated with the now famous Magna Carta of 1215, came to be seen as part of a "higher law" above the monarch. These kinds of rights—as civil rights—have been made central to most modern constitutions. They are the rights typically recognized in a basic law that stands above and qualifies all branches of government. And on the international stage, these rights are now touted as universal, standing above the claims of sovereign states but not enforceable by any authority other than the states.

The rights of citizens also expanded to mean more than mere passive immunity from government's arbitrariness. Citizenship now typically presupposes an open political community, open to the active influence of those who are subject to government and the law. Participation in parliaments and on juries, the creation of political parties as a means of nurturing and electing candidates for public office, and the use of a free press to voice criticism of government and to contend for popular causes—all of these represent a new kind of active citizenship.

And once again the question arises: what are the legitimate goals and aims of citizens in states? Should the aim be primarily to hold government in check, to keep it from interfering with individual freedom and with the non-government responsibilities of human society so that people can flourish in freedom? Or should citizens expect their governments to promote and advance various human aspirations and national goals? Should citizens try to shape the state primarily so it will recognize them as more than citizens and thus as persons who need freedom, or should they work to achieve the fulfillment of all the parts of human community in and through the state?

The Meaning and Purpose of the State

If the modern state is not a Greek polis or a Roman republic or a church-guided bearer of the earthly sword within Christendom, then what is it and what should it be trying to do or become? If the state does not exhaust the meaning of human life and the identity of human persons, what is its particular role and how should it play that role in relation to the roles of other institutions and organizations in law-governed societies? The emergence and development of the modern state has not given a single answer to these questions, and that helps to explain some of the dynamism and turmoil of the modern world in which the state is the dominant structure of governance.

Given the character of the new territorial states, the major questions of governance and interstate relations had to be approached in a new way. One might imagine that a monopoly of power by each monarch within a single state territory could have led to complete dictatorship or to what today we call totalitarian government. To be sure, some of the monarchs did assert the right to rule over everyone and everything without limit, imagining for themselves something of a ceasarlike role. But that pattern did not take hold or endure for long in the West. Europe was changing politically from a pattern of overlapping governance structures within a single Christian community into an arena of separate sovereign states. But within those states there was already a significant diversification of economic, academic, ecclesiastical, and legal institutions. So much so that the people would not for long yield to a type of government that tried to dictate or legislate every detail of every kind of human behavior in every sphere of life.

What actually developed over time, and in different states to different degrees at different times, was the specification of a nonabsolute, nontotalitarian sphere of public-legal jurisdiction for governments. Although the new states would permit no rival governments within their territories, and everyone within the state's territory would be subject to the laws of its government, the social jurisdiction of governments was not allowed to remain or become limitless; government's authority was not recognized as omnicompetent. Instead, the kind of responsibility that fell to the governments in most Western states, eventually to be codified in constitutions, was a distinct type of public-legal responsibility. That responsibility entailed the obligation to recognize and protect the independent responsibilities of churches, property owners, universities, scientists, trading companies, economic enterprises, and individual persons. Only one government in each particular territory could now monopolize force in order to compel everyone's compliance with public law, but the extensive, all-inclusive reach of public law could not be limitless with respect to everything human beings did. No longer would it be permissible for an emperor, prince, or feudal lord to say that his or her right to rule came from on high and thus could not be challenged in any way.

This is not to say that all of the new states quickly gained governments that governed more justly than any town, noble, king, or emperor had governed before. To the contrary, many governments ruled vengefully, arbitrarily, and unjustly. And we know from twentieth-century experience that totalitarianism was attempted again and again. But the fights to limit such arbitrariness and unjust rule within the modern state led in many cases to the differentiated qualification and accountability of government in a way that made possible the greater clarification of the freedom and competence of nonstate authorities and communities within the same territory.[28]

Finally, by differentiating and concentrating public-legal responsibility in one government per territory, government power itself was dispersed and diversified. This meant new possibilities for interstate trade and commerce, as well as for the balance of power. Of course, with the competitive imperialistic outreach of newly powerful European states between the seventeenth and twentieth centuries, the positive potential of the state just summarized was contradicted many times, eventuating in the two world wars of the last century. But those failures of the major European powers have made all the more clear the need for broadly dispersed governance around the world so that no single power can make its failures of governance the cause of injustice everywhere. Yet, this virtue of many dispersed states raises the old question about how states should be related to one another and whether there is any possibility of creating international and even transnational structures of governance that can make binding law above the states for the sake of international justice. For all the state's virtues, does its rise to world dominance portend anything other than perpetual conflict and warfare among states throughout the world?

CHAPTER SIX

⟋⟍

The American Republic:
Witness to the End of History

A Modern State?

The American state was founded as a republic, modeling itself in part on the Roman Republic. Its final *federal* constitution was a novelty, however, not anticipated at the start of the Revolution. Each of the federating states had hoped to become independent at the beginning, but the exigencies of the Revolutionary War drove them into a confederation. The confederation did not function adequately for unified military purposes, however, so representatives of the several states, meeting in special assemblies, reluctantly crafted a federal order with a stronger central government. This formation was indebted to the Swiss and Dutch experiences, for the *federal* government received its specific institutional authorization as a grant from the states below rather than from a church, or emperor, or God on high. The responsibility assigned to the federal government was largely that of protecting the states from foreign aggression and regulating commerce among them. The Constitution was designed to recognize the primacy of the states, each of which had its own legal, social, and economic order, its own government and constitution, and thereby its own relative autonomy. The authority of both the federal Constitution and the federal government was grounded in the rights of individuals and in the prior rights of the states that created the federation, not in the authority of God or a church.

The Declaration of Independence and the federal Constitution reflect the history of constitutionalizing civil rights, reaching back to the English Magna Carta;[1] they are also indebted to the Renaissance and Enlightenment revival of the Stoic idea of a universal higher law inherent in, or immediately available to, every rational creature. A single humanity stands before one God who endows every individual with the same rights and permits each nation to obtain its own "separate and equal station" in the world, independent of, but in free relation to, every other sovereign people.

> When in the Course of human events, it becomes necessary for one people to dissolve the political bands which have connected them with another, and to assume among the powers of the earth, the separate and equal station to which the Laws of Nature and of Nature's God entitle them, a decent respect to the opinions of mankind requires that they should declare the causes which impel them to the separation.[2]

The argument of the declaration to justify the American War of Independence is very much like the argument that individuals should be free and self-governing. The "political bands" that had united the colonies to Great Britain were being dissolved by the Americans unilaterally so that Americans could become properly joined (banded together) in accord with the "laws of nature." The laws of nature are the ultimate bands—the higher law—that legitimize individual freedom and "entitle" a people to assume its independent place among "the powers of the earth." On the one hand, this argument presupposes an extensive universal bond among all peoples: a single earth; the same laws and the same God of nature for everyone; the same rationality by which to offer justification for one's independent actions; and a universal moral obligation that any people should show a decent respect for the opinions of humans everywhere. On the other hand, the argument presumes the legitimacy of separate peoples establishing their own political bands in order to become "separate" from and "equal" to every other people. If the first part of the argument is indebted to the biblical tradition, Roman legal universalism, and the morally and religiously unified culture of medieval Christendom, the second part shows its indebtedness to the idea of the independent, self-sufficient polis or republic, updated by Aquinas and later thinkers as the natural polity or community in which human nature finds its most encompassing maturation. In the American case, however, indebted as Protestants were to the Augustinian tradition, the republic was constituted with a cautious, almost negative view of government, with priority placed on individual rights and freedom as the higher divine gift and commission.

There is a dilemma here in the American founding, however. The dilemma appears when we ask, which "people" or "powers" have the right of self-determination and before what court does a people make its case for independence? Less than a century later, the American federal union would not be willing to recognize the southern states as "a people" with their own right to dissolve their political bands with the United States in order to assume their "separate and equal station" among the "powers of the earth." Thus, despite the high view of a universal, rationally accessible law of nature, before which any people may justify its independence, the actual achievement of a nation's independent and equal station on earth depends on its military capability—and success—to make it happen. Whereas a universal natural law may exist in some ideal conception of reality, it has no institutional embodiment, no means of enforcement, no earthly court in which to hand down authoritative and enforceable rulings on rights and national sovereignty. In that sense, the higher universal law is not a law at all but only a moral standard to which a certain kind of reason appeals on behalf of the freedom of individuals and the independence of sovereign states.

Here we see the fruit of the moral and rational idealism of Plato, Aristotle, and Cicero and the influence of their modernizers in the Renaissance and the Enlightenment. Just as John Locke had emphasized the equality of rational individuals before the law of nature, so the founders imagined the equality of nations or peoples before the laws of nature's God. The supposed universality of the natural law grounds the autonomy of countless individuals, as well as the political independence of numerous peoples. But above the many sovereign states that monopolize the use of force, there is no transnational institution or governing authority to enforce the universal natural law. In the final analysis, then, the use of force among sovereign states will determine the degree to which freedom and independence, as well as harmony or disharmony, among them are realized.

What this version of the natural law universally affirms is the right of autonomy for individuals and nations, not the principle of any universal mode of governance for all. This is the Western basis for the sovereign state. And in this regard, the United States is the most modern of them all. The United States was the first to relinquish church, tradition, and divine sanction as the ground of its authority. Nature's god endows individuals with rights; it does not authorize governments. The laws of nature's god "entitle" a people to assume its position of independence; divine laws do not directly endow government with any power or authority. God is providentially observant of sovereign peoples; but the U.S. Constitution assumes that neither God nor the state is sovereign in political affairs. The people are sovereign. This was the most radical secularization of political authority in history, but as we will see, it went hand in hand with the sacralization of the American nation as a whole.

According to Daniel Lang, the modern "law of nations" and the "balance of power" among nations emerged "from a common opposition to religious war and to universal monarchy" and owed a great debt to Swiss diplomat Emmerich de Vattel, whose *Law of Nations* (1758) deeply influenced the American founders.[3]

> The principal lesson learned from the wars of religion and the Thirty Years' War was the inability of any single European state to conquer the others; instead they would have to reconcile themselves to one another's existence within a framework of equilibrium grounded in commonly accepted noneccle-siastical principles of legitimacy. Vattel's goal was to justify this lesson not simply in terms of necessity or expedience, but in terms of right. Thus he combined the universalism and categories of the just-war tradition with aspects of modern natural rights theory derived from Hobbes and praise for the balance of power system, making a new synthesis.[4]

In these brief comments we can see how clearly the modern state had, by 1776, become the unquestioned, institutionally actualized linchpin of the new international worldview. A universal higher law of nature and, when necessary, a balance of power among sovereign states appear to fit together, hand in glove, because each state may assume that its own independence is a self-evident *right*. Each state, being in the right, then needs to rely on warfare, diplomacy, and a *balance of power* with other states to achieve its foreign and defense policy goals.

However, in trying to run away from the religious wars and the monarchies of Europe, the Americans, and eventually other moderns, forgot the source of that peculiarly Western sense of the unity of humankind that they believed they were continuing to represent. They simply assumed that the independence of nations was morally and rationally right and that cooperation based on mutual recognition of equal, separate nations would follow. Yet, when philosophers and practitioners of international law like Vattel tried to ground this new order in nonecclesiastical principles of "right," they attempted a synthesis that could not be sustained. The actual court in which any state could appeal to international principles of right was none other than the array of surrounding sovereign states, each acting in accord with its own right of independence and, from time to time, in temporary balance-of-power coalitions with others. Consequently, from that time forward, those who would keep looking for ways to encourage states to abide by what is universally right, above and beyond the rightness of their sovereignty, would be called *idealists* because of their appeal to a moral standard that has no independent, institutional enforcing power on earth. Those, on the other hand, who would choose to focus strictly on the reality of relations among sovereign states would be called *realists* because in their view there can, at best, be only a balance of power among sovereign states as the means of preserving a modest tranquillity of order in this world. There is no reality of government in a law that cannot be enforced.

The parallel between free individuals and free nations is something the founders took for granted, drawing on Vattel and on their own experience. "Nations," Lang explains, "enter into treaty arrangements with others for reasons similar to those which drive men into civil society: security and comfort."[5] To sustain this parallelism, however, Vattel and the American founders would have had to argue that free and equal nations should enter into an international compact to create a trans-state federation for their mutual security and comfort. At the time of the founding, however, this was the last thing any American would want. It was difficult enough for most early Americans to accept a strong central government in their republic. Their goal was freedom not bondage. This is why the balance-of-power system that emerged in Europe seemed "right" and not merely "expedient." Vattel praised "the European balance of power system as a good in and of itself, by which modern Europe had become 'a kind of republic, of which the members—each independent, but all linked together by the ties of common interests—unite for the maintenance of order and liberty.'"[6]

What is fascinating here is how completely the modern worldview has displaced the medieval worldview while unconsciously depending on important elements of ancient and medieval political ethics. Vattel imagines that individuals and states, starting from a position of independence, somehow come together to form compacts for mutual benefit based on common interests. In fact, however, most of the moral and legal terms that made such cooperation possible derive from the community of medieval Christendom from which those states had emerged. The states never were autonomously separate from one another before coming together to form their balance-of-power agreements. Not acknowledging this, Vattel projects an imaginary bond like "a kind of republic," which he thinks the cooperating states are achieving through a balance of power because of their common desire to maintain order and liberty. But the analogy is entirely inappropriate because the autonomous individuals who supposedly come together to form a republic actually establish institutions of government whose laws and authority are binding on them. By contrast, sovereign states that enter into temporary balance-of-power arrangements and sign treaties of cooperation do not create or yield to any superior institutional government or law enforcer. They do not subordinate themselves to a trans-state government in the way that the new American states subordinated themselves in important respects to a federal government. The principle of sovereignty means that there is no political or legal authority superior to the state. To draw an analogy as Vattel does between the contract among individuals to form a state and the common-interest cooperation among states, which he calls a "kind of republic," is to draw no analogy at all. A temporary balance of power among relatively equal states is much more like the prepolitical anarchy of individuals in the "state of nature" (as Hobbes pictures it) than it is like a "kind of republic."

This mode of thought and imagination about modern state sovereignty and international relations would continue to guide American presidents and foreign policy makers up to the present day and helps to explain many of the international crises of our time. Near the end of World War I, Woodrow Wilson proposed a new league of independent states bound together more closely to secure peace and promote democracy and common interests. But the League of Nations was built on, and did not fundamentally challenge, the first principle of national sovereignty, particularly U.S. sovereignty. The United Nations, formed after World War II, also took as its first principle state sovereignty, with the hope that through it states would freely strengthen their common bonds. The League and the United Nations were mature versions of what Vattel might have described as a "kind of republic," but neither of them established any mode of trans-state governance.

Exceptional Nation

Having said this much about the founding of the American republic and its position in the world, we have covered only half of what is necessary for an understanding of the new nation and its sense of identity. For its identity came not solely from its constitutional republicanism and its insistence on having a separate and equal position among the peoples of the world. More important is the fact that the republic thought of itself as an exceptional polity from the start, unlike all others in the world. The earliest, most influential, American self-interpretation was, after all, that of the Puritan mission to New England. The inspiration behind the Puritan settlement was not modernized Stoicism or Ciceronian republicanism but a modernized covenantalism, a new-Israelitism. The Puritan goal was to gain release from the deformities of "Christian" Europe and to settle like a monastic community at the outer edges of human civilization where they could become a bright shining city on a hill.

This vision was obviously inspired by biblical stories, beginning with God delivering Israel from Egypt and establishing Israel in a new land as God's chosen people. The Puritan vision was also indebted to the long medieval Christian attempt to embody a community on earth that would both reflect and thereby point ahead to the city of God. Historian Mark Noll says that "the importance of Puritanism for American theological history is more easily grasped if it is regarded as an English Protestant extension of Christendom."[7] More specifically, the Puritan venture was like one of the monastic reform movements within Christendom.[8] The Reformation was an extension of earlier reforming missions, and its aim was to purify the church so it could more adequately manifest the work of the Spirit of God in fashioning a new community of people on earth. Calvinist Reformer John Knox, almost a century before the Puritans embarked on their mission, sought "to turn the Scots into God's chosen people, and Scotland into the New Jerusalem."[9] The idea of a "new Israel" or a "new Jerusalem" or a "new Zion" was not original with the American Puritans, though they found the opportunity to launch their experiment in a new (non-European) land.

There was even more to this Puritan vision. For the settlement of a community of faith in an exclusive territory was intended not as a retreat from ordinary society but as a light for the nations. The Puritans were part of an outward movement inspired by the Reformation to reclaim and reform the world. Their sense of mission was one of participating in God's providential, redemptive-historical trajectory, calling the lost to join in a reforming pilgrimage toward the city of God. Puritan divine Cotton Mather "promised that the Puritan calling anticipated 'the *Generall Restoration of Mankind from the Curse of the Fall*, and the opening of [the last stage in] that Scheme of *the Divine Proceedings*, which was to bring a blessing upon all the *Nations of the Earth*.'"[10] The Puritan mission to America was to fashion a new community. Thus, even with the Calvinist distinction between church and state, the Puritan colony was constituted as an encompassing unity. Like ancient Israel, the new city on a hill included priests and prophets, rulers and families, cities and rural clans, all bound together as the people of God. The Puritan mission was not a narrow ecclesiastical one. It was creationwide. As Richard Gamble summarizes it, "Worldwide renovation would begin in America—the Fall reversed, dominion restored, the earth renewed, paradise regained."[11]

In what sense, however, was the Puritan experiment compatible with anything in the Bible? The earliest Christian communities did not see themselves as territorial polities, as replacements for Israel in the promised land. The early church was an eschatologically oriented community of faith living in and among the cities and empires of the world. The Puritans were certainly not wildly utopian about what human government could achieve in this age. They were Augustinian Calvinists who emphasized human depravity and the dangers of power and idolatry. So they did not mistake their civil common-wealth for the New Jerusalem. Nevertheless, questions remain. Did the Puritans see their New England experiment as a branch of the one Christian community spread throughout the world? Or did they see their territorial polity as a replica of Israel and themselves as starting the covenanting process over again so that they would become the fount of the renewed church everywhere?

The ambiguities in the Puritan settlement that lie behind these questions have never been resolved. In the original Puritan commonwealth, voters were male church members, thus assuring a bond between the institutionally differentiated church and the state. But when a growing number of men in the second and third generations did not continue as church members, concern about the colony's future became as urgent as the concern about the health of the church. One influential proposal to resolve the problem was put forward by Solomon Stoddard (1643–1729). His interpretation helps to explain how the United States as a whole would take on the identity of a new Israel in covenant with God. Stoddard, according to Noll, believed that "a national covenant existed whenever any people subscribed in the aggregate to the Christian religion. . . . [He assumed] that New England was a Christian nation, or in his terms, 'the Commonwealth of Israel.'"[12] Not every citizen or voter, in other words, needed to be a Christian for the commonwealth as a whole to be considered God's chosen people. By this means the inspiration behind the Puritan attempt to found a new Christian commonwealth worked its way into the American experiment as a whole like leaven in a lump of dough. In the future, church membership would be reserved for confessing Christians while citizenship in the "Christian" commonwealth would be open to everyone without regard to church affiliation, though not without regard to various obligations to the commonwealth as God's chosen nation.

"Puritanism," says Noll, "is the only colonial religious system that modern historians take seriously as a major religious influence on the Revolution. During the War for Independence, a vibrant Christian republicanism and Real Whig political analysis, persuaded other colonists to think that the new nation in its entirety might be specially elect of God like a new ancient Israel."[13] It was that sense of identity, coupled with the Greco-Roman, Stoic-Enlightenment influences feeding the modern idea of an independent republic, that produced the peculiar state of the United States of America. Quite in contrast to the European and British pattern of antagonism between Christians and republicanism, Americans synthesized the two, as Noll explains.

> If for evangelicals during the Revolution "the cause of America" had become "the cause of Christ," as the Pennsylvania Presbyterian Robert Smith put it in

1781, then the achievement of independence meant that, for many patriots, "the cause of Christ" had become also "the cause of America." The belief that the United States was a land chosen and protected by God for special, if perhaps even millennial, purposes may not have been as widely spread during the War for Independence as is sometimes suggested. But it did flourish in the decades after the war.[14]

The heirs of the Puritans, says Gamble, quoting Sacvan Bercovitch, "'incorporated Bible history into the American experience—they substituted a regional for a biblical past, consecrated the American present as a movement from promise to fulfillment, and translated fulfillment from its meaning within a closed system of sacred history into a metaphor of limitless secular improvement.' The Puritan errand," Gamble continues, eventually "became secularized as temporal progress, social amelioration, material well-being, and the regeneration of society."[15] James Block makes the same point in developing his thesis that America invented itself as "a nation of agents." At the time of the Civil War, says Block, civil religion reached a high level of articulation. "If prewar religious activists burned with 'the gospel ideal of a righteous nation,'" then, says Block, the fashioning of a "new society as a single moral enterprise in the Civil War made that view a widespread conviction. . . . [T]he war became the ultimate test of the nation's religious destiny, of God's blessing upon the land as a whole."[16]

The nation's goals were to be regarded as sacred goals, its successes sacred accomplishments:

> Men in all walks of life believed that the sovereign Holy Spirit was endowing the nation with resources sufficient to convert and civilize the globe, to purge human society of all its evils, and to usher in Christ's reign on earth. *The nation's governance and direction would henceforth replace the fate of the churches as the strategic center of the mission* (emphasis added).[17]

Clearly, the United States was a state in the modern sense described in the last chapter. But it is also equally clear that the United States was a new kind of religious community—a civil-religious community—just as the Roman Republic and the Greek polis had been religious polities, and just as the new European states continued for some time to be Roman Catholic or Erastian polities. After the First Amendment was adopted with the Constitution, and after all the states disestablished their churches, the United States was certainly no longer a community defined by an exclusive *ecclesiastical* faith. The states and their federal government had been constitutionally delimited for a differentiated purpose, and citizens were free to associate independently in different ecclesiastical communities of faith. One could be a Presbyterian and an American, a Baptist and an American, and eventually one could also be a Catholic or a Jew or an atheist and an American. But there can be no doubt that a certain kind of civil religion also characterized the republic and membership in it. What kind of religion was (is) this?

Wilfred McClay recently revived the discussion of American civil religion, explaining that the phrase "civil religion" can mean several things at the same time.

> Civil religion is a means of investing a particular set of political and social arrangements with an aura of the sacred, thereby elevating their stature and enhancing their stability. It can serve as a point of reference for the shared faith of an entire nation. As such, it provides much of the social glue that binds together a society through well-established symbols, rituals, celebrations, places, and values, supplying the society with an overarching sense of spiritual unity—a sacred canopy, in Peter Berger's words—and a focal point for shared memories of struggle and survival.[18]

What is surprising, McClay writes, is that the Puritan-indebted American civil religion did not dissipate within a few decades of the founding. The "self-understanding of America as the Redeemer Nation" has persisted in part because the American civil religion incorporated elements from both the Enlightenment and Christianity. The synthesis that has persisted conveys "a strong sense of God's providence, His blessing on the land, and of the Nation's consequent responsibility to serve as a light unto other nations."[19]

There are, of course, many American Christians, such as Stanley Hauerwas and William Willimon, cited by McClay, who reject and criticize civil religion. And today they, too, can be full American citizens like everyone else. America can thus be thought of as God's chosen nation even if not all Americans share the dominant civil-religious faith, just as the Puritan colony after a few generations could still be thought of as a Christian commonwealth even if not all its citizens were members of the Congregational Church. A crucial question that McClay raises in this regard is whether the use of Christian symbols, like the cross, in America's civil religion subordinates "the Christian story to the American one" and thus traduces its Christian meaning?[20] His answer is ambiguous. On the one hand, he says, we should be able "to understand the disgust felt by many serious Christians and other believers toward civil religion." Yet, on the other hand, McClay doubts that critics of civil religion can "offer a serious and persuasive vision of what things could be like in this country, or any country, without it. . . . Indeed, there may be more to be feared from the continued weakness of America's civil religion than from its resurgent strength [after 9/11]."[21] "In a pluralistic society, religious believers and nonbelievers alike need ways to live together, and to do so, they need a *second language of piety*, one that extends their other commitments without undermining them" (emphasis added).[22]

McClay takes for granted that the United States, and probably every polity, needs a civil religion and that such a religion need not "undermine" the primary religion of its citizens. Yet, this assumption was challenged by Augustine and before him by the New Testament writers and the prophets of Israel. The fact that Christians refused to share in emperor worship did not make them bad citizens, Augustine argued, in responding to charges to the contrary. Jesus allowed that his followers should pay taxes to Caesar, but they were to do so only in dedicating their lives entirely to the one true God, using only one language of piety. And Paul could urge Roman Christians to recognize the God-ordained authority of governing officials and to seek to live at peace with all their neighbors while refusing to be part of any community of faith other than the one that followed the way of Jesus Christ. There is, in fact, a persuasive, biblically grounded, and enduring vision of how Christians can fulfill their civic responsibilities while rejecting all civil religions. There is no need for citizens to learn a "second language of piety," unless they are trying to practice more than one religion at the same time, and that is a contradiction of Christianity; in biblical terms it is called idolatry and will undermine Christian faith. The political community does not itself have to be a community of faith, supported by a civil religion, in order to have strong, differentiated *civic* bonds built of shared memories and, most importantly, a shared confidence that the constitution and the government are pursuing public justice.[23]

McClay's discussion of a persistent American civil religion and his own expression of support for its legitimacy are revealing. A differentiated modern state need not depend on a civil religion, and the new-Israelitism that characterizes the American civil religion distorts and challenges both Judaism and Christianity. But McClay is correct that the United States is a civil-religious polity to the core, and it is impossible to fathom America's self-understanding and its foreign and defense policies without taking into account its civil-religious character. One need not share the dominant faith to recognize its power and influence. By the end of the Civil War, writes Block, "Liberty and Protestant agency had been seamlessly meshed in 'the national religion, a religion of civilization' in which 'conflict between church and world seemed to be disappearing,' constituting a 'continuum of Christ and culture.'"[24]

In Sum

The Christian-republican consensus that gained dominance around the time of the American Revolution was complex in the way it differentiated government and society while holding them together in a commitment to new-Israelite nationalism. *Government* must be limited, restricted, and restrained because of sinful human tendencies and because it owes its existence to rights-bearing individuals who have granted government only limited authority. Government, particularly the central government, should be treated with a degree of suspicion because it has been charged only with the responsibility to protect the lives and properties of free individuals, not to become a self-aggrandizing behemoth, which all governments, particularly monarchies, tend to become. And with respect to government's limits, citizens should be free in private to practice their different faiths and belong to different churches.

However, at the same time, the people who thus organized themselves into that kind of republic believed that their project as a whole, including both its limited government and its free individuals, represented a unique, providential blessing and appointment of God in history. Consequently, the *nation* came to see itself as a chosen people called to serve as a light to the world. Thus, it would become possible in America's future for citizens to remain suspicious of government even while loving the nation. The newly founded republic could see itself, on the one hand, as merely one state among others, needing to calculate carefully and realistically how to negotiate its way in the world in order to preserve itself. On the other hand, it could act in the world with confidence that God had chosen it for a special mission that would bring blessing to the whole world.

America's purposes were never understood by its people and its leaders to be those of any ordinary state. To the contrary, Americans have believed from the beginning that their nation has a divine mission to fulfill, to bring light to the world, a light that was subsequently defined as the light of freedom, democracy, and prosperity rather than the light of biblical righteousness. But America was and remains, in its citizens' minds, a nation that is both righteous and right to be marching at the vanguard of history, leading all nations to their true destiny, to the true end or goal of earthly history. It is, as the Great Seal of the United States (printed on the back of the dollar bill) says, a *novus ordo seclorum*, a new order for the ages, a witness to the end of history.

CHAPTER SEVEN

⌐⌐

Wilsonianism: From Witness to Vanguard

America, in the experience of its citizens, is at one and the same time a particular, limited, federated, republican *state* and an exceptional *people*, or *na-*
tion, with a world-historical mission to fulfill. This national self-understanding
derives from the synthesis of Puritan new-Israelitism and Enlightenment
modernism. Americans see their nation as specially chosen by God to be a
light to the world, the leading witness to the true goal of political history.
This civil-religious identity, though indebted to Judaism and Christianity,
represents a corruption of the biblical story and shows the influence of the
secularizing and sacralizing influences of the Renaissance and the Enlightenment, as well as the influence of Christendom and the Reformation.

As the cultural visions and aspirations of the Enlightenment gained the
upper hand in the public life of the West, most Westerners, including Americans, increasingly infused their states with the public purposes of advancing
education, agriculture, industry, technology, economic growth, individual
freedom, and national greatness. From the Revolution to the Civil War,
Americans also privatized their traditional ecclesiastical religions even as
they united generally around the civil religion of American exceptionalism.
The religiously deep sense of identity and mission that came with the Puritans was infused into the political, economic, technological, and liberal purposes that the republic chose to promote as part of the nation's sacral mission
in the *saeculum* (secular history).

Because of the separation of church and state, one of the major illusions or
misunderstandings that took hold was that government, academic learning,

business, and diverse professions and occupations were no longer religious. A close look at the American experience makes clear, however, that religion and religiosity have never been partitioned off and confined to the activities associated with churches, synagogues, mosques, and personal piety. In the course of the nineteenth century, the dominant American civil religion may have amalgamated nationalism, liberalism, economic growth, and new-Israelitism into a social gospel and religion of democracy, but it functioned and still functions much the same as the religions of covenanted Israel, the polis, the Roman Republic, the Roman Empire, and Christendom functioned in earlier eras. Among the elite who carried and were carried by the American faith was President Woodrow Wilson.

Wilsonianism

Lloyd E. Ambrosius, the preeminent authority on Woodrow Wilson and his foreign policy, says that the World War I president identified "the United States with Christianity, and patriotism with religion." For Wilson, according to Ambrosius, "'America was born a Christian nation. America was born to exemplify that devotion to the elements of righteousness which are derived from the revelations of Holy Scriptures.' This view of the United States enabled Wilson to define the [First World War] as a crusade," and from that "theological perspective, the Presbyterian president decided to call the League [of Nations'] constitution a Covenant and to locate its headquarters in Calvinist Geneva."[1]

Ambrosius provides a detailed interpretation of Wilson's worldview and foreign policy that need not be elaborated upon here.[2] The important thing for our purpose is to show how thoroughly Wilson and the leading journalists and intellectuals of the day understood America's role in the world to be that of a messianic nation bringing redemptive political light and leadership to the world of nations. The goal was democracy, prosperity, and national self-determination for every people so that all could eventually work together harmoniously. As Wilson saw it, this would in many ways represent the fulfillment of the Christian hope for the fulfillment of history.

The United States, according to this interpretation, has no imperialist intentions, no selfish designs on the world. It is simply the servant of God's good for humankind. America's exceptional role in the world, Wilson believed, "served the common welfare of mankind rather than its own imperial ends. 'This is Pan-Americanism,' he explained. 'It has none of the spirit of empire in it. It is the embodiment, the effectual embodiment, of the spirit of law and independence and liberty and mutual service.'"[3] Confident that the

American experience was what every nation in the world wants and needs, Wilson "projected his conception of American nationalism onto the rest of the world, presupposing its universal validity," says Ambrosius. "Viewing the United States as the vanguard, he expected other nations to follow its example and develop in the same way. His vision of the future consequently combined both universalism and unilateralism. While proclaiming a new era of internationalism, the president actually expected others to conform to his particular understanding of American ideals and practices."[4]

Richard Gamble's impressive study of progressive Christianity and the Social Gospel at the end of the nineteenth and the beginning of the twentieth centuries also provides a rich picture of the mind-set of the times. President Wilson's final, reluctant decision to enter World War I, Gamble writes, was announced to the House and Senate on April 2, 1917. In that speech, the president called on America "to make the world safe for democracy"[5] (which reminds one of Emperor Constantine's aim in the fourth century "to make the world safe for Christianity").[6] Congressional debate about whether to back the president continued until Good Friday, when the war resolution was finally approved. Essayist Margaret Prescott Montague, writing in the *Atlantic Monthly*, found in that war resolution the same significance that Christians find in Christ's suffering on Good Friday.

> As Christ's resurrection had followed only after the pain "of Gethsemane, Golgotha, and the Crucifixion," she wrote, so the world's rebirth would require self-denial and even misery. To be worthy of the privilege of bearing the iniquity of mankind, America had to embrace the spirit of sacrifice, put aside every selfish motive, and demonstrate its compassion. . . . This analogy between the United States at war and Christ on the cross served the progressive church well throughout the war.[7]

The progressive clergy, says Gamble, "not only portrayed the United States as a righteous nation engaged in a modern crusade to liberate the worldwide 'Holy Land,' but also identified the war as the collective reenactment of Christ's crucifixion on Calvary."[8]

In 1918, with American soldiers engaged in battle, the *New York Morning Telegraph* editorialized on the relationship between Christianity and national service, noting, according to Gamble,

> that "loyalty to the flag swiftly is coming to be recognized as of equal or even greater virtue than fidelity to a church, a religious sect, or an ordained priesthood." The newspaper preached an amalgam of sacred and secular ideas that reveals much about the mentality of the war: "Soldiers of Moses, soldiers of

Christ, and soldiers of Democracy have become unified in the one Grand Army of Liberty, which is giving the only meaning worth while to . . . 'the Church Militant.'" Soaring even higher, the editors proclaimed that America and the church had become one—"the Bill of rights and the Bible are being reconciled, the Cross and the colors together top the towers of churches, and one of the high degrees of Holy Orders includes the priesthood of patriotism."[9]

Speaking to a reunion of Confederate veterans in June of 1917, Wilson "proposed that God had preserved the union through the Civil War to achieve His transcendent purposes, so that the nation might be 'an instrument in the hands of God to see that liberty is made secure for mankind.' The United States had been saved for this moment in the divine plan."[10] The *New Republic*, "which prided itself on hard-headed realism and practicality," also turned to the language of religious nationalism to convey support for the war. An editorial by Lyman Abbott "presented a righteous America, a pagan Germany, and a war inseparable from God's millennia-long redemptive history," writes Gamble. "True to his expansive progressivism, [Abbott] argued first that America, as a Christian nation, was obligated to serve the other nations. . . . America, representing 'organized Christianity,' understood God's system, while Germany, representing 'organized paganism,' ignored it."[11]

With respect to foreign policy decisions, President Wilson was, of course, the head of a particular state and was therefore compelled by his office to consider American interests and responsibilities first, even if his assumption was that American interests represented the whole world's best interests. The sense of responsibility to protect the pure and righteous American experiment over against a threatening, evil world led Wilson to advocate an expanded vision of the Monroe Doctrine. Prior to American entrance into World War I, he worked to encourage and compel the establishment of governments in Latin America and the Caribbean that would be friendly to the United States. This meant, says Ambrosius, that "the distinction between defensive and offensive acts disappeared as [Wilson] asserted American control over weak Latin American nations. The occupation of Haiti in 1915 and the Dominican Republic in 1916 exemplified this pattern. . . . Although [Wilson] spoke about constitutional liberty, the military intervention that he practiced in these countries overrode their own constitutions. His real objective was American control rather than democracy or merely order."[12]

If we take seriously the American civil religion as a national identity and a mission that established the terms of America's role in the world, we can see that the tendency toward isolationism, on the one hand, and toward internationalism, on the other hand, are two sides of the same coin. In order for America to retain its identity as light to the world, it must, above all, survive and protect its position on the hill: thus, isolationism. But insofar as the American witness and influence manage to extend farther and farther into the world, then America must follow up to protect the fruits of the success of its messianic calling: thus, internationalism. Defensive and offensive acts may amount to the same thing, depending on the opportunities and the dangers of particular situations. This is the context in which to understand Wilson's plan, developed during the war, for a future League of Nations. The League, writes Ambrosius, "represented the worldwide expansion of the Monroe Doctrine. 'I am proposing, as it were,' Wilson explained, 'that the nations should with one accord adopt the doctrine of President Monroe as the doctrine of the world: that no nation should seek to extend its polity over any other nation or people, but that every people should be left free to determine its own polity, its own way of development, unhindered, unthreatened, unafraid, the little along with the great and powerful.'"[13]

The difficulty is that the ideal of a world of free states, each assuming its "separate and equal station" "among the powers of the earth" fails to address the problems of international governance and dispute settlement, as well as the question of which "nations" should be allowed to become self-determining. The first of these problems was one of the most contentious in the negotiations to create the League. According to Ambrosius, Wilson's isolationist leanings help to explain his approach to negotiations. Wilson did not want the United States to be bound automatically ahead of time by obligations of enforcement. The United States needed to remain above the fray in order to make sure that the League worked and that America's own pure "light" was preserved. He therefore "hoped that the League could guarantee the national self-determination of its members through peaceful means rather than military force."[14] In the negotiations, the French wanted the League to have a built-in means of enforcing the peace settlement that would end the war. They criticized Wilson's proposed covenant for failing "to provide methods for an immediate military response" to illegitimate aggression. The Americans and the British, on the other hand, "argued that the League would maintain peace and prevent aggression primarily by providing for a cooling-off period during which moral suasion could operate."[15] This was Wilson the international idealist.

With regard to the question of national independence, Wilson's idea of national self-determination was more a matter of history than of ethnicity. Not every people who claims the right of self-government is actually prepared to be an independent, self-determining state, in Wilson's view. People need to develop in a political way to become self-governing before they deserve to be recognized as independent among the nations. American nationalism was, in fact, Wilson's "norm for the world."[16] According to Ambrosius, most interpreters of Wilson, including Henry Kissinger, have misunderstood Wilson on this point. "Instead of attributing primacy to ethno-cultural factors, [Wilson] understood nationalism as the consequence of historical development. A people's national consciousness, Wilson believed, was shaped by the historical process, and this process involved political leadership. Civic affinities were more important than primordial ones."[17]

For this reason, Wilson, the realist, did not rush to encourage the proliferation of new states at the end of World War I. He was willing to recognize as new nations only those "that emerged from the collapse of the Russian, German, Austro-Hungarian, and Ottoman empires. . . . Even there, he hesitated to recognize the governments of new nations until he was certain they possessed the historical qualities of nationality that he witnessed in the American experience."[18] For many former colonies of European empires Wilson advocated "mandates" under the League of Nations rather than independent statehood. For example, he approved the distribution of Germany's former colonies to the British, French, and others as mandates. This was simply "colonialism in all but name," says Ambrosius, but Wilson thought it was different from colonialism because the governments holding the mandates "would exercise mandatory instead of sovereign rights. He expected them to fulfill the same mission in their League mandates that the United States had assigned itself in the Philippines."[19]

There can be little doubt that American exceptionalism included the conviction that the American state structure and the historical process of achieving it were the model for all peoples in the world. Consequently, when we think of Muslim distress at the defeat of the Ottoman Empire, we need to recognize that the offense in Muslim eyes was not only the infidels' rollback of the *dar al-islam* but the imposition of the dominant Western model of governance on the fragments of the Ottoman Empire. The imposition of Western mandates and state structures in this instance was connected directly to the American-led reorganization of the world following victorious battle. And Wilson's identification of the war as a crusade for freedom and democracy made the offense all the more grievous.

Ambrosius sums up "Wilsonianism" in four principles: "(1) national self-determination, which affirmed both national sovereignty and democratic self-government; (2) Open Door economic globalization, which favored a competitive marketplace for trade and financial investments across national borders; (3) collective security, which found expression in the postwar League of Nations; and (4) progressive history, which undergirded the Wilsonian vision of a better future for the world."[20] Because Wilson thought of the peoples of the world as living under a single moral order, he believed that a League of Nations could become something like what Emmerich de Vattel called a "kind of republic."[21] The moral pressure of a pre-agreed international covenant, which articulated the ideal of self-determination for every state, would supposedly lead to the peaceful settlement of disputes and guarantee each state's sovereignty. But absent an international or transnational government or automatic means of enforcement, the League would, in the end, depend on American hegemony or a balance of power among major powers, to which Wilson was actually opposed. In 1917 Wilson said, "There must be, not a balance of power, but a community of power; not organized rivalries, but an organized common peace."[22]

Here was an idealist vision of internationalism based on Western commitment to sovereign states, an internationalism *without* a cosmopolitan, or even significant international, means of governance to enforce the self-evident norms written in the heart of every rational creature. There would be no institutional transcendence of the state, particularly of the American state. There would be only a growing moral consensus among the peoples of the world as they came to see the American vision of the world as the right one. However, if moral suasion, pushed upon recalcitrant peoples by the mature nations of the world, failed to keep a minimum tranquillity of order in this world, then serious war could break out again in the future. All the more important, therefore, that the United States keep itself free from entangling obligations in order to be able to preserve its sovereign purity as exemplar and reservoir of virtue and strength in the world.

Wilson's proposed League was the expression of a hope that America's example would draw people throughout the world to share the same faith and desire for freedom, leading them to develop democratic states like the American republic, so that all people could be free and satisfied governing themselves within their own borders. Force would seldom need to be used to keep the peace, but when used it would reaffirm the universal moral principles of the system. Wilson was either unconscious of, or simply unwilling to acknowledge publicly, the dependence of the entire system on American hegemony of the League.[23]

Making the World Safe for Democracy

The joining of Greco-Roman-Enlightenment influences to a Puritanized new-Israelitism had given shape to a small American republic, which, by the end of World War I, was on its way to becoming a colossus. Of course, the war among major empires that created the vacuum America helped to fill was not the result of American intentions and imperial designs. The international position of the United States at that time, and its even more formidable position today, came about not by the conquering achievements of Roman legions but by a combination of American participation with allies in wars it did not start and by building alliances and cooperative international organizations during and following the two world wars and the Cold War. Throughout the period from the Civil War until today, American strength has also grown because of economic, scientific, and technological achievements that outpaced those of other countries.

In certain respects, the outcome of World War I appeared to be a divine gift to the chosen nation, a confirmation of America's mission to the world. That perception may also help to explain why American citizens continued to think of themselves as nonaggressive, nonimperial innocents in a dark and dangerous world even as the United States continued to grow in worldwide strength. The federal government had been set up to protect and defend the freedom of the American people in their several states, which had joined together to free themselves from the unjust oppression of a colonizing power. Americans never wanted too strong a central government and certainly not a world government, even if such a government would be their own. The country as a whole had only commercial and communicative aims, not imperial, military designs.

Wilson tried for as long as he could to keep the United States out of Europe's war. When he finally decided to enter, it was, as he saw it, for purely defensive purposes to help save the world and the United States from disaster. In the League of Nations he believed the American federal government would continue to have only a defensive purpose: to protect free and self-governing peoples working to develop and express their freedom and independence. Every American military foray into the world would be, by definition, only a response to evil, a reaction to threats from the outside, in order to defend the good city on a hill.

This myth that the United States has never sought power but has had "greatness thrust upon it" is a dominant story line of American self-identity, according to Andrew Bacevich. Few scholars specializing in American diplomatic history today accept the idea, but "in practice, the [twentieth-century] myth of the 'reluctant superpower'—Americans asserting themselves only under duress and then always for the noblest of purposes—reigns today as the master narrative explaining (and justifying) the nation's exercise of global power."[24] The American federal government's early purchase of huge tracts of land to the West to expand the frontier and its later preemptive forays in Latin America, the Pacific, and Southeast Asia were not thought of as self-aggrandizing deeds. They were all intended to protect the zone of freedom—the innocent goodness of the chosen nation—in which political, economic, and religious freedom are, by God's providential blessing, being perfected so that America and all freedom-loving peoples can spread the light of progress to the whole world. It just so happens that by 2001, the front lines of America's defense forces could be found in the farthest corners of the globe. So much so that immediately after 9/11, the cry went up for "homeland defense" (later changed to "homeland security"), which was quite an irony given the hundreds of billions of dollars spent each year by the U.S. Department of Defense. Yet, America's major military forces are positioned so far away and in so many parts of the world that an American citizen could feel inadequately defended at the actual borders of U.S. territory.

What requires explanation is why the American people and leaders are blind to the imperial characteristics of their colossal global hegemony. The peculiarity originates in the earliest self-interpretation of the nation as a city on a hill, whose calling is to exemplify the political truth of universal history. America's calling is not to achieve that goal by military conquest. Yet, insofar as the civil-religious calling bears witness to a universal goal, the whole world must always be kept in American sights as both a field of opportunity for freedom's expansion and as a potential threat to freedom's survival. Nonimperial America must, therefore, be prepared to fend off all imperialist ventures of those who try to threaten the progress of freedom and who may thereby destroy America and its mission. Niall Ferguson calls this the "imperialism of anti-imperialism." When, at the end of World War II, the United States succeeded in helping Japan and Germany to rebuild, says Ferguson, the American aim was not altruistic and philanthropic. On the contrary, it was motivated by "the fear of a rival empire"—something that would continue throughout the Cold War. "For an empire in denial [the United States], there is really only one way to act imperially with a clear conscience, and that is to combat someone else's imperialism. In the doctrine of containment, born in 1947, the United States hit on the perfect ideology for its own peculiar kind of empire: the imperialism of anti-imperialism."[25]

The peculiarity of America's exceptional mission to make the world safe for democracy can be highlighted by comparing and contrasting it with the two most important parallels of recent and current history. The first is (was) the Soviet communist mission, which took hold with the 1917 revolution during World War I, and the second is the mission of Islam, which experienced perhaps its greatest crisis at the same time. The parallel is not in the content of communist ideology, Islamic jihad, and the American mission. Rather, the parallel is to be found in the common conviction that history is moving toward the fulfillment of a universal human destiny and that the primary carrier of the means to reach that destiny is a specially chosen vanguard that must overcome diametric opposition.

Communist ideology is a secularized version of Christianity that sacralizes the proletariat for a world-historical revolution. For Christianity, the mission of Christ's disciples is to bear witness through their way of life to the coming of Christ's kingdom. For the Russian Orthodox Church, which supported the tsar headquartered in Moscow (the Third Rome), movement toward the city of God was supported by a centralized, hierarchical, caesaropapist empire. In Lenin's and Stalin's hands, Russian caesaropapism was transformed into the Communist Party's dictatorship, which stood in for the proletariat, the substitute for the church and its Messiah. The proletarian revolution was supposed to produce the "new man" as an outcome of the final judgment— the communist revolution. That final judgment was supposed to come about through the revolutionary liberation of the proletariat and would bring an end to the state as well as to capitalism. Western capitalist countries, like the United States, were judged to be reactionary bastions of oppression that had to be kept at bay or destroyed because they threatened the progress of socialism moving toward communism.

Given the reality of modern states, the Russian attempt to foment a worldwide communist revolution was not directed, as it should have been, by the working classes in all countries but rather by the Russian imperial state, renamed the Union of Soviet Socialist Republics (U.S.S.R.) after Lenin's Bolsheviks took over. Consequently, contradictions and inconsistencies appeared in the Soviet Union's actual practices because the effort to advance Russian state interests in a global, balance-of-power system frequently ran counter to the communist ideology's goal of uniting the working classes throughout the world and dissolving the state altogether. The communist proletarian vision was not carried by an independent, working-class organization on earth but by the powerful Soviet-bloc states and revolutionary movements supported by those states. The Soviet Union and its allies were confronted chiefly by American and European states that cooperated to deter and contain the Soviet Union. In the end, a worldwide proletariat never materialized and thus did not prove capable of substituting for the biblical Messiah and church. With the collapse of the Soviet empire, communist ideology suffered a major, if not fatal, setback.

Now consider Islam. Muslims, as we saw earlier, anticipated the progress of Islam as an unstoppable expansion of the *dar al-islam*—the territory in which submission to Allah is observed—which would eventually overcome the oppositional *dar al-harb*—the territory of conflict in which submission to Allah is not observed. The forward movement of history would be powered and defended by jihad in its broad sense of a personal and social struggle for God. For Muslims, including radical Islamists, the human struggle is clearly a divine mandate. What has never been clear, however, is the specific normative responsibility of political rulers for the advancement of Islam. Prior to the rise of the Western state, Islam was carried by various regimes—Umayyads, Abbasids, Ottomans—and resisted by others, including the Holy Roman and Byzantine empires. In modern times, Islam has been carried or resisted by states: Turkey, Egypt, Iran, India, Greece, Great Britain, and the United States, to name only a few. The Muslim obligation of jihad, or holy war, continues to be upheld even without a general consensus among Muslims about when and how force should be used against enemies. Consequently, the meaning and identity of the *dar al-islam* has become fragmented and threatened both from within and without. There is still no Muslim consensus about the normative identity and role of the state, which Islam had no hand in creating. Thus, even though Muslims throughout the world now live and work in the context of states, Muslim understanding of personal responsibility and eschatological destiny does not yield a clear notion of what the state's role should be in the achievement of the *dar al-islam*. This is part of what has given an opening to the Islamist radicals, whose tactics are not approved by Muslims in general.

In comparison with Russian communism and contemporary Islam, the American identity and sense of mission fall somewhere between the other two. For many, if not most, Americans, Providence (not the biblical Trinity) is somehow both behind and ahead of vanguard America, just as Allah is behind and ahead of the progress of Islam. But the goal trumpeted as the public mission of the United States now has a this-worldly character, namely, freedom, democracy, and prosperity, rather than an otherworldly character. The goal of American messianism is quite clearly that of a world filled with differentiated, limited, independent, and democratic states, trading freely and living prosperously in peace with one another. American civil religion does not strive for a final renovation of the world by means of a holy war or a proletarian revolution. Moreover, the American civil religion is tied to a particular polity—the United States. Americans believe in political liberty and democracy (and thus in a modest and limited state) and many want liberty precisely in order to exercise their personal faith in the coming, transstate kingdom of God. American opposition to Nazi and communist totalitarianism arose in large measure because of antagonism toward the universalist, undifferentiated, revolutionary, aims of those ideologies. The American mission is, therefore, quite distinct from both the Russian communist and the Islamic missions.

These three movements toward history's goal have been borne along by different sacral *carriers*. Islam is represented by a religious community whose crisis today is due, in part, to the fact that it has been without a primary political carrier at least since the end of the Ottoman Empire. It is not clear whether Muslims are ready and willing to be satisfied with an "ecclesiastical" or "synagogal" form of identity inside territorial states that may be religiously pluralistic and thus unconcerned about a clear line between the *dar al-islam* and the *dar al-harb*. Communism, as a comprehensive, religiously deep ideology, was supposed to be carried by a united, worldwide proletariat but was instead picked up by a small Russian vanguard on behalf of a global proletariat that never materialized. The American civil-religious mission is carried by one state in particular on behalf of the whole world's political destiny. In contrast to the carriers of the communist and Muslim missions, the American carrier is still very much intact with a definite state identity.

The *realm* in which these three missions have expected to find their fulfillment is nothing less than the whole earth; they are all universalistic and thus destined to conflict with one another. Prior to the triumph of the universal good, each visionary movement has expected conflict between good and evil, truth and error. The realm of truth, goodness, and righteousness for Muslims is the *dar al-islam*. The realm of truth, goodness, and righteousness for the Soviet socialists is (was) the *dar al-communism*. And for the American republic, the earthly realm of truth, goodness, and righteousness is the *dar al-freedom* or the *dar al-democracy*. Each of these "holy lands" is challenged or threatened by a diametric antagonist—a *dar al-harb*—that needs to be converted, transformed, set aside, conquered, or destroyed. Historically speaking, Islam's *dar al-islam* kept expanding for several centuries but subsequently suffered setbacks of major proportions. Islam remains a compelling way of life for millions of people today even if many Muslims are perplexed and angry about why Islam has lost ground and become fragmented. The *dar al-communism* projected by the U.S.S.R. expanded rapidly (in the guise of state socialism and Soviet imperialism) into vast territories but collapsed almost as quickly, all in one century; there are very few communities of communist faith left in the world. The American-sought *dar al-freedom* began its expansion much later than Islam's *dar al-islam* yet more than a century before the rise of Russian communism. Today, it is the progress of the *dar al-freedom* that appears to be the most rapidly expanding political realm in the world, having withstood Russian communist imperialism and, thus far, the most threatening of radical Islamist forces.

Is it correct, however, to identify the United States as the vanguard of the *dar al-freedom*? Is that not the mistake of American exceptionalism rooted in the new-Israelite myth updated by Wilsonianism? There are, after all, many other democracies in the world, interdependent with the United States in NATO, the United Nations, and various international economic organizations. Moreover, as was evident in Wilson's foreign policy, the American state does not always have as its first priority the advancement of freedom and democracy in the world. Sometimes the United States chooses to work with and support illiberal and even antidemocratic states (like the Soviet Union in World War II, Iran under the shah, and Pakistan, Egypt, and Saudi Arabia today) in order to advance its own interests, which, from its point of view, are always ultimately good for the world and for the ultimate advancement of freedom and democracy. Here again we see the extent to which the real responsibilities of practical state governance necessarily restrict America's ideological mission to lead the world to the global kingdom of freedom and democracy.

The vanguard of world progress, in American eyes, is certainly the United States, whose state interests and balance-of-power politics must often take precedence over the promotion of democracy elsewhere and may also take precedence over American support of other self-governing states, including other democratic states. After all, from the viewpoint of American civil religion, if the United States were ever to be dealt a lethal blow, then democracy and freedom everywhere would be threatened. All of history would be in doubt. If the messianic nation fails, from whence comes salvation and the fulfillment of history? Yet, this pride of preeminence keeps Americans from seeing the extent to which they are dependent on others, tied up in mutual obligations, and merely one state among many in the world.

The Post–Cold War Challenge for America

In the last fifteen years, the rise of the United States to the position of sole superpower may have radically changed the international balance of power among states. Are those changes also now transforming American self-identity and the American mission? There is no longer a relative equality among a variety of powerful states such that balance-of-power strategies can be counted on to keep a tranquillity of order in this world. Nor does there appear to be any significant counterempire at work, requiring the exertion of America's anti-imperial imperialism. That may be one of the reasons why the threat of terrorism now looms so large in the American imagination. Anti-imperialism requires a *major* threat to the United States. Thus, American defense expenditures continue to rise, preventive wars are in the works, and fears of global threats to freedom and democracy are as strong as ever.

Does any or all of this suggest that the United States should, on its own, seize the moment and try as aggressively as possible to expand the *dar al-freedom*, as defined by America's view of the world's destiny? Should the United States attempt to do this modestly by making sure it uses "soft power" as well as "hard power," as Joseph Nye argues,[26] and by trying to exercise "global leadership" rather than "global dominance," as Zbigniew Brzezinski urges?[27] Or should the United States do this with much greater boldness and aggressiveness, even purposefully building an "empire of freedom," as John Lewis Gaddis and Ferguson suggest may be legitimate and as Charles Krauthammer believes is imperative?[28]

Or should the United States perhaps retreat from international projections of power and concentrate on trying to reform its own city on a hill so it can become a better exemplar for the world? In view of the limits of America's military and economic power, even at the height of its influence, Paul Kennedy's lessons from history suggest caution about empire building. The United States, says Kennedy,

> cannot avoid confronting the two great tests which challenge the *longevity* of every major power that occupies the "number one" position in world affairs: whether, in the military/strategical realm, it can preserve a reasonable balance between the nation's perceived defense requirements and the means it possesses to maintain those commitments; and whether, as an intimately related point, it can preserve the technological and economic bases of its power from relative erosion in the face of the ever-shifting patterns of global production. . . . [T]he United States now runs the risk, so familiar to historians of the rise and fall of previous Great Powers, of what might roughly be called "imperial overstretch": that is to say, decision-makers in Washington must face the awkward and enduring fact that the sum total of the United States' global interests and obligations is nowadays far larger than the country's power to defend them all simultaneously.[29]

Or, as yet another alternative, should the United States perhaps relinquish its myth of new-Israelite exceptionalism and adopt a different, more cooperative, pluralistic, and multilateral mission in the world? Clyde Prestowitz urges his fellow citizens to "rethink American exceptionalism."[30] "We have an admirable democracy, but it is not the only possible democracy and not always the best possible democracy," writes Prestowitz. "We have a very successful economy, but so do others, and ours is not in all ways the best. We have a good system of justice with much to admire, but so do others, and ours is not always the best."[31] If Americans turn away from pridefulness on those counts, they might find it possible to construct a new basis for their sense of exceptionalism, Prestowitz seems to suggest. "An America that stressed its tolerance rather than its might, its tradition of open inquiry rather than its way of life, and that asked for God's blessing on all the world's people and not just its own, would be the America the world desperately wants."[32]

How should America now take its stand with or against the world?

CHAPTER EIGHT

Another American Century?

"What is this thing called hegemony?" asks Niall Ferguson. "Is it merely a euphemism for *empire*, or does it describe the role of the primus inter pares, the leader of an alliance, rather than a ruler over subject peoples?"[1] There have been different kinds of empires, says Ferguson, many of which do not involve the direct governance of subject peoples. Once this is understood, the term "hegemony" can be dropped, and the United States can be recognized for the kind of empire it is: an informal one that prefers indirect to direct rule. Taking into account an even greater number of characteristics, Ferguson characterizes the American empire this way:

> It goes without saying that it is a liberal democracy and market economy, though its polity has some illiberal characteristics and its economy a surprisingly high level of state intervention ("mixed" might be more accurate than "market"). It is primarily concerned with its own security and maintaining international communications and, secondarily, with ensuring access to raw materials (principally, though not exclusively, oil). It is also in the business of providing a limited number of public goods: peace, by intervening against some bellicose regimes and in some civil wars; freedom of the seas and skies for trade; and a distinctive form of "conversion" usually called Americanization, which is carried out less by old-style Christian missionaries than by the exporters of American consumer goods and entertainment. Its methods of formal rule are primarily military in character; its methods of informal rule rely heavily on nongovernmental organizations and corporations and, in some cases, local elites.[2]

With regard to the "informal" and "indirect" character of the American empire, Ferguson adds, "It conspicuously lacks the voracious appetite for territorial expansion overseas that characterized the empires of the West European seaboard. It prefers the idea that foreigners will Americanize themselves without the need for formal rule."[3]

Security in Freedom

How can we explain the emergence of this peculiar kind of "hegemony," which most Americans are reluctant to call an empire? U.S. preoccupation with its own security is related not only to the fact that it is a state, like other states, with an obligation to protect its own citizens; the United States is also, in its own eyes, the exceptional nation with a world-historical mission, and its security is of paramount importance. Given America's view of history, there is also nothing surprising about its expectation "that foreigners will Americanize themselves without the need for formal rule." If the goal of history is democracy and freedom for all people, and if America is the model, then people throughout the world need to build their own states. As a matter of principle, *direct* rule of the world from the top, by a single imperial authority, violates the American view of human nature, self-governance, and its own responsibility. Yet, it is also clear that in order for the goal of freedom and democracy to be reached by all peoples, America must remain unassailable as both exemplar and vanguard. This explains the American preference for military rule even if the defense of freedom requires American military posts on the other side of the globe. The United States does not want direct control of, and responsibility for, other nations' territories, but rather defense of the *dar al-freedom*, in which America is positioned at the center. Furthermore, precisely because the United States sees itself as a democratic state with a free economy serving as the exemplar nation, it must be able to communicate globally, to trade freely, and to allow its economic and technological achievements to enliven the world. In the United States most of society's functions are carried out by means of free enterprise and nongovernmental organizations, so that is the kind of society the United States will try, informally, to promote elsewhere in the world.

None of what Ferguson describes is considered to be imperialistic by most Americans because, by definition, a liberal state—a free and democratic state—imposes nothing. Democracy is simply the expression of people working together in freedom and needing protection from a government they can hold accountable. The United States, in other words, is at the service of (and itself the leading exemplar of) the freedom that God (or Nature) has implanted in every people as their own true aim and desire. This is why one of the primary "public goods" the United States wants to provide to the world is, in Ferguson's words, a form of conversion, which he calls "Americanization." This is a universal public good in the eyes of Americans because they have taken into their own identity that which they are convinced is the universal standard for all. Many Americans interpret the U.S. Constitution this way, not as one among many basic laws but as the clearest articulation—the very representation—of the natural and universal law for any political order. Thus, they do not think of their hegemony as a matter of forcing American will and interests on others. Instead, they believe America is merely helping others to actualize the universal law of freedom for themselves.

This was the mind-set of the founders; this was Wilson's vision for the League of Nations; this was the substance and the hope that American leaders invested in the United Nations; this is the spirit of George W. Bush's 2002 National Security Strategy (NSS). "Freedom," says President Bush in his introduction to the NSS, "is the non-negotiable demand of human dignity; the birthright of every person—in every civilization." In its present position of power, he writes, "the United States will use this moment of opportunity to extend the benefits of freedom across the globe. We will actively work to bring the hope of democracy, development, free markets, and free trade to every corner of the world."

Does this sound globally imperialistic? It certainly may sound like that to many people in other countries who know that the speaker behind these words is the president of the most powerful state in the world, who happens to believe that his country has the obligation "to extend" freedom to the others. Nevertheless, the ideology fueling this morally charged language insists that America itself is but the servant of a larger subject acting in history, namely, freedom (which earlier Americans would have called Providence and the Puritans would have called God). The Bush vision is nothing less than freedom-idealism. The opening words of the president's NSS make it clear that America is but a vehicle, albeit the leading vehicle, at the service of the expanding *dar al-freedom* as it works to overcome the *dar al-oppression* of totalitarianism, dictatorships, and terrorism. "The great struggles of the twentieth century between liberty and totalitarianism ended with a decisive victory for the forces of freedom—and a single sustainable model for national success: freedom, democracy, and free enterprise," Bush says. That single sustainable model and leading force for freedom just happens to be what America believes itself to be—the privileged recipient of freedom's first prize, the prize that everyone else also surely wants to win.

How does this "empire of freedom" fit together with what Ferguson describes as the "peculiarity of American imperialism—perhaps its principal shortcoming," namely, "its excessively short time horizon"?[4] Americans do not expect that others should need much time to actualize self-government and freedom once they have the opportunity to do so. Once people have liberated themselves from their oppressors or have been liberated with the help of others, they should rise to self-governing freedom rather quickly because that is only natural. Their histories and predemocratic cultures should be as unimportant to them as they are unimportant to Americans. It may have taken the United States and other Western states a relatively long time to become independent and democratic and to develop their free economies. But now that these self-evident expressions of a universal human nature—particularly the American model—are available for all to see, relatively little time should be required for others to learn from them and to develop their own institutional equivalents. The American military, therefore, does not exist for the purpose of exercising sustained rule over others or for nation building but rather for the purpose of liberation—removing impediments to freedom.

Moreover, Americans are not prepared to pay a high price for what others should do for themselves. President Bush asked very little of the American people to fight the war in Iraq. The freedom of Americans to buy, sell, and enjoy tax relief so they can have an even greater measure of freedom should not be interrupted by war, even a war on terrorism that might never end. The war is something the military can handle because of its preeminent power and advanced technology. The American people need not be overly burdened by those responsibilities. In fact, the reason for overthrowing Saddam Hussein was to protect American freedom and to liberate others. Since others should do their own nation-building once they have been liberated, the time horizon in the American psyche for foreign engagements is very short indeed.

Not surprisingly, this view of the world is an extension of the American idea of its own liberal state. The government of a free republic should act primarily to protect the lives and properties of its citizens, using military force only when necessary to do so. There is, in this view of the state, not very much of a public commons that needs maintenance, enhancement, and heavy investment. Citizenship means the right to enjoy freedom and economic opportunity, not the burden of paying for large public bureaucracies that become a drag on freedom even as they try to solve problems that individuals and nongovernmental organizations should solve by themselves. Consequently, the idea that the American government should be involved for an extended period of time in nation-building elsewhere in the world, when that is not even its job at home, is a foreign concept. If the U.S. military must be huge and requires heavy public investment, that is legitimate because the military is essential for the disposal of tyrants and the defense of freedom from aggression.

The way most Americans see it, the twentieth century confirmed the correctness of their view of the world. Throughout the century the United States expanded economically, endured the Great Depression, and led the world in scientific and technological development. When its military had to reach across the oceans on behalf of the world, it was primarily to defend allies. Hitler's regime and the Soviet Union are now relics of the past, and America remains free, prosperous, and growing. Therefore, Providence continues to validate the American experiment, urging Americans to maintain their leading mission in and for the world. The twentieth century was the American century, and there is no reason why we should not expect the twenty-first century to be more of the same. It may be true that Americans tend to overestimate the extent to which they *achieved* or *earned* their global hegemony. The wealth of natural resources within the borders of what is now the United States; the protection provided by the two oceans; the energy of millions of immigrants; the collapse of European empires; and two world wars that left a huge vacuum of power for the United States to fill—all of these factors are more like endowments to, rather than achievements of, the United States. Yet, even these unearned "gifts" are typically interpreted as a providential sign confirming American exceptionalism. And to say this is not to underestimate the cost of American lives and the investment of American dollars and military might in the two world wars and the Cold War.

If America's preferred method of formal rule is military, as Ferguson argues, that is due, in large measure, to what transpired in the twentieth century's two world wars and the Cold War. The United States was a late, reluctant entrant into both wars. The outcome in both cases was a greatly increased American military capability. Furthermore, the structure of both the United Nations and NATO presupposed America's military presence throughout the world. The United States became the originator, the dominant organizer, the leading supplier, and the chief authority of an international defense establishment for Europe, the Far East, and the high seas throughout the world. Even after Japan and the Europeans, with help from American investments, recovered and became the world's second and third major economic regions, the American military establishment remained. Simply by looking at a map of military positions in the world, including the high seas, one can see the extent of the American empire. But to Americans, those military forces were either invited by allies or required for defensive reasons, and they now contribute to the defense of many nations. This is not an empire; it is just good neighborliness, and Americans pay more attention to their own "good works" than they do to the fact that they are beneficiaries of the cooperative efforts of many others.

In this informal empire, freedom is primary, meaning that self-government comes first. Security is secondary—the means by which a free people protects its freedom. Military security exists *for* the sake of freedom. Yet, there is another sense in which Americans believe that security is found *in* freedom. Unfree people, tyrannical oppressors, aggressive imperialists, and terrorists are the ones who destabilize the world and make everyone insecure. If all peoples were free and self-governing in their own states, then security would be found *in* that freedom. This is part of American idealism—freedom-idealism—articulated so clearly in Wilson's view of the League of Nations. The United States does not want to build or run an empire but only to help make the world safe for democracy, because in democracy the whole world will find security. When all people are free and self-governing, every country's military forces will be kept within its borders and will be drawn down to practically nothing. Nevertheless, until security materializes *within* that kind of freedom, then the forces of those who are already free, led by America, must help establish security *for* freedom. And that may require a very strong military indeed.

It is not so easy for Americans to see the tension here between the "for" and the "in" of security because the two are interdependent in our *identity* and our not-yet-fulfilled *mission*. It is easier to see the tension similar to this one that existed in the former Soviet Union, the tension between the reality of totalitarian governance and the ideal future that communist ideology promised. The communist goal was the classless, stateless society of the future; the reality of the Soviet Union was a heavily armed, dictatorial, class-structured society. A harsh, dictatorial regime was needed, said the Leninists and Stalinists, in order to defend against the enemies of communism, namely, the United States and its European allies, until the communist order could be realized. Soviet leaders believed that they were defending the inevitable future from the dangerous present.

Americans do not believe in dictatorship or socialist totalitarianism as a means of building a world filled with democratic states. But the tension between ends and means exists in the American way of life nonetheless. In the end, ideally, there will be little or no need of security *for* freedom because everyone will be enjoying security *in* freedom. But until that day comes (assume forever), the vanguard of freedom's future may need to operate a massive security force in the present.

Explaining it this way helps to account for why we Americans cannot see our hegemony as having imperialistic characteristics. Our military is simply working to secure the future of freedom against the present lack thereof. Since our identity and mission are as much about the ideal future as they are about the concrete present, we see ourselves in some respects as operating from out of the future—a future that we already claim as part of our present identity, but a future that is not yet. This public mind-set derives from the secularization of the Christian view of history via Puritan new-Israelitism and Enlightenment modernism. Christians believe, as the apostle Paul explained in his letters, that their ultimate citizenship is in the city of God and that because of Christ's resurrection they can, by *faith*, live proleptically in the present world as if already raised with Christ. The Puritans interpreted their New England experiment as a proleptic participation by faith in the city of God. Their city on a hill, if ordered properly, was an anticipatory sign of the eschatological city. When that sense of identity was taken over by the new republic as a whole, it infused Americans with the conviction that their city on a hill was illumined by a beacon shining back from the end of history. This is why Americans live oriented toward the future and do not live from out of the past. The national identity comes from the way Americans see their republic as both representing and anticipating the fulfillment of a freedom that has not yet been fully realized. And since in the end all nations will live in freedom, the exercise of American military leadership to stave off threats to freedom is not imperialism but merely the defense of the certain future against the dangerous present. To rework Ferguson, what appears to be America's anti-imperial imperialism is its anti-imperial freedom-idealism. The American republic is wired—constituted—as a community of proleptic, civil-religious faith.

A Force for Freedom

One of the especially striking things about the Bush administration's NSS is how much its articulation of a plan to defend America is a plan to secure the entire world for a very long time to come. The document proposes nothing less than an American military imperium as the long-term, though still temporary, order of "freedom" for the whole world.

Because the primary theme of the NSS is the strengthening of American military forces to face contemporary global realities, one might assume that its aim would be to recover a realist approach to foreign policy. To the contrary, the NSS is an *idealist* tract, calling for the shaping of a new world order. America will be secure only after the whole world is free. The word "freedom" is never defined with legal and political precision in the document, and that allows it to refer to many things. It stands for American independence and sovereignty, as well as for the opposite of regimes like Saddam Hussein's. Freedom stands for the target that terrorists want to destroy as well as for the substance of the new international order as a whole. The NSS presents freedom as a transcendent mission, a supranational standard, a universal eschatological goal, and a world-historical spirit, to which the United States and other countries must simply subordinate themselves. This is freedom-idealism at its grandest, immunizing American sovereignty and vanguard leadership against any conceivable kind of subjection to international and transnational governance. The universal ideal is the American particularity universalized. But the language of idealism makes the American pretension seem humble. The United States is merely a humble servant of the world-historical spirit of freedom, which is the higher subject of history now ushering in the final order of the ages.

But how is freedom working its will in history? Why is the Bush administration so confident it has divined the future? The implied answer to these questions is as old as America: the United States is the leading representative, defender, and messianic vanguard of freedom's universality. We know the future because we know ourselves and our mission. The NSS presents freedom as simultaneously America's own national interest and every person's and every nation's birthright. The United States is the ambassador of freedom, and therefore what America does militarily in the world will ipso facto advance the freedom of all. What is good for the United States is good for the world because the chief mediator of freedom is leading the world to its true destiny, to the triumph over all its foes. The NSS authors believe that a truly free international system will be one in which all states serve the same master. Freedom is lord, and America is its prophet. The following paragraph from the document's concluding section, "Transforming America's National Security Institutions," summarizes in a nutshell the case for America as the leading force *for* freedom:

> The presence of American forces overseas is one of the most profound symbols of the U.S. commitments to allies and friends. Through our willingness to use force in our own defense and in defense of others, the United States demonstrates its resolve to maintain a balance of power that favors freedom. To contend with uncertainty and to meet the many security challenges we face, the United States will require bases and stations within and beyond Western Europe and Northeast Asia, as well as temporary access arrangements for the long-distance deployment of U.S. forces (29).

There is not even a hint here that America's global military dominance might be viewed by other countries as something less than a welcome gift or a confirmation of their own identities and missions. The certainty of President Bush's conviction does not require even a nod in the direction of asking for the consent and cooperation of other nations. The United States *will require* bases and stations wherever and whenever it needs them.

Furthermore, in addition to the build-up of American military strength "beyond challenge," the Bush administration will brook no outside legal interference either: "We will take the action necessary to ensure that our efforts to meet our global security commitments and protect Americans are not impaired by the potential for investigations, inquiry, or prosecution by the International Criminal Court (ICC), whose jurisdiction does not extend to Americans and which we do not accept" (31). It is fine for other countries to subscribe to the ICC, which the United States even helped to design. But America must remain independent of all international bonds, even if other nations of the world would like to see us submit to such bonds for the sake of their security and interests. From the point of view of the NSS, freedom for any and all will be defined within the bounds of American military preeminence and American sovereignty.

This approach to the world is exactly what is needed today, affirms Tod Lindberg. The White House is "firmly aligning itself with Francis Fukuyama's universalist 'end of history' vision of the spread of the recognition by human beings of each other as free and equal."[5] President Bush's speech at West Point in June 2002, a forerunner to the NSS, "is nothing less than the founding document of a new international order with American power at its center and the spread of freedom as its aim."[6] Lindberg even goes so far as to say that what President Bush "is now promoting with this liberty doctrine is not [just] a model. It is the answer and it is final."[7] On the one hand, according to Bush at West Point (sounding like Wilson and many other American presidents), "America has no empire to extend or utopia to establish. We wish for others only what we wish for ourselves—safety from violence, the rewards of liberty, and the hope for a better life." On the other hand, as Lindberg happily explains, the president made this statement from a position of unprecedented strength and with "chilling implications": "America has, and intends to keep, military strengths beyond challenge—thereby making the destabilizing arms races of other eras pointless, and limiting rivalries to trade and other pursuits of peace."[8]

The message could not be more imperial. Now that the United States has the power to do so, it must fulfill its mission, ordained from on high, to protect the *dar al-freedom*, which belongs to the entire human race. John Lewis

Gaddis describes this strategy and its view of history as "Fukuyama plus force: the United States must now finish the job that Woodrow Wilson started. The world, quite literally, must be made safe for democracy, even those parts of it, like the Muslim Middle East, that have so far resisted that tendency."[9] In other words, the new world order of peace and freedom will be made possible and sustained by American force. The unstated implication is that the world will henceforth know only one truly sovereign state—the United States. Or to put it another way, President Bush's security strategy aims to reconstitute something like a pre-Westphalian international order, but in our era it will be the United States, not the Holy Roman Empire or the Roman Catholic Church, that will serve as the transnational guardian of freedom's canon law.

The problem inherent in the NSS, which is inherent in America's self-understanding generally, shows up in the familiar form of hypocrisy. When American self-protective interests do not correspond to the freedom interests of others, U.S. actions to advance its own interests will contradict its rhetoric about aiding the freedom of others. Realists say this is an inherent problem of idealism. From a realist point of view, the actions of states in the international arena are expected to be self-interested and each state takes the measure of the others accordingly. Each recognizes the sovereignty of the others. Evil, injustice, and greed can lurk anywhere, in every state, so each state should act cautiously and realistically in its own interests, without idealism, without even trying to subordinate its interests to a supposedly transnational moral good. Diplomacy is the preferred means through which self-interested states should work realistically to reach agreements on how to achieve their diverse and sometimes competing interests. When conflicts arise that cannot be resolved peacefully, say the realists, each state has the internationally recognized right to defend itself. Insofar as the United States acts realistically to protect its own interests and security, few states will object to its military actions.

However, if U.S. security is not immediately threatened, then an American decision to make itself permanently preeminent in the world militarily or to use its military force to destroy another regime, even when done in the name of freedom, can only be viewed as imperial aggression, which violates, or potentially violates, the sovereignty of other states. The rush to war in Iraq was interpreted in this way by many other countries, writes Gaddis, because "the absence of a 'first shot' or a 'smoking gun'" fueled "a growing sense throughout much of the world that there could be *nothing worse* than American hegemony if it was to be used in this way. For if Washington could go against the wishes of the United Nations and most of its own allies in invading Iraq, what could it *not* do? What were to be, henceforth, the constraints on its power?"[10]

By means of its NSS, the Bush administration believes it can help to bring about a new era of global peace and freedom and will thereby overcome the weakness of the United Nations itself. However, the means the Bush administration has chosen may encourage negative anarchy rather than ordered freedom. By deciding unilaterally to take distance from various international and multilateral means of cooperation that the United States once supported and helped to create, the Bush administration may be offering justification to other states to do the same, namely, to use preemptive force unilaterally when they choose to do so against their neighbors in pursuit of their own interests. Walter Russell Mead thinks that in our rapidly changing world "angels everywhere are being thrown out of their whirlwinds," and the United States cannot preserve its global leadership in this kind of atmosphere

> if our image of primacy is that we are the angel directing the whirlwind of the world. While keeping our eye on our core national interests we are going to have to reinvent some of the ways we think about power and influence and we are certainly going to have to repackage our leadership for a world that we ourselves are working to make increasingly antiauthoritarian and suspicious of elites. Part of the culture clash between the administration of George W. Bush and the rest of the world was that the administration presented an old-fashioned vision of leadership to a world that is looking for a new approach.[11]

By its rhetoric and its actions, the Bush administration has begun to take independent steps to establish not simply a better strategy for American security but a new kind of international system, different from the UN system as well as from NATO, both of which it helped to create. But if the new initiatives are not taken in cooperation with the nations who cooperated in creating those organizations—particularly major democratic states—the initiatives will inevitably be interpreted as an exercise of American imperialism. This is William Galston's point, expressed before the storming of Baghdad in 2003.

> What is at stake [in Bush's leaning toward unilateralism] is nothing less than a fundamental shift in America's place in the world. Rather than continuing to serve as first among equals in the postwar international system, the United States would act as a law unto itself, creating new rules of international engagement without the consent of other nations. In my judgment, this new stance would ill serve the long-term interests of the United States. . . . [Moreover], it is an illusion to believe that the United States can employ new norms of action while denying the rights of others to do so as well.[12]

The Limits of States

President Bush, like most presidents before him, has knowingly or unknowingly run up against the limits of the state—any state—including the United States. The modern state, even a democratic state with economic freedom, cannot by itself provide an answer to the question of international order. The state came into existence as a territorial polity of domestic law under a single, sovereign government, whose authority to enforce law does not extend beyond its territory. One may hope that a world of well-defined, democratic states, in which the citizens of each state are relatively satisfied with their government, will be a more peaceful and healthy world than it is today. But even that hopeful picture of the future describes a world of separate states, each governing its own territory. It does not begin to say anything about how the relations among states should be ordered so that the peoples of the world will also be relatively satisfied with the well-being of the world. Even if all states were democratically governed, there would still be no additional means of tending to the international commons, including its environmental sustainability, rules of trade, and security against terrorism perpetrated by internationally mobile groups. As soon as one takes up these issues, one is confronted with questions that cannot be answered by referring to the responsibilities and enforcement capabilities of the separate states within their own territories.

Furthermore, one of the longest standing testimonies of history is that states typically act to defend and advance their own interests, whether or not their actions enhance the freedom and well-being of other peoples. The government of each state is responsible first of all for its own citizens, not the citizens of other countries. There is no evidence that the U.S. government will be able to design a strategy that can abrogate this law of state limits. As one state among many, the United States is not now and cannot become, *simultaneously*, the advocate of its own interests, the servant of the interests of other states, and the impartial arbiter of justice for the international order. Other peoples in the world, whether or not they have reasonably responsible governments of their own, have no voice, no representation in the American government. Consequently, unilateral American action on behalf of freedom for the world will be either paternalistic or imperialistic.

This dilemma of how to establish a just international order based on the sovereignty of separate territorial states has remained with us ever since the Peace of Westphalia in 1648. Every proposed resolution of the dilemma has in practice been initiated by sovereign states: by going to war with one another; or by trying to develop mutually agreeable rules of diplomacy; or, under duress, by negotiating temporary balances of power; or, from positions of either strength or weakness, by negotiating international treaties and alliances for diverse purposes; or, for longer-term aims, by collaborating to establish international courts and other permanent organizations to deal with the enduring issues involved in ordering the international commons. States have necessarily had to face the challenges of resolving or not resolving international disputes, overcoming or not overcoming trade barriers, and strengthening or weakening existing international law, to name only a few of the problems that arise between states when there is no transnational structure of governance. Not surprisingly, the most powerful states or alliances of states have the most to say about the outcome of all these relationships and decisions. And also, not surprisingly, wars are frequent.

Ever since the two world wars, and especially since the second, the dominant conviction among most states, including the United States, has been that international law and organizations should play a larger, even if still subordinate role, in cooperatively defining and protecting the international common good. Yet, the Cold War, followed by the post–Cold War rise of the United States to global hegemony, and now international terrorism, have demonstrated not only that states face limits but that existing international organizations also face limits. The limits of the latter derive largely from the subordination of almost all international law and organizations to the first principle of state sovereignty.

The most creative way out of the state-sovereignty dilemma—though not an absolute guarantee of success—is one that the United States knows firsthand, namely, federalism. To be sure, the American federal experiment was initiated before the colonies had had any extended experience of sovereign independence. Moreover, the federated republic was unable to resolve peacefully the internal conflicts that led to the Civil War. Nevertheless, learning from the Dutch and the Swiss, the United States charted a federalist path that other countries followed, and the Europeans may soon show how to make it work on an even grander scale. Federalism builds on and reinforces the relative autonomy of solidly governed states by a process that lodges sovereignty of a limited kind in a federal government, which in turn is held accountable both by the member states and by all the people in the union. There is no reason why this historical experience and the principles of federalism should not play a bigger role in the future of international institution building.

An important ingredient of America's global hegemony that keeps Americans from thinking of international federalism and from recognizing the informal imperialism of their actions is that the NATO alliance, formed for the "temporary" purpose of containing the Soviet Union, turned into a long-term, multilateral (almost federal) defense establishment. The same thing emerged in the Pacific with the long-term disarmament of Japan. Instead of recovering the status of ordinary sovereign states, each with its own defense capabilities, the European states (with the partial exception of Great Britain and France) and Japan became partners in the American military umbrella. Consequently, after forty years of the Cold War, American defense responsibility around the world became relatively permanent. In essence, the Monroe Doctrine had been extended far beyond this hemisphere as a permanent, anticommunist, "do-not-cross-this-line" doctrine. The distinction between American security and western European and Far Eastern security became ever more difficult for Americans to see.

Most evidence from the Bush administration's actions and rhetoric suggests that the terrorist attacks drove the president to think more narrowly about American security (inside American borders), while taking for granted his freedom to use U.S. military forces throughout the world for American unilateral purposes. The president's immediate frustration was with limits to his freedom to act in order to protect the American homeland. Yet, the limits on unilateral American military action throughout the world are limits that the United States itself helped to create when it was taking a more multilateral approach in setting up the United Nations and NATO. President Bush's desire to defend the sovereign American state appears to have driven him to try to break through the limits that the alliance system placed on the United States. Within the state system, governments must negotiate, make joint decisions, and enter into mutually agreeable alliances when they want to cooperate for security and other purposes. That is how NATO was formed. However, the American military stands under the president's direct authority, and today it just happens to be positioned almost everywhere in the world, with little to challenge it. After 9/11, the president wanted to command the military to act in America's own interests and defense. What dropped from sight in the months that followed was the fact that America's military is positioned the way it is because of countless diplomatic agreements, treaties, and alliances that positioned it to cooperate with others in mutual defense. And those countries believe they ought to have some say in the way American military operations outside the United States will affect them and the larger world in which they also live.

The direction in which the president started to move after 9/11 took for granted the unrestricted sovereignty of the United States and appeared to be headed toward the construction of a new kind of international order different from that envisioned by the UN system. The new order that the president's NSS has in mind would be *international*, but only in the sense that it would be *global*. For the American military would, by U.S. decision and authority alone, become ever more independent, or unilateral, in exercising responsibility for *global* security. President Bush and future American presidents almost certainly would not try to consolidate a formal, authoritarian empire over the whole world because they would not want the burdens of such an empire. Moreover, as a matter of principle, they would not want American military supervision to interfere with the many kinds of autonomous decision making and competition that nations ought to be free to initiate in the areas of trade, cultural and technological achievement, and much more. Other nations, if not threatening the world with weapons of mass destruction, would be free to govern and protect their own domestic affairs as the Westphalian principle of state sovereignty prescribes. The Bush administration seems only to want to solidify what, in many respects, is already a fact, namely, American military preponderance throughout the world, making the United States the unchallenged, supranational security force of the world.

The NSS suggests that the president would like to remove any remaining hindrances to the unilateral action of the American military as concerns both American and global security. Under its imperial security umbrella, all legitimate states (in the eyes of the United States) would continue to have their own domestic administrations, court systems, local police, economies, businesses, schools, and so forth. Yet, the implication of all this, as already indicated, is that only the United States would remain fully sovereign, while all other states would, in principle, be reduced to positions of relative autonomy within America's new "international," imperial system of global security.

Somewhat like President Wilson's expectation that maturing nationhood anywhere in the world would follow the American pattern, President Bush seems to have an idea of a new global order that would look like the American federation enlarged. But in this case the U.S. government would act as international federal head. The American federal government (represented primarily by its military forces) would oversee the security of the world so that relatively autonomous states would be free to govern themselves and participate freely in international commerce in much the way the fifty American states enjoy free commerce among themselves and govern themselves relatively autonomously within the federal system.[13] With respect to global security and military forces, only the United States would be sovereign atop the security federation. Since most other states, during the last fifty years, have reduced their defense spending and none have kept up with American military expenditures, the world would, on Bush's terms, eventually settle into the new world order. The militarized American "federal security apparatus" would secure the world and guarantee to every other state, along with the fifty American states, the freedom each would need to maintain its relative autonomy.

The problem with all of this, however, is that while the new arrangement would hypothetically put an end to the limits of the current state system with respect to global security, it would do so by elevating the government of one state to the position of military imperator over all. Not only would the U.S. government be accountable to no one other than its own citizens; it would, in the end, be the sole judge of the world's security needs. This would do nothing, however, to establish better international means of dealing with globalization and the concerns of the international economic, social, technological, and environmental commons. Consequently, as conflicts arose, the imperial government would, in all likelihood, have to make more and more judgments about all things international simply to be able to maintain order and to make sure it had access to all the resources (such as oil) it needed to maintain its economic growth, which would be necessary to sustain its hegemonic military position. To the extent that other nations in the world decided, either separately or jointly, that they could not accept the restrictive and oppressive judgments being made by the United States, they would probably try to force changes in the system that would reach all the way to the top, and those pressures could be perceived by the United States as a threat to global security. That, in turn, could lead either to warfare and chaos or to ever-tighter controls by American "security" forces. All of this would violate the means and the end of America's stated mission to serve as the vanguard of freedom in the world. What kind of "American century" might this one turn out to be?

CHAPTER NINE

Justifiable Warfare and Visions of Peace

The subtitle of Robert Kaplan's book *Warrior Politics* is "Why Leadership Demands a Pagan Ethos." His intention is to show that since "progress often comes from hurting others," a pagan rather than a Christian ethic is necessary to back the use of force. "Christianity is about the moral conquest of the world," he writes, but "while virtue is good, outstanding virtue can be dangerous."[1] The moral idealism of U.S. foreign policy, influenced in part by Christianity, has often led to inconsistent, hypocritical, and dangerous outcomes because, in Kaplan's view, Christian idealism is incompatible with realistic power politics. "While a foreign policy with no moral intent will be cynical," he writes, "a policy that seeks to guide, justify, and glorify its every action with moral imperatives risks being extremist."[2] This is why Kaplan agrees with Machiavelli that "religion leads to extremism when its otherworldliness impinges too much on worldly affairs. . . . We must be careful not to return to such absolutism, for if there is such a thing as progress in politics, it has been the evolution from religious virtue to secular self-interest."[3]

Clyde Prestowitz is also a critic of America's moralistic and often hypocritical idealism. On many occasions the United States has intervened in the affairs of other countries by overthrowing democratically elected governments or propping up dictators, even while trumpeting its moral crusade for democracy and freedom.[4] Yet, Prestowitz sees this as an expression of this-worldly, self-interested politics, not of otherworldliness, and he does not see it as a sign of progress. Though he is not a pacifist, Prestowitz calls

Americans and American leaders to the kind of humility that is more deeply Christian rather than less Christian.[5] He and Kaplan could not be further apart.

The contrast between Kaplan and Prestowitz raises again the old question that Augustine and Aquinas asked: can war, from a Christian point of view, ever be justified? Do the great love commandments—to love God above all and our neighbors as ourselves—ever permit the use of force? Isn't it inevitable that even the official use of force for a good cause will violate the love commands? Can the kind of humility that Prestowitz calls for go hand in hand with support for government's careful and considered use of force, or must humility lead to the renunciation of force altogether? Even if war can sometimes be justified, is it legitimate to call the fight against terrorism a war? If the United States, under the Bush administration, is trying to solidify America's global military imperium, will that not lead inevitably to the violation of just war principles?

Kaplan seems strangely ignorant of the long Christian tradition of reflection and experience that produced a Christian *public* ethic (and not only a private ethic) for Christendom. Nor does he recognize the influence of that tradition on the modern state and relations among states. For even when Kaplan applauds Augustine, Richelieu, Bismarck, and Reinhold Niebuhr for their "Christian Realism," he does so by saying that they were groping for "a way to use pagan, public morality to advance—albeit indirectly—private, Judeo-Christian morality."[6] For Kaplan, in other words, Christianity offers nothing but a private ethic. But his judgment ignores the influence of both Augustine and Aquinas, as well as Christian experience over centuries, which made the case for the legitimacy of an official, restricted use of force held accountable to the requirements of love. Despite their dependence on Cicero and Aristotle, the two church fathers developed a *Christian* public ethic—concerned with the governance of life in the *civitas terrenae*. Central to their thinking was the conviction that Christian love requires action that aims to bring about earthly peace insofar as possible. Christians, they argued, may exercise the responsibilities of public office out of love for neighbors in order to restrain violence and criminality and to uphold a tranquillity of order among sinful creatures. That responsibility does not permit the indiscriminate use of force, but it does *entail* the use of force. Self-aggrandizing aims cannot justify warfare, but upholding the common good calls for just governance, which depends on police and military forces.[7]

In trying to assess America's role in the world today, the question of justifiable warfare is as urgent as it was when nuclear weapons and the nuclear deterrence strategy of mutual assured destruction (MAD) were being debated.

Yet, given the peculiar amalgam of constitutional republicanism, Puritan new-Israelitism, and Enlightenment rationalism that defines the United States, and given America's hegemonic position in the post–Cold War world, it is not a simple matter to make judgments about the just use of force. It should come as no surprise, then, to discover that in American circles today a strong movement is emerging that calls into question the long-standing accommodation of the Christian way of life to the American way of life. Those leading the charge of critical questioning want to break with what they judge to be the mistaken synthesis of Christianity and American nationalism. America is not God's people, a new Israel, but a state like all states. The church should no longer support the myth of a Christian America, a myth that only corrupts the church and keeps it from being what God called it to be. Revealing their indebtedness to Augustine's description of the antithetical motives of the city of God and the city of this world, these contemporary reformers are urging the church to become a genuine counterpolis to militaristic states like the United States. America, they believe, depends on the ungodly manipulation of Christian and other religious symbols to justify the government's use of force for self-interested, self-aggrandizing ends. The Christian community needs to renounce the use of force and stand boldly against the pagan ethos of modern American imperialism.

Violence, Love, and Justice

John Howard Yoder, Stanley Hauerwas, and Richard Hays are the leading theologians of the contemporary Christian purification movement that identifies any cooperation with the use of force—particularly nationalistic warfare—as a violation of the Christian way of life. They stand in a long tradition that reaches back through the Reformation-era Anabaptists and the medieval monastic communities to the Augustinian antithesis and the early Christian communities that resisted Rome. They judge most, if not all, American crusades for democracy, the war in Vietnam, and Bush's war in Iraq to be exhibitions of non-Christian hypocrisy and violence that contradict the law of love. Moreover, the ideologies of nationalism and statism are idolatrous. In an important way, thinkers and activists of this stripe agree with Kaplan: even the official use of force is designed to "hurt others," and Christians have been called to do the opposite, to love their enemies. Government and politics as we know them—even in the liberal, democratic tradition—reflect a pagan ethos. Christ called his followers to something else entirely.

Is it possible, as Yoder, Hauerwas, and Hays contend, that for centuries Christians in the West have misunderstood Christianity and failed to recognize that the only grounds for the use of force are to be found in a pagan ethic? Could it be that the Christian compromise with Roman imperialism, followed by the accommodations inherent in Christendom, in divine-right monarchies, and in Christian-republican America, had no *Christian* basis? Would it be best, therefore, both for Christian authenticity and for American security to separate once and for all the community of Christian love from the realities of hard-nosed government actions that require a pagan ethos? If so, how? And if not, why not?

To pursue these questions, we need to reconsider several biblical texts, starting with the interpretation offered by Hays, a New Testament scholar at Duke University. Hays devotes a central chapter of his book *The Moral Vision of the New Testament*[8] to a discussion of violence, and by these means he lays out his distinctive argument for the separation of the church from the state. Throughout the chapter, he makes an exegetical case in support of arguments by Yoder and Hauerwas against the use of force.[9] Hays's argument depends, however, on an equivocal use of the word "violence." When he asks, for example, "Is it ever God's will for Christians to employ violence in defense of justice?"[10] the question is rhetorical. The word "violence," much like Kaplan's phrase "hurting others," generally connotes an unloving, unjust use of force that does injury to another. How could God call Christians to commit harmful, unloving acts in defense of justice? The answer is an obvious "no." Yet, Hays gives no attention to the different biblical words that convey different meanings of "the use of force." With the words "violence" and "use of force," he encompasses acts initiated by one person to harm another, as well as acts by governments and soldiers, as if all uses of force amount to the same thing.

If, by contrast, Hays had phrased his opening question, "Is it ever God's will for Christians to employ *vengeance* in defense of justice?" he would have put the question of Romans 12–13 on the table and would have used the Greek word *ekdikesis* or *ekdikos*, which has a retributive ring to it, a word that has to do with *responding* to a prior, unjust act of harm or violence. Words like "vengeance," "retribution," and "punishment" reflect a different context than does the word "violence" when the latter is used to signify an initial act of harm, hurt, or murder. The single word "violence" cannot be used unequivocally to refer both to an initiation of physical harm and to the response to such an act, whether by means of personal vengeance or by means of official retribution. The Bible witnesses clearly to God's appointment of officials to carry out official punishment for various crimes. The Bible does not speak of God commanding murder or the initiation of violence against one's neighbor in order to serve oneself or to satisfy one's hatred or lust or greed. More than one word is needed, therefore, to express the various ways in which the Bible refers to the use of force.

The main burden of Hays's interpretation of Matthew 5:38–48, Romans 12, and a few other passages is the argument that "from Matthew to Revelation we find a consistent witness against violence and a calling to the community to follow the example of Jesus in *accepting* suffering rather than *inflicting* it."[11] What Jesus did and taught exhibited God's intention that the redeeming work of Christ and the calling of a new community to follow him would not and could not be built on violence against others. By contrast, the church today "is deeply compromised and committed to nationalism, violence, and idolatry," according to Hays.[12] Our culture "is deeply committed to the necessity and glory of violence," which is why Hays reasons that truly committed Christians "would have to relinquish positions of power and influence insofar as the exercise of such positions becomes incompatible with the teaching and example of Jesus."[13]

With regard to one meaning of the term "violence," Hays is quite right about the teaching of the New Testament. The people united through faith in Christ were not called to a mission of self-aggrandizement, of advancing their cause by stepping on and destroying others. Quite the opposite. Moreover, Jesus did not try to re-gather Israel into its own territory as an armed state, the way the zealots and even some of the disciples still expected him to act (Acts 1:6). Nor did Jesus call his disciples to build the Christian community as a territorial polity that would need to protect itself by means of force. The community of Christ's followers, by the power of the Holy Spirit, was to grow and spread out across the world like grain mixed with weeds in the field of the world (Matt. 13:24–30) or like leaven in a loaf of bread (Matt. 13:33). Christ's kingdom embraces the whole earth, and he will not be satisfied with anything less than a worldwide kingdom. The good news of the messianic kingdom must be taken to the whole world. But the responsibility of Christ's followers under his authority is not to try to build God's global kingdom by force, as if it were a human polity or empire like the Roman Empire. The biblical vision of Christ's kingdom was what Augustine interpreted as the city of God.

Matthew 5:14–15 uses three metaphors to suggest that the followers of Jesus should be strong and visible witnesses to the world. Jesus said, "You are a light of the world. A city [polis] on a hill cannot be hidden. Neither do people light a lamp and put it under a bowl." Hays uses the reference here to the "polis on a hill" to argue that the church is to be a new kind of polis, the "most salient feature" of which is that it will transcend violence.[14] Nothing in these allusive metaphors, however, suggests that Jesus was calling his

followers to become a counterpolis. Jesus did not say, "My church should become a polis on a hill." That is what the American Puritans incorrectly read
into the scriptures about their project and what the new American federation eventually adopted as its own self-interpretation. Jesus did not ask his
disciples to become a "new Israel." Jesus did not try to set up a pacifist city—
of the kind the Quakers at first tried to establish in Pennsylvania—and call
it his church. It seems quite evident from the text that Jesus was using similitudes to tell his followers that they were to be *like* light to the world; *like* a
city clearly seen on a hill rather than a city hidden in a valley; *like* a lamp
held up to give light rather than a lamp hidden where it cannot give light.
The "likeness" is to be found in the church's visibility, in its light-giving witness, not in the structure of the polis or the lamp.

If we look at Jesus's use of similitudes and metaphors, there are many others. His church will be the bride of Christ, a household of faith, God's
dwelling place made up of living stones, the family of God, a holy priesthood,
the sheep of the shepherd, and more. If the polis is taken as one such
metaphor, then it, too, has a primary referent. This seems to be what the
book of Revelation is conveying with John's vision of the New Jerusalem,
the city of God. But do the similitudes provide the basis for saying that the
church in this age should turn away from marriage to become Christ's bride,
or turn away from natural families to become God's family, or turn away from
life in earthly cities to become God's countercity? The more natural reading
would be to understand that marriage, the family, and life in a city are not responsibilities to turn away from, but part of human experience (even if now
marred by sin) given by the Creator to relish and cherish as partially revela-
tory of the meaning of the family of God and the city of God. This is what
many of the Psalms convey about the kingdom of Israel. With regard to life
in this age, until the city of God appears in its fullness, the New Testament
seems quite clear about urging Christians to give themselves in love to one
another and to their neighbors by taking seriously their earthly marriages,
families, and cities.

How then should Christians live as light-giving servants of God in and
among the empires and states of this world? How should they serve all their
neighbors, including their non-Christian neighbors, under the judicial, police, and military systems of the empires and states in which they find themselves? These are the questions asked by Augustine, Aquinas, and the church
in a way that produced, among other things, the just war doctrine. Hays, by
contrast, argues that the most basic part of an answer to the question about
the identity of the Christian community is that it should not participate in
the use force. He admits that no text in the New Testament says explicitly

that Christians may not hold the office of a military or police official. Nevertheless, he judges that "the place of the soldier within the church can only be seen as anomalous."[15] There is, therefore, no place for a public ministry of justice—of the kind that states administer—under Christ. The soldier who fights in a war and the judge who passes a judgment of capital punishment, for example, are committing acts of violence, which are contrary to the way the Christian community should act. Consequently, from Hays's point of view, there is indeed no possibility of developing a *Christian* public ethic that can justify the government's use of force.

That is why Hays reads Romans 12–13 the way Yoder does.[16] The end of Romans 12 is a close echo of the Sermon on the Mount in Matthew 5–6 and tells Christians they should not exercise personal vengeance on their own behalf or return evil for evil. Hays, like Yoder, believes this means that Christians may not hold the human office of government that Paul discusses in Romans 13, for God appoints the governing authority to exercise vengeance as a servant of God. This reading, however, makes Paul in Romans 13 sound like one of the Pharisees whom Jesus demotes in Matthew 5, since Paul is giving an account of the origin of governmental authority that seems to coincide with the Old Testament's teaching. From Hays's point of view, Paul in Romans 12 is following Jesus, while Paul in Romans 13 is apparently falling back on older traditions and modes of reasoning that are not fully compatible with Jesus's teaching. In fact, this contrast would appear to drive the incompatibility between "vengeance" and "turning the other cheek" all the way back into the Godhead. On the one hand, Jesus, the Son of God, calls Christians to live as a community whose members refuse to hold any office that exercises forceful retribution. On the other hand, "outside the perfection of Christ" (as the 1525 Schleitheim confession of the Anabaptists would later describe it), God the Father establishes offices to which he apparently calls only non-Christians to serve in exercising a measure of divine vengeance. On this interpretation, only non-Christians can carry out the acts of violence that fulfill the Father's will for punishment of the evildoer and for the protection of the innocent. Christians would disobey Christ, the Son of God, if they did what God the Father appointed governments to do.[17] Hays and Kaplan appear to be very close together at this point.

There is, however, another way to read Romans 12 and 13, a way that allows for a distinction between offices of responsibility in the world and a distinction between the motivating spirit of Christian love and the contrary spirit of self-love. The alternate reading calls, in fact, for a *Christian* rather than a pagan *public* ethic, an ethic that demands of governments compliance with normative principles of justice in a way that will not contradict the

Christian way of life. This interpretation certainly calls into question the American civil religion and the synthesis of Christianity and secularized new-Israelitism. Yet, unlike Hays's interpretation, the interpretation that follows lays the basis for a normative view of public governance that neither identifies all public use of force with unloving violence nor conflates the Christian community with a particular state, like the United States.

Paul in Romans 12 does, indeed, affirm that the people of God must not try to preserve themselves and their interests by exercising personal vengeance against those who have harmed them. That kind of vengeance not only violates the love command but only begets more violence. Yet, Paul teaches in Romans 13 that God established governing authorities to keep the peace, to encourage the good person, and to punish the evildoer. There is nothing incompatible here with Romans 12. The reason is that public officials (not just in Israel) have the responsibility as God's servants to carry out a certain measure of the very vengeance that humans are supposed to leave in God's hands (Rom. 13:4). The governing authority that "does not bear the sword for nothing" (Rom. 13:4) is a divinely established office, not a coordinating executive of human vengeance.

The contrast, as well as the relationship, between Romans 12 and 13 could not be clearer, therefore, and it is not the contrast that Hays draws. Romans 12 speaks of personal vengeance, the kind of reaction against evil that would involve a person in usurping the divine prerogative to authorize just punishment. That authority over enemies and potential enemies does not belong to the individual Christian or to the Christian community. That authority and prerogative belong to God. To live as an obedient, loving Christian requires, among other things, leaving vengeance in God's hands. What God has done, however, as Paul explains, is to appoint specific offices of *human* responsibility to serve as *God's* servants for this purpose. Consequently, there is no reason why Christians may not hold public offices of the kind Paul considers in Romans 13 as long as they exercise the responsibilities of the office in accord with God's standards and purposes. When governing authorities carry out just recompense, they may not *initiate* violence, or perpetrate *personal vengeance*, or try to give an advantage to Christians over their enemies, or try to bring in Christ's kingdom by force. The implication of what Paul is saying here is precisely to put government in its place under God's sovereignty. Rome or any other empire or state may not be the total community in which Christians find their meaning. Nor do Christians find their identity by turning away from their specific, limited responsibilities as citizens, family members, friends, laborers, and more. The all-encompassing lordship of Christ constitutes a community of faith whose members and local congregations and larger bodies will continue to bear civic responsibilities in a wide variety of different political systems throughout the world. Therefore, God the Father does not stand in conflict with Jesus; nor does the love command stand in conflict with the authorizing of governing authorities to do justice. Normative Christian living coheres with obeying God in normative patterns of public governance. This is not to suggest that Christians will never sin or fail. In any area of life, including public-office holding, they will continue to be sinners and thus may fail to meet God's high standards of love and justice. But that demonstrates human frailty and depravity, not the inherent illegitimacy of government.

When official police, judicial, and military systems are established with proper accountability, they may, therefore, in biblical terms, be recognized as divinely authorized institutions for the sake of doing justice, breaking the cycle of violence, and giving both the perpetrator and the victim of crime what they justly deserve. The use of force by a government official in keeping with legal norms of impartial justice, is, in terms of Romans 13, a gift of God's grace, a means whereby the officeholder serves as a minister of God for the public well-being of all neighbors. The proper exercise of such responsibility, quite in contrast to its improper exercise, can be an expression of love: love for God and love for civic neighbors.

This view of government obviously and quite clearly requires very definite and severe strictures on governments and states. It is in this regard that Christianity has made one of the most significant contributions to Western government and the structure of the modern state. If the state should be a differentiated, nontotalitarian, public-legal community, which may rightfully monopolize and use force only for the purpose of upholding justice for all, then it may not, with any legitimacy, be the kind of community that uses force arbitrarily or for any crusade or ideology that its leaders and citizens choose. Governing authorities, in terms of Romans 13, are not authorized to make themselves leaders of a new Israel; or the final judge of humankind; or the messianic inaugurator of the kingdom of God; or the servant of the vanguard of the proletariat; or the servant of Nazi ethnic cleansing; or the power to rid the earth of evil. Expectations of final judgment and peace without end will be fulfilled only when the city of God appears as God's gift in the fullness of time. The task of human government, in biblical terms, is a very modest one, a humble duty of administering public justice, always limited in its domain of competence. Exercised properly, government authority will help to preserve public peace and make it possible for humans to fulfill the wide variety of responsibilities God has given them, most of which are not governmental and political. The church as depicted in the New Testament—the people of God in Christ—is a community that extends throughout the world and cannot be confined or reduced to any state. But the Christian community does not exist apart from or outside of states, any more than it exists apart from or outside of families and every other kind of human vocation and institution. From this point of view, Christians in America have a civic responsibility as citizens in the United States, but America may not be identified as God's chosen nation.

Just Governance and the Tranquillity of Order

Justifying the use of force by means of just war reasoning can only be done adequately, therefore, within a broader framework of judgments about the institutional responsibility and accountability of governments. This is where a Christian *public* ethic has made its contribution. The office of government exists *not simply* for the purpose of making war and using police force. Just war criteria were developed, in other words, out of a concern with the legitimacy of government—about whether the exercise of governmental responsibility is compatible with the calling of Christians to serve God and their neighbors in love. Consequently, any attempted justification of war and police actions must be offered as part of the justification of right government. That is why, for example, the just war tradition arrived at the criterion that a military response to foreign aggression must be made officially, by a rightful authority, and not by a private person or a gang. Moreover, a decision to go to war in response to foreign aggression must be made as a last resort because just and healthy relations among people ordinarily require peaceful means of resolving conflicts and disagreements. The use of force, even by governments, should not be initiated too quickly, so as to cut off the possibility of finding peaceful means of dispute settlement. Likewise, just war argumentation insists that the end in view, when a government decides to go to war, must be the restoration or establishment of peace, meaning a situation in which good governance can be recovered or established. War may never be initiated merely to destroy an enemy, or to engage in fighting without end, or to test a country's military capability. Not every act of destruction by foreigners, such as the acts of terrorists, calls for a military response of war.

Questions about the just use of force, consequently, always come back to the prior question of just governance. This means that the wider horizon of our concern about America's role in the world today must be about the justice of its governance and its contribution to the strengthening of just governance abroad. That is a much wider concern than simply the right of states to maintain their sovereignty. What is helpful about Kaplan's book is that his call for a pagan ethos puts the heat on sloppy, synthetic civil religions and nationalist idealisms. Many American Christians believe that the U.S. government has a right to do whatever it takes to keep the country strong because they believe this is a good, democratic country, or that it is God's chosen nation, or that inside its territory many Christian virtues are still evident and worth preserving. Kaplan's argument exposes this as a type of means-to-end reasoning, and if one assumes that the end justifies the means, then there will be no limits in principle to the use of force as a means to supposedly good ends.[18]

The kind of reasoning that justifies government's use of force as a means to the end of preserving American exceptionalism or of advancing freedom and democracy in the world can easily lead to the transgression of every boundary of justice with regard to the means being used. That, in turn, undermines the very principle of just governance. It is not surprising, then, that many Christians are attracted to pacifism and the appeal of living in a pure counterpolis. In many ways that was the original appeal of America to the Puritans and to many generations of immigrants. Today's talk of "just war" in a militarized America may sound increasingly like nothing more than a cover for self-aggrandizing, nationalistic actions. Christian pacifists are certainly justified in wanting to avoid complicity with evil and hypocrisy, but are they correct to believe that governments, by their very nature, will act contrary to God's standards for the Christian way of life?[19]

With regard to the contemporary American situation since 9/11 and the arguments being made by Christians such as Hays, Jean Bethke Elshtain is helpful, though narrowly focused, in her recent defense of the just war tradition.[20] In an introductory discussion of terrorism, Elshtain emphasizes the distinction between a response of revenge and a response that seeks justice. The distinction, she says, is as clear as that "between the actions of a lynch mob and a conviction by a jury in a first-degree murder case arrived at after a fair trial and hours of careful deliberation."[21] The implication is that the achievement of justice requires impartial offices of public governance. However, Elshtain does not draw out that implication at the outset and gives too little attention to the meaning of just governance—both domestic and international—throughout her book. This is particularly problematic when it comes to assessing America's global military imperium, the "war" on terrorism, and the criticism of the United States coming from Christian reformers like Hays.

Elshtain begins her introduction to the just war tradition with a comment made to a friend after 9/11: "'Now we are reminded of what governments are for.' The primary responsibility of government is to provide basic security—ordinary civic peace. St. Augustine calls this form of earthly peace *tranquillitas ordinis*."[22] Yet, Elshtain does not speak of justice or of the broader context of government's responsibility at this juncture, and she reduces the scope of "basic security" to "those minimal conditions that prevent the worst from happening."[23] This is a very severe Augustinianism and even more severe than Kaplan's view of government, for while Augustine certainly did not anticipate the more positive and ample "common good" that Aquinas thought possible in the political community, Augustine did argue for government to do more than merely try to prevent the worst from happening. When Elshtain picks up the theme of justice again further on, it is only to discuss the decision to go to war and the means of conducting war, not to consider the wider responsibility of just governance, or the limits of the modern state, or the problem of ideologies that so often distort the exercise of governmental responsibility today. She emphasizes that justifiable warfare requires an official decision by a government—"at the behest of *right authority*."[24] But by this time her focus has narrowed to warfare alone.

In all of this, Elshtain does not give sufficiently serious consideration to the reason for the challenge presented by today's new pacifists. They are, like the prophetic and monastic reformers of the past, concerned with the truthful witness and health of the church; they see the uncritical support of nationalism among Christians as an unhealthy sign. Elshtain dismisses those who think the early church was primarily pacifist by saying that the early "Christian mainstream" supported just war. But since when does an argument for truth follow from identifying the norm with what the mainstream does or believes? In addition, Elshtain says that since Jesus himself distinguished between "serving God and serving Caesar, Christians were obliged to take the measure of earthly rule and dominion rather than condemn it or its necessities outright."[25] However, Hays does not deny Jesus's acknowledgment of caesar's authority; he simply argues that Christians should not hold offices that support public violence because to do so violates the identity and calling of the church. The question about caesar in that biblical passage (Matt. 22:15–22) has to do with whether and how the responsibilities of earthly government fall *under* God. And we might extrapolate from there to ask whether government also falls "under" Christ. Elshtain, however, makes it sound as if the text offers a fairly simple distinction between two terrains, God's and Caesar's, that lie *alongside* one another. But Jesus told his disciples after his resurrection that all authority in heaven and on earth now belongs to him (Matt. 28:18). Does this mean that Jesus Christ is the one to whom Caesar is somehow accountable under God, or does earthly government fall "outside the perfection of Christ" as the Christian pacifists contend?

When Elshtain takes up the discussion of Romans 13, she interprets it as affirming "the *rightful authority* of earthly kings and kingdoms to punish wrongdoers," and since "Christians believe evil is real," she says, "both justice and charity may compel us to serve our neighbor and the common good by using force to stop wrongdoing and to punish wrongdoers."[26] However, this passage in Romans says something more about government than that it should punish wrongdoers. There is a broader role that Paul envisions for government, a role of commending those who do what is right and of being "God's servant to do you good" (Rom. 13:3–4). Even more important, the "rightful authority" of government to use the power of the sword, according to Paul, comes because it is an office of *divine* appointment, called to exercise a measure of divine vengeance; it is not a humanly organized means of exercising human vengeance. Thus, it is not, as Elshtain says, because Christians believe that evil is real that they may decide to use force to oppose wrongdoing; rather, God has called governments to exercise the peculiar responsibility of restraining and punishing those who do wrong and that responsibility belongs to the office of government, not to Christians or people in general who believe that evil is real. In connection with the brief comment on Romans 13, Elshtain then offers an equally brief introduction to the just war tradition, including the principles that warfare must have a just cause; that it "must be a response to a specific instance of unjust aggression"; that it must be initiated as a last resort; and that it should not be undertaken without a reasonable chance of success.[27]

Given the small platform she has built, Elshtain's subsequent consideration of the American "war" against terrorism remains too narrowly focused. For example, she does not question the president's commitment to a "war on terrorism" in response to 9/11 and the Taliban in Afghanistan. (Her book was written before the war in Iraq.) But how, on just war terms, as Elshtain herself presents them, can the response to terrorism be called "war" (and considered a *just* war) if two of the criteria for justifiable warfare are (1) that war is "a response to a specific instance of unjust aggression" and (2) that there must be a "reasonable chance of success"? In another essay, Elshtain makes more of the latter point: "Before you intervene, even in a just cause, be certain that you have a reasonable chance of success. Don't barge in and make a bad situation worse."[28] Much of what concerns us about terrorism is its seemingly ubiquitous and nonspecific nature and the fact that even with improved intelligence and international cooperation, terrorism may never be stopped altogether. All the military power in the world may prove to be entirely inadequate to defeat terrorism. Working to stop terrorism, in other words, cannot justifiably be called war if one is making careful use of just war criteria.

Another goal or outcome of justifiable warfare is supposed to be peace and legitimate governance after the war, not chaos or such a degree of destruction that war might continue indefinitely or soon recur. Even if we judge that the United States entered warfare justifiably against the Taliban and Al Qaeda in Afghanistan, the American responsibility, in just war terms, must be to bring about a peaceful order under a more just government. Later in her book, Elshtain quotes Afghan President Hamid Karzai asking for more troops to be sent to his country "for as long as we need . . . to fight terrorism, to fight warlordism, to fight anarchy . . . until we have our own institutions—a national army, a national intelligence, national police and so on."[29] At the time of this writing, the United States and other countries were continuing to fight Al Qaeda leftovers in Afghanistan, but it is not at all evident that the United States is fighting very hard against warlordism and a resurgent, illegal drug trade or investing enough resources to build a truly national government with the capabilities Karzai was asking for. If those tasks (along with the responsibility the United States now bears to help build a stable order in Iraq and to help stop terrorism throughout the world) require the cooperative effort of many countries, as well as an American readiness to pay the price of its engagement for many years to come, then there are serious questions about whether current American operations and its "war" on terrorism meet the demands of the just war tradition.

Later in her book, Elshtain does touch lightly on the matter of just governance, even commenting that "just war thinking is not only about war but about politics."[30] She writes that "the only defense against terrorism in the short run is interdiction and self-defense. The best defense against terrorism in the long run is building up secure civic infrastructures in many nations. That is why a number of policymakers have spoken about a contemporary version of the great Marshall Plan that rebuilt Europe after the catastrophe of World War II."[31] This is precisely the point at which a discussion of just governance is urgently needed, particularly to consider the kinds of responsibilities that legitimate governments in the past have agreed to bear jointly through organizations such as NATO, the United Nations, the World Bank, and the World Trade Organization, responsibilities, that is, to protect and help to build up secure civic infrastructures and to stabilize the international order. But Elshtain does not move in that direction. Her emphasis is not on international cooperation in nation building and international governance but on the right of the United States to go to war. "The track record of nonstate organizations as effective bodies to interdict violence and punish aggression is not impressive," she says. With respect to security, the United States, which is "the world's only superpower, " bears a disproportionate responsibility and therefore must be free to take initiatives on its own.[32]

The question about stopping terrorism, however, is not narrowly about whether the United States bears a disproportionate *military* responsibility in the world. The question is whether terrorism should even be considered an act of war and whether the proper response to it should be military in nature. The question is how best to fight terrorism and to deal with rogue states so that the result will be greater peace and just governance. This means a fight that goes hand in hand with efforts to build institutions for just governance, just policing, and just defense around the world so that terrorism cannot easily flourish. These responsibilities may well require the reform of ineffective international organizations and the creation of new ones, and Elshtain is right in saying that "First comes the state. Then comes transgovernmental and international connections."[33] But the word "first" should not be used here to imply that nothing can be done internationally and transgovernmentally until all the necessary states have been built and secured or to imply that in the meantime the United States should feel free to take military action in unilateral disregard of long-standing treaties and agreements with other countries. The building process must go on at both the state and the international levels simultaneously. Unjust actions by states can interfere with the development of healthier international bodies and cooperative efforts, just as ineffective or malformed international organizations can hinder the development and responsible action of states.

When Elshtain concludes by saying that today "the possibility of international peace and stability premised on equal regard for all rests largely, though not exclusively, on American power,"[34] she is defending America's war against terrorism as a just war, launched from its position of global hegemony. But that argument all but ignores the shape of the current international *tranquillitas ordinis* that the United States helped to construct by building NATO, leading in the development of the United Nations, and binding itself to other international organizations. Simply emphasizing America's right to use force does not do much to advance moral reasoning about how and when justifiable warfare does or does not fit into the larger cooperative responsibility that governments bear to stop international criminal behavior, to fight terrorism, to strengthen accountable governments in states where they are now weak or nonexistent, and to strengthen just governance of the international order itself. Elshtain's somewhat quick dismissal of international organizations and America's obligation to them might make sense if the consideration is only about America's defense of its own territory against the kind of active or imminent aggression that can be justifiably opposed by military force. But with respect to the larger responsibility of dealing with worldwide terrorist organizations and dangerous rogue states, America's global military hegemony gives the United States no right, in just war terms, to decide unilaterally if and when it will cooperate with other states to re-order global security arrangements and to set up or knock down the governments of other states.

War may indeed be justified under certain circumstances, but the larger question today is about the conditions of just international governance in a shrinking world where states must cooperate to an increasing degree to deal not only with terrorism but also with economic and other dimensions of globalization. What kind of world should the United States be helping to shape?

CHAPTER TEN

◡

What Role among the Nations?

The international role the United States should play in the decades to come is one that gives *priority* to helping to reform, strengthen, and create international organizations for the better governance of the world. This is essential not only to fight terrorism and to strengthen national security, though Michael Ignatieff demonstrates why terrorism "presents a very powerful argument for the reinvigoration of all forms of multinational and multilateral cooperation."[1] Beyond security, the priority of international institution-building is essential because of the way in which the world is simultaneously shrinking and expanding. Human societies are rapidly becoming ever more interdependent, especially economically, which is bringing to light for all to see the diversity of human cultures, religions, and ideologies, different levels of human development, and the wide range of economic, vocational, and political ambitions of the people in this one world. Consequently, as Walter Russell Mead says, part of America's response to the magnitude of current changes in the world "must be a new and more creative approach to issues of global governance."[2]

This priority does not call for revolutionary action or sudden policy shifts on the part of the United States. To the contrary, it calls for long-term political, economic, social, and defense policies that build out carefully and historically from contemporary domestic and international realities. Nevertheless, if the stated priority were to be adopted by successive American administrations, it would depend on and lead to significant changes in the American view of the world and to changes of considerable magnitude in American foreign and defense policies.

The American people need to gain a deeper understanding of what it means that the world's people and states share a single global commons, the governance of which is becoming more and more difficult with each passing decade. The current international system, even with American military supremacy, is inadequate to deal with global crises such as terrorism, migration of peoples, spread of disease, degradation of environments, the maldistribution of basic resources, and the consequences of bad governance in many states and internationally. Democratic states depend, for example, on capital markets, says Ignatieff, but a free market in everything, including weapons of mass destruction, threatens democracy itself. "Economic globalization could become the means of our own destruction, unless globalization is accompanied by a steady expansion of regulatory capacity on the part of states, companies and international institutions. Yet no single state," argues Ignatieff, "not even the global superpower, has the resources to police a global market in lethality. Hence all states have an interest in devising effective regimes of multilateral regulation."[3]

At this time, the states of the world bear different degrees of responsibility for promoting the just ordering of the international commons. Some states are negative contributors because their governments do more harm than good. Many states are torn by civil war or by fractures so deep that their governments can hardly contribute to the just ordering of their own territories much less to the just governance of the global commons. The richest, most stable, and most powerful states clearly have the greatest potential and the greatest responsibility to lead in reforming, strengthening, and creating new institutions that are essential for the present and future governance of the world.

There already are many sound international organizations and an extensive body of sound international law; there are also many inadequate or failing organizations and laws that need to be reformed or replaced. In addition, there are many gaps that need to be filled by new international efforts and institutions. Nothing about these arrangements prior to 9/11 suggested that the United States had reason, after 9/11, to pull back from close cooperation with other states just in order to defend itself and to protect its essential interests. To the contrary, the United States was in a position in the 1990s and after 9/11 to do even more than it did before the end of the Cold War to help build a better international order both for its own benefit and for the benefit of others. In the decades ahead the United States should place a premium on working bilaterally, multilaterally, and through international organizations to help strengthen what is good, to reform what is deficient, and to fill gaps where new organizations are needed, all in order to improve the prospects of a more stable and just world in the future. Not to do this would be to jeopardize America's own long-term best interests. It would also be to waste America's potential for helping to build institutions of democratic governance and the rule of law, a potential that will dissipate all the more quickly if other states become convinced that the United States is now concerned only with its own security interests.

Nothing said in what follows aims to lessen the quality of American life by calling for the relinquishing of any U.S. capability. To the contrary, the aim is to show that American failure to think and act cooperatively over the long term for the international common good is part of what threatens even America's future. Mead comments that unless the United States and its allies "find ways to promote orderly and peaceful development in much of the world, the ideologies and organizations of terror will flourish and our security at home will be endangered."[4] At this turning point in history, the United States needs to hold on to most of what it knows about democratically accountable and constitutionally limited states, but it needs to change considerably its view of what makes for a sound and sustainable international public order.

The Problem of America's Civil-Religious Mission

The relatively modest role the United States has played in the world since its founding is tied directly to the fact that it is a particular, constitutional state, not a totalitarian empire or an undifferentiated revolutionary movement that aimed to take over the world. Yet, despite its constitutionally differentiated and limited structure, the United States has, from the beginning, been the carrier of a national mission that is too expansive and undifferentiated for a constitutional state to fulfill. Ignatieff says of the Iraq war, for example, "oil is not the whole story, as capitalist interest has never been [for America]. From Teddy Roosevelt to George W. Bush, moral feeling has made a real difference to the timing and scope of interventions." Compared to his father, the younger Bush "is more a hotblooded moralist. Bringing freedom to the Iraqis seems to matter to him, which is why, perhaps, he rushed to Baghdad not caring whether he had a coalition behind him or not."[5] Ignatieff's phrase "moral feeling" is not strong enough, however, to convey the American civil-religious purpose that carries Bush and most Americans.

Criticism of the Bush administration's resort to "unilateralism," particularly in the case of the Iraq war, has arisen because, as Jeffrey Record explains, the unilateralism reinforces the image abroad of an "overbearing 'hyperpower'"[6] instead of a respected lead nation. Record quotes John Ikenberry to the effect that "America's nascent neoimperial grand strategy threatens to rend the fabric of the international community and political partnerships precisely at a time when the community and those partnerships are urgently needed. It is an approach fraught with peril and likely to fail," says Ikenberry. "It is not only politically unsustainable but diplomatically harmful. And if history is any guide, it will trigger antagonism and resistance that will leave America in a more hostile and divided world."[7]

Nurtured on American exceptionalism, it was nearly impossible for American citizens to experience the 9/11 terrorist attacks as anything less than the violation of freedom's holy land—the world's democratic holy of holies. Consequently, the American response rose (or fell) to the level of a "war against evil," a civil-religious crusade that no human military could possibly accomplish. For neither Al Qaeda's terrorists nor U.S. military forces are capable of destroying the evil they see in the other. One can make sense of the president's quick call to war only by understanding its source in Puritan new-Israelitism, a divine mission belonging to this particular city on a hill and to none other. The early sacralizing of America as the civil-religious community chosen to lead the world to its true destiny explains why Americans tend to believe that all people on earth really are destined (and should desire) to become like us: free, self-governing, and prosperous. Yet, according to the American self-understanding, the future cannot come to pass except through American leadership. Therefore, if anything threatens America's leadership of the global mission for democracy and economic freedom, then the whole world may be lost. The city on a hill must be defended at all costs and by every means. Consequently, every grave threat seems to call for war.

If it is necessary to recognize the religious depths of the Islamist ideology in order to understand Al Qaeda's actions, even if the religion of Osama bin Laden is not that of traditional Islam, so, too, is it necessary to recognize the religious depths of the American exceptionalist ideology, even if that civil religion is now two or three times removed from original Puritanism. It is their national civil-religion that leads Americans to overestimate their own leadership in the development of democracy and the protection of freedom throughout the world. The exceptionalist self-understanding is what drives Americans to interpret antagonism toward the United States (whether terrorism or allied criticism) as evil or a threat to America's righteous purpose and thus a threat even to God's purposes. American leaders then tend to pit America against the world, trusting only themselves to be the dependable defenders of the *dar al-freedom*. The contribution of other countries to the promotion of democracy and to the defense against terrorism is played down and even overlooked. The civil-religious exceptionalist ideology also explains why Americans view any potential limitation to their own sovereignty as anathema, even as they are willing to allow for the subordination of all other nations to America's military hegemony. America's strategy of joining *with* the world is, as much as possible, carried out only on American terms, meaning that the United States must be prepared to stand *against* the world whenever the world does not join America in its cause and in its approach to the world. The resort to war may come reluctantly, but when the United States is threatened, a decision to go to war may come quickly, even if without sufficient forethought or planning for the consequences.

If my estimation is correct that the ambition and zeal of America's new-Israelite mission has always exceeded the capability and responsibility of the American state, then there are at least two fundamental prerequisites for the future constructive engagement of the United States in the world. First, public officials must concentrate with a high degree of discipline on what governments and international organizations can and should do in governing. And second, public officials and the American people together must work to disestablish the civil religion that functions as the primary moral dynamo of U.S. foreign and defense policies. Only by disconnecting normative policy-making from our politically debilitating civil religion is there a possibility for government leaders to get a proper estimate of the United States as a state and of its potential for contributing constructively to a world that America cannot govern or steer on its own.

The Reality of States

Almost everyone in the world today experiences life in a state, even if the states in which some people live are highly unjust and terribly malformed. The nearly two hundred states that exist throughout the world encompass a vast number and diverse range of peoples and cultures, none of which is universal, while the supposedly universal human rights that have been articulated in UN documents carry no guarantee of being enforced, for there is no cosmopolitan government or court that can enforce human rights within the states or in international relations. The question that remains, then, is how the world's single humanity can experience a more healthy, just, and sustainable international order while being governed by a diversity of sovereign states that cooperate far too inadequately to serve the common good of all.

Part of the answer to this big question about international justice is to be found, perhaps surprisingly, in the value and achievements of the state itself. If the central challenge is to govern seven, going on eight, billion people in one world, then it is remarkable that all of those people live in fewer than two hundred states, many of which are quite small. Moreover, since two of the major threats to the governance of so many people are, on the one hand, complete anarchy and perpetual crime and warfare and, on the other hand, the rise to global dominance of a single, omnicompetent, and totalitarian regime, it is a healthy feature of the contemporary world that there are many strong and relatively well-governed states. Regardless of what kind of global harmony among peoples one might hope for in the future, it is quite evident that healthy, just, and sustainable governance will require many experienced, trusted, and accountable local and regional governments. And that is one of the things that states provide to a relative degree. Within borders usually recognized by other states, governments uphold public order for those living in their territories. Most of the arguments and negotiations (and many of the limited wars) being carried on today are about the injustice, inadequacy, and oppression of existing states and modes of governance. But the very fact that there can be such debates, negotiations, and limited warfare is a positive thing compared to either worldwide anarchy or global totalitarianism.

This positive affirmation of the value of the state—and the state system—should not be mistaken for an expression of optimism about the world getting better and better through the redemptive efforts of sovereign states. The twentieth century was the bloodiest in history. States, many of them empires, were the cause of much of that conflict, including the first two worldwide wars in history. The state as a structure offers no automatic guarantee of healthy, just, and sustainable governance either for the people in them or for the relations among them. Things could get worse rather than better in this century as people fight for limited resources, lay hold of highly destructive weapons, and fail to find ways to resolve conflicts peacefully or to share resources. And tragic scenarios could turn out to be even worse if various civil religions and revolutionary ideologies drive people to demand of their states the impossible. But since humans do engage in conflict and go to war with one another, as they have always done, the fact that a diversity of states now provides a huge public governance capacity for most people means that there is an important structural basis for ongoing efforts to restrain conflict and to work toward better governance for everyone in the world.

It also happens to be the case that the development and articulation of universal humans rights has emerged, in part, because of the growth and development of states. Whether the occasion was to stipulate the civil rights that citizens should enjoy within a state, or to draft rules of warfare (including how prisoners should be treated), or to articulate UN principles for international justice, the process of state building has necessarily involved a process of articulating certain human rights, along with the concomitant limits of government. Consequently, the formation and endurance of the modern state partially embodies the age-old wisdom, often ignored, that humans are not ultimately sovereign in human affairs; they are not the measure of all things; their governing capabilities and responsibilities are highly limited; their wisdom is never adequate; their theoretical achievements and ideals always fall short. In view of so many human limitations and deformities, the formation of the state has been one of the positive outcomes of the historical struggle to limit the power and reach of any single government, to stipulate the limits of government with respect to a host of nongovernmental responsibilities, and to hold governments accountable to standards of good governance and to the people they govern.

Despite all the critical things said in the foregoing chapters about American foreign and defense policies, it is important to emphasize that one of the best restraints on American hegemony in the world today comes from the fact that the American vision of how the world ought to be governed is a vision of many separate states, each governing itself independently and democratically. The American mission of advancing worldwide freedom and democracy does entail a chauvinistic projection of the American way of life onto the rest of the world, and the actual implementation of American foreign and military policies has often thwarted rather than aided the development of well-governed states. But the sound part of America's hope for the world serves as part of a normative apparatus that encourages both domestic and international criticism of American policies and practices. However incompatible the civil-religious ambitions of American exceptionalism may be with the constitutionally confining limits of the United States as a state, the expansive messianism of the former remains tethered to the structural limits of the latter. This is more than can be said for the ideological ambitions of those peoples and states that have set themselves on a course of conquest, radical revolution, or sheer destruction. The latter have seldom been held accountable by those whose resources they have commandeered and whose lives they have ruined or snuffed out.

The Limits of Realism

The modern state's endurance as the almost universally adopted mode of organizing large numbers of people under government is the basis for the *realist* approach to modern international relations.[8] States, through their governments and citizens, can understand their own interests, their own power, and what they need to sustain themselves, say the realists. States cannot have a similar understanding of, commitment to, or responsibility for the people of other states. They cannot know what "justice for all" could possibly mean at the international level. That is why the government of any state should assume that states everywhere, just like people, act in their own interests. The most likely possibility of achieving mutual understanding and stability in the relations among states, therefore, is for each to be accurately aware of its own power and limitations, to work diligently for its own interests, and to recognize that others are doing the same. On that basis, each state can make realistic assessments of why other states are acting as they are and react accordingly. On a realistic basis, diplomacy, trade, and decisions about entering into treaties and participating in balance-of-power arrangements can be carried forward with the greatest likelihood of sustaining one's own state and the state system.

What is inadequate about traditional realism, ironically, is its insufficient attention to political *reality*, not its lack of idealism. Human and state interests are not as narrow as realists have often assumed. Debates about the normative responsibilities of government are part of what constitutes a polity and state crafting. Realists typically do not take the contentions over "right" as seriously as they take the struggles over "might." Nor have they adequately assessed the power of religions (including civil religions) and ideologies as motivating drives of nations and governments.[9] State-focused realists have often paid insufficient attention to the reality of growing international interdependence at many levels, not just politically. Human relationships and institutional bonds of great importance to people increasingly transcend the borders of the states in which they live. As George Soros says, "Globalization has rendered the world increasingly interdependent, but international politics is still based on the sovereignty of states."[10]

States are certainly the central political institutions monopolizing force today, but their adequacy as institutions has to be measured by more than the quantity and quality of their military arsenals, their GNP, their industrial capacity, and their relative dependence on imported resources. Insofar as realists stand opposed to idealism, they tend to discount the meaning of normative principles of justice and injustice, morality and immorality. Yet, right at the heart of governance and its legitimacy in the minds of citizens (and of foreigners) is the question of when, how, and even whether military force, or trade sanctions, or diplomatic sanctions should be employed. As Thomas Pangle and Peter Ahrensdorf said of Thucydidean realism, it "sees through the moralism of states that claim to fight for justice, but that realism simultaneously discerns the benefits of, and the truth hidden in, such moralism." To realists, the "moral and religious passions may be unreasonable, but since we human beings are far from being simply reasonable creatures, those passions have a real power in the world. Justice is a concern that no state or statesman can escape."[11]

Realism's weakness at this point helps to explain why Niall Ferguson's estimation of the potential for the success of America's informal empire is
largely negative. America's vision of what the world should become and of
its own role in bringing it to pass is generally incompatible with the kind of
imperial order that Ferguson believes is needed and that he thinks the
United States could establish and administer. As I would put it, the American self-identity and sense of mission does not allow for a full-bodied global
imperium—even an informal one. Among other things, says Ferguson,
Americans do not want to pay for an empire because they don't even want
to pay for adequate social security and health care for the American public.
It's not that by so-called objective measures the United States is incapable
of squashing every rogue state and compelling a degree of order in the world.
But Americans do not want to do that. Furthermore, says Ferguson, the
United States is headed for a massive economic crisis because it is living on
borrowed money, as its citizens, individually, are also doing. But even beyond the economic (and manpower) deficit that Ferguson highlights, Americans do not have the commitment necessary to sustain a long-term, liberal-
imperial reordering of the world.[12]

Ignatieff contends that President Bush's intervention in Iraq in 2003 "fit
into America's long history of intervention" because the president believed
it "would increase both his and his country's power and influence. . . . The
Iraq intervention was the work of conservative radicals, who believed that
the status quo in the Middle East was untenable. . . . They wanted intervention to bring about a revolution in American power in the entire region."[13]
All of this may sound like the epitome of realism. But behind the actions was
Bush's freedom-idealism based on American military superiority and posi-
tioning as laid out in his National Security Strategy (NSS). The immodest
idealism rather than realism is what produced the false expectations about
what would result from the mere dislodging of Hussein. It was the immodest
idealism that kept the administration from squaring with the American people about why it was doing what it did. "Because the *casus belli* over Iraq was
never accurately set out for Americans," says Ignatieff, "the chances of
Americans hanging on for the long haul . . . have been undercut. Also dam-
aged has been the trust that a president will need from his people when he
seeks their support for intervention in the future."[14]

Philip Heymann observes that an essential ingredient for a constructive
American role in the world is "our reputation among our allies. That, in
turn, is determined in part by a very long history but in part by the more
salient activities we engage in currently. For leadership, reputation is critical: reputation for wisdom, for steadfastness, for boldness in using economic

and political powers, for willingness to share decision-making in the world, and for caring for those who feel left behind."[15] Most realists would agree that a country's reputation and perceived status in the world must be taken into account in arriving at realistic policies, but, like Machiavelli, they often contend that a state should want others to fear it, not necessarily to love or respect it. The fact is, however, that the world is no longer governed by states operating largely as autonomous entities, like separate billiard balls rolling around on the same table, engaged with one another only when they choose to be or when they bump into one another. Many of the human endeavors that states have helped to set in motion by encouraging science, technology, communications, trade, and economic development have produced networks of interdependence among states so thick and intricate that the realities of globalization are being forced on them, not chosen by them. There is more to sound statecraft than realist calculations, including balance-of-power strategies, particularly if we recognize that the shrinking world, failed states, and radically conflicting ideologies are increasingly shaping the circumstances that are making it impossible for states to meet the demands of governance.

The Limits of Idealism

Israel and the biblical prophets, as well as the early Christians and Augustine, were not idealists. The oneness of the world and of humankind, they believed, comes from the Creator. The divisions and brokenness of the world are due to human sin. Thus, there will be no unification of the world in peace until God finally establishes the city of God. People of many cultures have been able to imagine a universal higher law, or a transcendent order that holds for everyone, or a world of nations united in peace, because, in biblical terms, the creation is a single order, and God is sovereign over all. The human obligation to do justice to one's neighbors, to repair the world, and to try to build peace among the nations comes from the Creator. Apart from God's guidance, judgment, and blessing, therefore, universal peace on earth is out of the question. A utopia, arising from human imagination and sought by human efforts alone, will prove to be exactly that—an unrealizable "no place."

From a biblical, Augustinian point of view, therefore, international idealism is the product of an imagination and an overconfident rationality that absolutize one feature of reality. For example, it is true that there is but one creation order in which God commands all humans to do justice and love their neighbors. For this reason it is possible to imagine, as the Stoics did, that there is a universal rational order of law that holds for everyone and that ought to be realized on earth. It is also possible for people to sense that the normative truth about political reality somehow transcends the actual cities and states and empires of our historical experience, and that is why some, like Plato, Aristotle, and Cicero, sought to discover the higher truth by way of a disciplined rational quest. As another example, it is possible to imagine a future when all nations are living in peace, as idealists of different stripes have done, even if the means of realizing such a world are not at their disposal.[16]

The element of truth in the various idealisms and utopianisms is that humans are indeed bound together by more than national self-interest, greed, and suspicion or hatred of foreigners. There is but one humanity in only one world. The meaning and purpose of political order is about more than calculations to protect national interests in keeping with realpolitik. Political life entails some kind of political-legal moral obligation, and there is but one world, not merely a large number of self-interested states. Governing is about *right* and not only about *might*, and therefore the question of what is right for my neighbors and for the whole world, as well as for me and my state, will not go away.

There are, however, two major limitations inherent in international idealism, understood as the rational quest for an ideal state, or for a global society, or for an all-encompassing international legal order, or for a worldwide peaceful order of free and democratic states. First, idealism fails to take sufficiently into account the human deformities of selfishness, hatred, and a willingness to use violence for ends that inhibit or destroy the very possibility of peace. Second, idealism fails to take seriously enough the need for an enforcing authority if an international bond of peace is to be upheld. The *universal* cannot be left in the heavens (or in the theoretical mind), or it will be used as the moral ground to justify the absolutization of some *particular*, such as the Roman Empire, the sovereign state, national socialism, Soviet communism, or any number of other particular vehicles that promise to bring universal peace on earth.

As for the first limitation, many political movements that have taken over large parts of the modern world have been motivated by visions and missions that could not possibly lead to peace without large-scale slaughter and destruction. Think of Napoleon's imperial ambitions, or of Hitler's, or Stalin's, among others. These attempts to bring final peace to earth were motivated by dangerous idealisms. It is not only peace-loving people who have grand ideals. Part of the reason for the failure of the League of Nations was the impracticality of some of its ideals, arising undoubtedly from the sense of divine political mission that was shared by many delegates to the Paris Peace Conference of 1919. British diplomat Harold Nicolson, speaking "for many of his generation," wrote of the conference, "We were journeying to Paris, not merely to liquidate the war, but to found a new order in Europe. We were preparing not Peace only, but Eternal Peace. There was about us the halo of some divine mission. We must be alert, stern, righteous and ascetic. For we were bent on doing great, permanent and noble things."[17] Good intentions and grand hopes by enlightened people are not enough to bring peace and good governance to earth.

As for the second limitation of idealism, a lawfully ordered world requires a law-enforcing authority. At present, modern states monopolize force and are recognized as sovereign in the most important international treaty organizations, such as the United Nations. Consequently, the only internationally enforceable laws are those that the states agree to submit to or to enforce on themselves. Anne-Marie Slaughter writes that since international law is without a central enforcement authority, "it lacks even the hint of coercion that's implicit in every encounter with a domestic police officer." However, when she then goes on to explain the UN Charter, writing that Article 2(4), "required all states to refrain from 'the use of force in their international relations against the territorial integrity or political independence of any state,'" she does not underline the fact that the word "require" has no enforceable meaning if the member states do not agree to restrain themselves. There is no international "police officer" to compel compliance with what the UN Charter required.[18]

The Bush administration's freedom-idealism, which is deeply indebted to Wilsonianism, tries to combine a commitment to realpolitik with an idealistic commitment to international peace and order. Peace and order are supposed to arise as an indirect and almost automatic consequence of nations becoming free and democratic. The "realism" lies in refusing to subject the United States to any international authority that the administration thinks would undermine the ability of the United States to govern itself and to achieve its goals in the world. The "idealism" lies in imagining that international peace and justice will arise almost automatically as a consequence of every state becoming free, democratic, and sovereign in a way that America finds acceptable. "The interesting question," says Slaughter, "is why the United States, the overwhelmingly dominant power at the end of World War II, would choose to embed itself in a web of international institutions." John Ikenberry, she says, "argues compellingly that the United States pursued an institutional strategy as a way of entrenching a set of international rules favorable to its geopolitical and economic interests."[19] Considered from a realist perspective, Ikenberry may be right, but the American motive was also to use those kinds of rules and institutions (which did not fundamentally challenge U.S. sovereignty) as a means of fulfilling its idealist mission to advance freedom, democracy, and prosperity for everyone in the world. That the United States, along the way, was, as Ikenberry puts it, "compelled to accept real restraints on American power in order to assure weaker states in its orbit that it would neither abandon nor dominate them" was part of U.S. condescension to help weaker states recognize the legitimacy of America's mission and to follow its example by growing up into American-like maturity. Today, the Bush administration believes that many of the international legal and institutional entanglements of the past fifty years have become too restrictive for the United States if it is to be able to protect itself and fulfill its exceptional mission in the world. The United States must, therefore, according to the NSS, fall back on the deeper, prior principle of its own sovereignty and providential calling to serve freedom.

According to Jeb Rubenfeld, when the United States helped to build the United Nations, it saw itself "bestowing the gifts of American liberty, prosperity, and law, particularly American constitutional law, on the rest of the world. The 'new' international human rights were to be nothing other than the fundamental guarantees made famous by the U.S. Constitution."[20] But the enforcement of such rights depended on the sovereign states. Nothing about the United Nations would be allowed to trump American sovereignty. "Our willingness to promote and sign on to international law would be second to none—except when it came to any conventions that might require a change in U.S. domestic law or policy."[21] Rubenfeld calls this approach to building international order "national constitutionalism."

By contrast, "international constitutionalism" (more of a European idea) assumes that the universal authority of law resides "in a normative domain above politics and nation-states," thus allowing unelected judges to interpret it and "to countermand all governmental actions, including laws enacted by democratically elected legislators."[22] The incompatibility between these two "constitutional" views is exposed by the fact that Americans understand the universality of the "laws of nature" as entailing the right of self-government, which means that American sovereignty and the U.S. Constitution may not be trumped or overruled by any other human interpreter of nature's laws. If the United States were to submit to the rulings of international judges, it would violate the higher law of freedom itself. On the other hand, "international constitutionalists" tend to view the higher law as having a kind of trans-state "constitutional" validity. This would be true, however, only if all states submitted themselves voluntarily (with various moral, financial, and big-power pressures) to the international court system and to international law generally. That would be somewhat comparable to the way governments in western Christendom submitted to papal authority and to the Catholic Church's canon law. However, without a strong and sustained voluntary commitment on the part of all states to yield to the moral and legal authority of some body of universally recognized judges who have no independent enforcement authority, this ideal of "international constitutionalism" is impractical, unrealistic. Without institutionalized law enforcement, state sovereignty is not transcended.

Normative Statecraft

If the moment of truth in the best of realism is its recognition of the reality of states in an imperfect, competitive world, the moment of truth in the best of idealism is the recognition of ineluctable normative obligations that states and international organizations ignore at their own peril. If realists tend to overlook or discount trans-state norms of justice, idealists tend to overlook or discount the necessity of institutional enforcement of transnational law. If realists hope that international stability can best be achieved and maintained by means of each state basing its foreign policy decisions on its own interests with carefully calculated balances of power, idealists hope that human beings who desire peace rather than war will increasingly influence their respective governments so the latter can see that, even out of self-interest, they should voluntarily abide by international law. Realists tend to focus attention on the state because of its historical endurance in monopolizing force for the sake of governing. Idealists tend to underestimate the tenacity and durability of states because they see so clearly what states have failed to do, namely, avoid war, and in the long-term, war cannot serve the interests of people who want to live in peace.

The challenge for the United States today is to pursue "normative statecraft," which necessarily entails the building of trustworthy international and transnational organizations. This means taking seriously the importance of real governing institutions, which today are mostly states, while recognizing that the normative demands of justice increasingly require more than the governance of states by states. To the extent that justice holds for the domestic obligations of states, their governments have real responsibilities to act for the public protection and well-being of their citizens, including the responsibility to defend their countries against unjust aggression (in accord with just war principles). To the extent that justice calls for upholding the common good of the international public order in ways that cannot be adequately achieved by separate states acting alone or merely in cooperation, justice requires the building of international and transnational governance capabilities that improve the quality of state responsibilities while also building out beyond state sovereignty.

The fact that states—especially the most powerful states—are generally unwilling to relinquish some of their autonomy to help create necessary international and transnational institutions does not prove the invalidity or meaninglessness of transnational norms of justice. It is a sign, on the one hand, of a proper caution that any state should have about subjecting its citizens to rules and regimes that it does not control by itself. On the other hand, and at the same time, the reluctance of states to relinquish degrees of sovereignty confirms the limitations of the state system to achieve what will increasingly be needed for the just governance of a shrinking world and the well-being of states.

Furthermore, the fact that there is so much international injustice, particularly for the poor and for those in weaker and malformed states, does not prove the invalidity or the meaninglessness of the state as a means of governance. Some aspects of international injustice simply demonstrate the need for better and newer forms of governance that transcend the limits of states. Yet, the building of those institutions will have to be done in the same way that states were (and are still being) built, namely, by the gradual efforts of states and other institutions to act in a normative fashion to achieve just governance.

"The signal failure of American foreign policy since the end of the cold war," says Ignatieff, "has not been a lack of will to lead and to intervene; it has been a failure to imagine the possibility of a United States once again cooperating with others to create rules for the international community."[23] As human societies grow in complexity and become more and more interdependent internationally, the demand for international justice grows in urgency. According to Michael Sandel, "In a world where capital and goods, information and images, pollution and people, flow across national boundaries with unprecedented ease, politics must assume transnational, even global, forms, if only to keep up. Otherwise," he says, "economic power will go unchecked by democratically sanctioned political power. Nation-states, traditionally the vehicles of self-government, will find themselves increasingly unable to bring their citizens' judgments to bear on the economic forces that govern destinies."[24]

Development of the European Community into the European Union (EU) is one dynamic illustration of the tension inherent in international institution building. Questions about the welfare, health, and education policies of the EU require answers of a normative kind about the plural structure of society and the proper distribution of governmental responsibilities between national and EU-wide institutions. The more the EU becomes a publicly integrated entity beyond a mere trade zone, the greater becomes its need for transnational governance, including strong legislative and judicial branches of government at the federal level in which all the people living in EU states are adequately represented through elections.[25] The same thing can be said for international integration in other regions and on a global scale. The more that issues of global finance, trade, the environment, terrorism, war and peace, and human migration determine the conditions of political life both inside and among the states, the greater the normative demand for different kinds of international and even transnational governance with adequate representation of the people in achieving the rule of law.

Through both its strengths and its weaknesses the United States has helped to magnify the partial vacuum that exists in this one world of many states experiencing the growth of interdependence. That vacuum concerns international governance for the sake of both the many states and the global commons. The United States has been instrumental in contributing to the development of international law and organizations over the last century, primarily in response to global military and economic crises. At its founding, the United States pioneered a unique experiment in confederalism and then federalism that has considerable relevance for the strengthening of transnational governance in the future.[26] Nevertheless, in almost every instance in the twentieth century, international institutions were designed primarily to uphold the principle of national sovereignty, and particularly to preserve U.S. sovereignty. What is increasingly needed now are designs and commitments that strengthen trustworthy international governing capabilities.

Some criticisms of the Bush administration have been naive because they simply call on the president to fall back into patterns of the first Bush and the Clinton administrations. However, the international status quo was not adequate prior to 9/11. The distribution of political power and authority had changed to such an extent during and immediately after the Cold War that it had become incompatible with the structure and aims of the UN system itself, not to speak of the security interests of the United States and of the security and economic interests of other states. John Kelsay points out that the emphasis on state sovereignty when the United Nations was established was intended in part to provide protections for new states from the more powerful states as the former were emerging from colonialism.[27] But now that the principle of state sovereignty has been established for all states, the wider concern about what makes for international peace and order must be reconsidered, including questions of humanitarian intervention and interventions to stop terrorism and to guard against the development and use of weapons of mass destruction. The United Nations' undergirding of the principle of state sovereignty, according to UN Secretary General Kofi Annan, was never intended to protect small and weak states in a way that would make room for them to cloak the violation of human rights.[28]

We may well be facing a crisis of international law and order today more profound than the crisis that emerged with World War II and the loss of the European empires and more profound than the crisis that gave birth to the Treaty of Westphalia. The United Nations does not represent states among which power is relatively evenly distributed and among which a political-moral consensus about international obligations is universally shared. James Traub reminds us that back in 1948, U.S. Secretary of State George Marshall predicted that "should there be 'a complete lack of power equilibrium in the world, the United Nations cannot function successfully.'"[29] Not only is there no power equilibrium in the world today, but the United Nations does not even represent a consensus about the kind of political and legal systems its member states should have.

If the United States were to dedicate itself to the priority of helping to build stronger international institutions for the sake of better governance of the world, what might that entail? With regard to terrorist and other serious threats, such as a regime's attempt to conduct ethnic cleansing within its state borders, Ignatieff argues that America not only needs "its own doctrine for intervention but also an international doctrine that promotes and protects its interests *and* those of the rest of the international community."[30] To accomplish this, he argues, the United States should work with allies to reform the UN system in order to bring it into line with today's realities.

> The United States should propose enlarging the number of permanent members of the [Security Council] so that it truly represents the world's population. In order to convince the world that it is serious about reform, it ought to propose giving up its own veto so that all other permanent members follow suit and the Security Council makes decisions to use force with a simple majority vote. As a further guarantee of its seriousness, the United States would commit to use force only with approval of the council, except where its national security was directly threatened.[31]

If that move sounds improbable and difficult enough to achieve, the next step Ignatieff proposes would be even tougher. For he thinks the United Nations should change its first principle. The protection of state sovereignty should not be the chief reason for the United Nations to exist. For in maintaining that first principle, "it ends up defending tyranny and terror [by some sovereign states]—and invites a superpower to simply go its own way."

Instead, the United Nations should establish as its first principle the defense of human rights and protection against the wanton use of force by regimes as well as nonstate actors. There are five clear cases, says Ignatieff, when the United Nations could authorize intervention in states:

> [1] when, as in Rwanda or Bosnia, ethnic cleansing and mass killing threaten large numbers of civilians and a state is unwilling or unable to stop it; [2] when, as in Haiti, democracy is overthrown and people inside a state call for help to restore a freely elected government; [3] when, as in Iraq, North Korea and possibly Iran, a state violates the nonproliferation protocols regarding the acquisition of chemical, nuclear or biological weapons; [4] when, as in Afghanistan, states fail to stop terrorists on their soil from launching attacks on other states; and [5] finally when, as in Kuwait, states are victims of aggression and call for help.[32]

A new international charter like this, says Ignatieff, "would put America back where it belongs, as the leader of the international community instead of the deeply resented behemoth lurking offstage."[33]

However sound the details of Ignatieff's proposal may be, he does not go far enough. Giving an enlarged Security Council more flexibility and clout with a simple majority vote may allow decisions to be made that any number of countries—not least the United States—could find unacceptable. In those instances, why wouldn't the United States just "go its own way" if it didn't like the outcome of Security Council decisions, as it is inclined to do now? Moreover, if action by the "new" Security Council were to depend on troops and finances from the several states, as it does now, the United States and others may simply refuse to support certain interventions mandated by the council. A proposal to redesign the Security Council, if it does not address the fundamental question of sovereignty, may not be the best or the first thing the United States should do to begin concentrating more vigorously on strengthening the international order.

Eventually, a revised UN Charter needs to include some clear criteria and requirements for membership. Of course, to say this is to raise the most basic question about the source of the criteria that should be codified to define a legitimate, "civilized" state and to stipulate its obligations to the international order.[34] Yet, that is precisely the challenge today. The EU has criteria for membership. NATO has criteria for membership. Apart from serious criteria and requirements, an international organization will never be able to act meaningfully, or keep the confidence of its members, or hold its members accountable. The several UN declarations on human rights articulate some of the important criteria that should qualify the responsibilities of governments toward their citizens, and those declarations are nearly universally recognized. But they remain statements of norms, pointing to an ideal. The challenge is to place greater actual demands on member states in the United Nations to uphold the norms of good government. This is not the place to lay out an agenda for three or four successive American administrations on how to contribute, cooperatively with other states, to the reform and strengthening of international organizations for the sake of greater international justice and order. But with detailed proposals like those of the recent International Commission on Intervention and State Sovereignty,[35] against the backdrop of more than fifty years of successes and failures in building organizations, the argument of this book does not come as a call from out of the blue or as something altogether new.

In the early 1990s, according to Ferguson, "it seemed as if the United States had established a unipolar order. Yet today's transnational threats such as terrorism, nuclear proliferation and organized crime—to say nothing of disease pandemics, climate change and water shortages—put a premium on cooperation, not competition, between states."[36] Heymann stresses that American leadership requires the trust of others. It can't be forced on the world. "Great power can lead to great resentment as readily as to admiration."[37] All the more reason, then, for the United States to concentrate on working with other states to build trustworthy international institutions. Stanley Hoffmann argued almost twenty-five years ago that to develop a better world order "we need a statecraft that stresses long-term collective gains rather than short- or long-term national advantages; that accepts the need for a large measure of institutionalization in international affairs, and for important commitments of resources to common enterprises; that shows great restraint in its use of means; and that goes, in its choice of ends, far beyond the realm of interstate relations."[38]

None of this should be taken to suggest that I have sympathy for what Hedley Bull called "global centralism"[39]—a single, centralized, world state. Instead, with Sandel and Michael Walzer I am leery of a type of centralization of government in the world that would, in Walzer's words, lack the "capacity to promote peace, distributive justice, cultural pluralism, and individual freedom."[40] Sandel and Walzer both want to avoid centralized oppression as well as anarchy. For Sandel this means that sovereignty needs to be "dispersed" rather than "relocated."

The most promising alternative to the sovereign state is not a cosmopolitan community based on the solidarity of humankind but a multiplicity of communities and political bodies—some more extensive than nations and some less—among which sovereignty is diffused. Only a politics that disperses sovereignty both upward and downward can combine the power required to rival global market forces with the differentiation required of a public life that hopes to inspire the allegiance of its citizens.[41]

For Walzer, even a "federation of nation states" would be too uniform and centralized because it would probably "make its peace with material inequality" and would be too oligarchic. A global federation would more likely "be reached and sustained by pressure from the centre than by democratic activism at (to shift my metaphor) the grass roots."[42] Walzer proposes something looser and more pluralistic than a global federation, namely, "the familiar anarchy of states mitigated and controlled by a threefold set of nonstate agents: organizations like the UN, the associations of international civil society, and also regional unions like the European Community."[43] Walzer, however, does not adequately distinguish governmental from nongovernmental organizations. If there is not to be a single global federation, then undoubtedly the stronger states will have greater control of the United Nations, the European Community, the World Trade Organization, and other regional and global organizations, as is now the case. The most important normative question, it seems to me, is not how people and nongovernmental institutions can manage to thwart anarchy and centralization, but rather how governments and international organizations can do justice to individual rights, nongovernmental institutions, and the resources and networks of the global commons. The question is what just international governance requires, not what should it avoid.

Ultimately, the questions about government around the world today are questions about norm-responsiveness. The answers to these questions will not be found simply by noting that democracy is better than totalitarian communism, or that democracy leads to greater happiness and prosperity for more people than does dictatorial government, or that a middle way needs to be found between anarchy and centralization. The answers will not be found simply by fighting to retain the supposedly sovereign state at all cost, and particularly the sovereignty of the United States. Rather, the United States should persist in a long-term commitment to cooperation with other states to build stronger, more trustworthy and sustainable international institutions that can lead, demonstrably, to a more just ordering of the international commons.

Of all the "certainties" that have been proposed and fought for in the world, one in particular has proven very durable over the centuries, namely, that there is but one world. The fact that human cultures and languages are many and that there has been more war than peace has not undermined this certainty. As the world continues to shrink with respect to the density of human interdependence, its oneness becomes all the more apparent. Yet, it is also clear that the world has not been unified by human efforts—whether imperial or democratic—even though many efforts have indeed been made to try to bring the entire "known world" under the roof of a single authority. Neither the pharaoh nor the Roman Empire, neither the Middle Kingdom nor Christendom, neither Islam nor the modern state has been able to constitute the world as a political unity. An American imperium, even if only a military security umbrella, will also fail. The modes of human government have been plural and often in conflict. Nevertheless, the world as a single globe continues to shrink even as human societies continue to expand and become more complex. The system of states that has been developed since 1648 is of crucial importance, but it is insufficient for the just governance of the world. The unavoidable challenge to all states, and especially to the United States, at this point in history is to decide how to cooperate in governing themselves and in building the right kind of international and transnational institutions.

Notes

Chapter 1

1. There were only two previous surprise attacks on U.S. soil, the British burning of Washington in 1814 and the Japanese bombing of Pearl Harbor in 1941, both of which were military attacks. See John Lewis Gaddis, *Surprise, Security, and the American Experience* (Cambridge, Mass.: Harvard University Press, 2004), 10–11, 35–37.

2. For several different interpretations of modern Islamism, see Gilles Kepel, *Jihad: The Trail of Political Islam* (Cambridge, Mass.: Harvard University Belknap Press, 2002); Paul Berman, *Terror and Liberalism* (New York: W. W. Norton, 2003); Ian Buruma and Avishai Margalit, *Occidentalism: The West in the Eyes of Its Enemies* (New York: The Penguin Press, 2004); Bernard Lewis, *What Went Wrong? Western Impact and Middle East Response* (New York: Oxford University Press, 2002); and Max Rodenbeck, "Islam Confronts Its Demons," *The New York Review of Books*, April 29, 2004, 14–18. Buruma and Margalit, like Berman, emphasize the influence of Western romanticism and antirationalism on the radical Islamists. However, that is only part of an explanation of the ideology. Islamism's "depiction of Western civilization as a form of idolatrous barbarism is an original contribution to the rich history of Occidentalism," by which the authors mean a view of the West as having become so rationalistic and materialistic that it has lost its soul along with the deep spiritual and organic meaning of life (Buruma and Margalit, *Occidentalism*, 102).

3. Quoted in Paul Marshall, Roberta Green, and Lela Gilbert, *Islam at the Crossroads* (Grand Rapids, Mich.: Baker Books, 2002), 95.

4. Quoted in Reuel Marc Gerecht, "The Gospel According to Osama bin Laden," *The Atlantic Monthly* (January 2003): 48.

5. Ethan Bronner, "Collateral Damage," *The New York Times Book Review*, February 22, 2004, 11.

6. Bronner, "Collateral Damage," 11.

7. Philip B. Heymann explains that "we have a tradition going back well over a century of keeping the military out of domestic law enforcement, both because it is trained for war and not policing, and because we fear the centralization of power that would come with domestic control managed by the commander in chief or the secretary of defense. We also have a tradition since the 1970s of keeping the Defense Department out of intelligence gathering about domestic activities, and that tradition has served well both the military (by preserving public respect) and the public (by providing more confidence in the privacy of political activities" (*Terrorism, Freedom and Security* [Cambridge, Mass.: The MIT Press, 2003], 32–33).

8. Robert Kagan, "America's Crisis of Legitimacy," *Foreign Affairs* 83, no. 2 (March/April 2004): 66–67.

9. For detailed discussion of legitimate and illegitimate changes in security laws, see Heymann, *Terrorism*, 87–157, and Michael Ignatieff, *The Lesser Evil: Political Ethics in an Age of Terror* (Princeton, N.J.: Princeton University Press, 2004), 1–53.

10. Fareed Zakaria, "Terror and the War of Ideas," *The Washington Post*, April 10, 2004. Michael Howard made this point just a few weeks after 9/11. He argued that Western states are facing a transnational conspiracy. "In dealing with it the rhetoric and expectations of 'war' are counter-productive and much military experience irrelevant. With skillful political management and patient police-work, backed up where necessary by armed force 'in aid of the civil power,' this particular conspiracy can, perhaps, be eradicated," Howard affirmed. "But 'the war against terrorism' cannot be won, for terrorism will always be available as a weapon in the hands of people desperate and ruthless enough to use it" (*The Times* [London], October 2, 2001).

11. George Soros, "The Bubble of American Supremacy," *Atlantic Monthly* (December 2003): 65.

12. Lee Harris, "Al Qaeda's Fantasy Ideology," *Policy Review* (August–September, 2002): 32–33. Samuel P. Huntington tries to skirt the issue of equivocal language by speaking of the strife between the West and Islamist extremists ever since the 1979 Iranian Revolution as an "intercivilizational quasi war," noting simply that both sides have "recognized this conflict to be a war" (*The Clash of Civilizations and the Remaking of World Order* [New York: Simon and Schuster Touchstone Book, 1997], 216.

13. Heymann, *Terrorism*, 27.

14. Ivo H. Daalder and James M. Lindsay, *America Unbound: The Bush Revolution in Foreign Policy* (Washington, D.C.: Brookings Institution Press, 2003).

15. Clyde Prestowitz, *Rogue Nation: American Unilateralism and the Failure of Good Intentions* (New York: Basic Books, 2003).

16. Charles Krauthammer, *Democratic Realism: An American Foreign Policy for a Unipolar World* (Washington, D.C.: The AEI Press, 2004), 18. Niall Ferguson agrees that 11/9 did more to change the world than did 9/11. "The fall of the Berlin Wall on November 9, 1989, changed the context of American power far more profoundly than the fall of the World Trade Center" (*Colossus: The Price of America's Empire*

[New York: The Penguin Press, 2004], 27). But Ferguson has a different view than Krauthammer of the American empire and its prospects for survival.

17. Krauthammer, "Democratic Realism," 16.

Chapter 2

1. Paul Marshall, Roberta Green, and Lela Gilbert, *Islam at the Crossroads* (Grand Rapids, Mich.: Baker Books, 2002), 81.

2. John L. O'Sullivan (1839), quoted in Richard M. Gamble, *The War for Righteousness: Progressive Christianity, the Great War, and the Rise of the Messianic Nation* (Wilmington, Del.: ISI Books, 2003), 18.

3. Gamble, *War for Righteousness*, 18.

4. "Religion, Culture, and International Conflict After September 11: A Conversation with Samuel P. Huntington," *Center Conversations*, a publication of the Ethics and Public Policy Center, Washington, D.C. (June 2002): 13. Later in the conversation, Alan Cooperman added, "I think that a certain messianism is implicit in our idea that we need to protect not only ourselves but also representative democracy, and capitalism, and globalization, and if people in other cultures don't want this package of things, that's only because they don't know enough, or are uneducated, or have a false consciousness. They *should* want it and they *will* want it, and ultimately they'll thank us for it" (15).

5. In a fine essay on Robert S. McNamara's ongoing attempt to come to grips with America's failure in Vietnam, Lloyd E. Ambrosius explains that McNamara wanted both sides to admit that they had missed opportunities and made mistakes based on mutual misunderstanding and lack of knowledge. But, says Ambrosius, McNamara avoided

> more probing questions about responsibility for the war and its consequences. . . . In his explanation of the war, McNamara did not ask how, even if all of Vietnam had fallen to Communism, it would have directly threatened U.S. security. He did not ask why the United States, as the world's most powerful nation, had been so afraid of such a small, relatively weak nation in Southeast Asia. He did not ask whether, given this vast disparity in power, Washington had been more responsible than Hanoi for the war and its consequences. Nor did he ask what answers to these questions might reveal about the Wilsonianism of American political culture. . . . McNamara refused to acknowledge that U.S. goals in Vietnam in the 1960s had been unrealistic. Although recognizing then that the United States probably could not achieve its goals by military means, he could not at the time— and still could not in the 1990s—bring himself to draw the logical conclusion that Washington policy makers needed to reconsider their goals." [*Wilsonianism: Woodrow Wilson and His Legacy in American Foreign Relations* (New York: Palgrave McMillan, 2002), 166]

For an in-depth comparative study of American wars in Vietnam and Iraq, see Jeffrey Record and W. Andrew Terrill, *Iraq and Vietnam: Differences, Similarities, and Insights* (Carlisle, Pa.: Strategic Studies Institute, U.S. Army War College, May 2004), also available at www.carlisle.army.mil/ssi.

6. Michael S. Doran, "Intimate Enemies," *The Washington Post*, February 18, 2004.

7. Gamble, *War for Righteousness*, 21.

8. Gamble, *War for Righteousness*, 6.

9. Gamble, *War for Righteousness*, 6.

10. For some background on the American "civil religion," see Russell E. Richey and Donald G. Jones, eds., *American Civil Religion* (New York: Harper and Row, 1974), and the essay by Ruth H. Bloch, "Religion and Ideological Change in the American Revolution," in *Religion and American Politics: From the Colonial Period to the 1980s*, ed. Mark A. Noll (New York: Oxford University Press, 1990), 44–61. Jason Boffetti explains how even a thoroughgoing secularist like contemporary philosopher Richard Rorty has returned to embrace American civil religion in the spirit of John Dewey and Walt Whitman. "[D]ispensing with theism altogether and replacing devotion to God with devotion to one's fellow man," Rorty wants an American civil religion that "enshrines solidarity as its defining public virtue rather than holiness." The American essence, says Rorty, "is our existence, and our existence is in the future. Other nations thought of themselves as hymns to the glory of God. We redefine God as our future selves." Boffetti, "How Richard Rorty Found Religion," *First Things*, no. 143 (May 2004): 29.

11. Samuel P. Huntington, *The Clash of Civilizations and the Remaking of World Order* (New York: Simon and Schuster Touchstone Books, 1997), 11.

12. Huntington's article, "The Clash of Civilizations?" was published in *Foreign Affairs* (Summer 1993) and later expanded into the book we have been citing, *The Clash of Civilizations and the Remaking of World Order*.

13. Huntington, *Clash*, 255.

14. Saad Eddin Ibrahim, *Egypt, Islam and Democracy: Critical Essays* (Cairo: The American University in Cairo Press, 1996, 2002), 81.

15. See, for example, Clyde Prestowitz, *Rogue Nation: American Unilateralism and the Failure of Good Intentions* (New York: Basic Books, 2003), 186–87, and for all the details, Steve Coll, *Ghost Wars: The Secret History of the CIA, Afghanistan, and bin Laden, from the Soviet Invasion to September 10, 2001* (New York: Penguin, 2004).

16. Prestowitz, *Rogue Nation*, 187–90. See also Mark Pythian, *Arming Iraq: How the U.S. & Britain Secretly Built Saddam's War Machine* (Boston: Northeastern University Press, 1997). Ibrahim, writing in 1995, comments that "not only does the legacy of Western colonialism lurk in Muslim collective memory, but it is easily invoked with every contemporary Western act or policy which smacks of double standards. . . . The Western pressure on Arab and Muslim countries to sign an unlimited Nuclear Non-Proliferation Treaty (NPT), without asking their archenemy Israel to do the same, is to them a blatant double standard. . . . The West has long been on the best of terms with Muslim despots, such as Saudi Arabia, Iran's Shah, and Pakistan's Zia ul-Haq." *Egypt, Islam, and Democracy*, 90–91.

17. Jason Burke, "Think Again: Al Qaeda," available at www.schwartzreport.net.

18. Marshall, Green, and Gilbert, *Islam at the Crossroads*, 25. For a detailed and elaborate discussion of the Muslim meaning of jihad in comparison with the early Christian idea of "holy war," see James Turner Johnson, *The Holy War Idea in Western and Islamic Traditions* (University Park: Pennsylvania State University Press, 1997). Some modern Muslims vigorously protest the misuse of the word "jihad" by both Islamist radicals and westerners. Writing recently in the Arabic-language daily *Al-Sharq Al-Awsat* out of London, Islamic law professor Abd Al-Hamid Al-Ansari wrote that "From the beginning, Jihad has been defined by two goals: The first was a response to aggression and oppression. . . . The second is the liberation of the persecuted peoples from tyrannical regimes, as happened to the Persian and Byzantine peoples." There is no basis in Islamic law, he says, for the distortions that led Islamists to call for jihad to oppose the liberation of Kuwait from Saddam Hussein's aggression; to oppose the liberation of Afghanistan from the Taliban; to oppose the American-led war on Saddam's regime; or to support the recent terrorist bombings in Saudi Arabia. "The truth is that there is no explanation for the distortion of the concept of Jihad, except for the fact that there is an aggressive ideology embedded in the hearts of some people." From an electronic release (No. 699) on April 22, 2004 by the Middle East Media Research Institute (memri@memri.org), Washington, D.C.

19. Marshall, Green, and Gilbert, *Islam at the Crossroads*, 63.

20. On the end of the Ottomans and other consequences for the Middle East resulting from the Paris Peace Conference that followed World War I, see Margaret MacMillan's *Paris 1919* (New York: Random House Trade Paperbacks, 2002, 2001), 366–455. MacMillan says of the deals finally made at the conference, "The Arab world as a whole never forgot its betrayal and Arab hostility came to focus on the example of Western perfidy nearest at hand, the Zionist presence in Palestine. Arabs also remembered the brief hope of Arab unity at the end of the war. After 1945, those resentments and that hope continued to shape the Middle East" (409).

21. See Roger Scruton, "The Political Problem of Islam," *The Intercollegiate Review* (Fall 2002): 5–6.

22. Marshall, Green, and Gilbert, *Islam at the Crossroads*, 64. Johnson explains that the Ottoman rulers "sought consciously to connect their rule with that of the classical conception of the caliphate and to incorporate the *shari'a*, Islamic law, into the governance of the empire. Yet they proceeded from first establishing political control through the exercise of power, and their religious claims functioned to bolster their right to rule. The Ottoman sultans were not 'holy personages' by blood; their claim to religious leadership was actually derived from their exercise of ruling power through the *ghaza* or holy war" (*Holy War Idea*, 142).

23. According to Ibrahim,

The idealized history which Muslims learn in school and hear about in mosques has a simple, unidimensional message: Islam in the days of the Prophet Muhammad and the Guided Caliphs (A.D. 610–61) enabled Muslims to be virtuous, just, prosperous, and

strong. The true believers conquered the world and built the greatest civilization humanity had ever known. When Muslims strayed away from the straight path of Islam, they became decadent, poor, and weak. The culprits are sinful rulers at home and enemies of
Islam abroad. To restore on earth the "paradise lost," it is the duty of every good Muslim
to strive by deeds and words to restore the true Islamic societal-moral order. [*Egypt, Islam,
and Democracy*, 85]

24. Huntington, *Clash*, 174–79.
25. Johnson, *Holy War Idea*, 137–43. According to Johnson, "even in the early
years of Islam and throughout the classical age of Islamic jurisprudence, the ideal of
statecraft by which the *dar al-islam* was understood as a single religio-political entity
under unitary rule, opposed only by the non-Muslim *dar al-harb*, did not correspond
to the actual political shape or governance of the Islamic world" (139).
26. Johnson, *Holy War Idea*, 151.
27. Johnson, *Holy War Idea*, 160.
28. Paul Berman, *Terror and Liberalism* (New York: W. W. Norton, 2003), 87.
29. Buruma and Margalit, *Occidentalism*, 117. Berman, representing Qutb, says,

The people of God had come under insidious attack from within their own society, by the
forces of corruption and pollution [from the West]. In Qutb's version, these were the false
Muslims, the "hypocrites." The enemies from within were backed by sinister and even
cosmic enemies from abroad. These were the Crusaders and Jews. There was going to be
a terrible war against them, led by the Muslim vanguard. It was going to be the jihad. Victory was as always, guaranteed. And the reign of God, which had once existed in the long-
ago past, was going to be resurrected. It was going to be the reign of shariah. And the
reign was going to create a perfect society, cleansed of its impurities and corruptions. [*Terrorism*, 99]

30. Scruton, "Political Problem," 13.
31. Buruma and Margalit, *Occidentalism*, 69.
32. Gilles Kepel, *Jihad: The Trail of Political Islam* (Cambridge, Mass.: Harvard
University Belknap Press, 2002), 375.

Chapter 3

1. The following introductory overview of the biblical tradition is indebted to
William J. Dumbrell, *The Search for Order: Biblical Eschatology in Focus* (Grand
Rapids, Mich.: Baker Books, 1994); N. T. Wright, *The Climax of the Covenant: Christ
and the Law in Pauline Theology* (Minneapolis, Minn.: Fortress Press, 1991); Abraham
Joshua Heschel, *The Prophets* (New York: Harper and Row, 1962); Eric Voegelin, *Is-
rael and Revelation*, vol. 1 of *Order and History* (Baton Rouge: Louisiana State Uni-
versity Press, 1956); Geerhardus Vos, *Biblical Theology: Old and New Testaments*
(Grand Rapids, Mich.: Eerdmans, 1948). See also James W. Skillen, *A Covenant to
Keep: Meditations on the Biblical Theme of Justice* (Grand Rapids, Mich.: CRC Publications, 2000).

2. In addition to other works to be cited, this brief overview of the Greco-Roman tradition is indebted to S. E. Finer, *Ancient Monarchies and Empires*, vol. 1 of *The History of Government from the Earliest Times* (New York: Oxford University Press, 1999, 1997); Eric Voegelin, *The World of the Polis*, vol. 2 of *Order and History* (Baton Rouge: Louisiana State University Press, 1957); and Mario Attilio Levi, *Political Power in the Ancient World*, trans. Jane Costello (New York: New American Library, 1965).

3. Robert D. Kaplan, *Warrior Politics: Why Leadership Demands a Pagan Ethos* (New York: Random House, 2002), 45.

4. Kaplan, *Warrior Politics*, 47.

5. Thomas L. Pangle and Peter J. Ahrensdorf, *Justice Among Nations: On the Moral Basis of Power and Peace* (Lawrence: University Press of Kansas, 1999), 29, 31.

6. Eric Voegelin, *The Ecumenic Age*, vol. 4 of *Order and History* (Baton Rouge: Louisiana State University Press, 1974), 226.

7. Voegelin, *Ecumenic Age*, 227.

8. Pangle and Ahrensdorf, *Justice Among Nations*, 45.

9. Pangle and Ahrensdorf, *Justice Among Nations*, 48.

10. Pangle and Ahrensdorf conclude, "The more one ponders the severe restrictions on international community indicated by the Greek thinkers, the more one wonders to what extent they hope through their influence to bring about a relaxation of those restrictions, and to what extent their brief but pregnant reflections on foreign and war policy are meant to indicate some of the sharpest limits on and questions about the justice of which cities are capable. This would mean to say that their teaching is intended chiefly as a liberation for select wise, or potentially wise, individuals" (*Justice Among Nations*, 49–50).

11. F. Parkinson, *The Philosophy of International Relations* (Beverly Hills, Calif.: Sage Publications, 1977), 10.

12. Parkinson, *International Relations*, 11.

13. Parkinson, *International Relations*, 12.

14. Cicero, *On the Commonwealth* (*De re publica*), trans. George H. Sabine and Stanley B. Smith (Indianapolis, Ind.: The Bobbs-Merrill Co., 1976), 216 [Bk. III, 22].

15. Voegelin, *Ecumenic Age*, 47.

16. Voegelin, *Ecumenic Age*, 47.

17. Abraham Joshua Heschel writes that "the prophets of Israel had no theory or 'notion' of God. What they had was an *understanding*. Their God-understanding was not the result of a theoretical inquiry, of a groping in the midst of alternatives. To the prophets, God was overwhelmingly real and shatteringly present. . . . To them, the attributes of God were drives, challenges, commandments, rather than timeless notions detached from His Being." "The God of Israel and Christian Renewal," in Heschel, *Moral Grandeur and Spiritual Audacity*, ed. Susannah Heschel (New York: Farrar, Straus and Giroux, 1996), 269. Thorleif Boman concludes his comparative study of Hebrew and Greek experience by saying, "The Greek most acutely experiences the world and existence while he stands and reflects, but the Israelite reaches his zenith

in ceaseless movement. Rest, harmony, composure, and self-control—this is the Greek way; movement, life, deep emotion, and power—this is the Hebrew way" (*Hebrew Thought Compared with Greek* [New York: W.W. Norton, 1950], 205).

18. Pangle and Ahrensdorf, *Justice Among Nations*, 63.
19. Quoted in Pangle and Ahrensdorf, *Justice Among Nations*, 65.
20. Pangle and Ahrensdorf, *Justice Among Nations*, 66.
21. Pangle and Ahrensdorf, *Justice Among Nations*, 66–71.
22. Pangle and Ahrensdorf, *Justice Among Nations*, 72
23. Parkinson, *International Relations*, 13.

Chapter 4

1. On the influence of Christians in the early centuries after Christ, as well as their accommodation to the cultural and political patterns of life in which they were immersed, see, for example, Charles N. Cochrane, *Christianity and Classical Culture* (New York: Oxford University Press, 1944); Paul Veyne, ed., *From Pagan Rome to Byzantium*, vol. 1. of *A History of Private Life* (Cambridge, Mass.: Harvard University Belknap Press, 1987); and Robin Lane Fox, *Pagans and Christians* (New York: Harper and Row, 1986).

2. Harold J. Berman, *Law and Revolution: The Formation of the Western Legal Tradition* (Cambridge, Mass.: Harvard University Press, 1983), 3.

3. Cochrane, *Christianity and Classical Culture*, 178. This was a result of the Edict of Milan, and Cochrane reminds us that through most of the fourth century this meant a new pluralism, not the privileging of Christianity as the exclusive imperial religion. "Toleration, or rather complete religious neutrality, was embraced, not merely as a political expedient, but as a fundamental principle of public law; so to remain until the accession of Theodosius in 378" (179).

4. Cochrane, *Christianity and Classical Culture*, 197.
5. Walter Ullmann, *A History of Political Thought: The Middle Ages* (New York: Penguin Books, 1965), 33.
6. Ullmann, *Middle Ages*, 35.
7. F. Parkinson, *The Philosophy of International Relations* (Beverly Hills, Calif.: Sage Publications, 1977), 65–66.
8. Michael Grant, *Constantine the Great* (New York: Scribner's, 1993), 116–22.
9. O. Edmund Clubb, *China and Russia: The Great Game* (New York: Columbia University Press, 1971), 8.
10. Clubb, *China and Russia*, 8.
11. Ullmann, *Middle Ages*, 40.
12. Ullmann, *Middle Ages*, 41–42.
13. Ullmann, *Middle Ages*, 38.
14. Ullmann, *Middle Ages*, 47.
15. Ullmann, *Middle Ages*, 47.
16. Ullmann, *Middle Ages*, 47–48.
17. Ullmann, *Middle Ages*, 48.

18. Judith Herrin, *The Formation of Christendom* (Princeton, N.J.: Princeton University Press, 1987), 8.

19. Herrin, *Christendom*, 477.

20. Herrin, *Christendom*, 477.

21. Herrin, *Christendom*, 480.

22. Herrin, *Christendom*, 480. For a thorough treatment of governance in Byzantium, the Islamic world, and western Christendom, see S. E. Finer, *The Intermediate Ages*, vol. 2 of *The History of Government from the Earliest Times* (New York: Oxford University Press, 1999, 1997).

23. Augustine did not write a treatise on politics and government as such, but his most important major work for our consideration is his *City of God* (*De civitate Dei*).

24. Thomas L. Pangle and Peter J. Ahrensdorf, *Justice Among Nations: On the Moral Basis of Power and Peace* (Lawrence: University Press of Kansas, 1999), 75.

25. Pangle and Ahrensdorf, *Justice Among Nations*, 75.

26. George Weigel, *Tranquillitas Ordinis: The Present Failure and Future Promise of American Catholic Thought on War and Peace* (New York: Oxford University Press, 1987), 28–29.

27. This message of caution about the ambiguity of earthly politics is the burden of Jean Bethke Elshtain's *Augustine and the Limits of Politics* (Notre Dame, Ind.: University of Notre Dame Press, 1995).

28. Christopher Dawson, *Religion and the Rise of Western Culture* (New York: Doubleday, 1950), 46, 122.

29. Dawson, *Religion*, 133.

30. Dawson, *Religion*, 215.

31. See the study by Oliver O'Donovan, "The Political Thought of *City of God* 19," in Oliver O'Donovan and Joan Lockwood O'Donovan, *Bonds of Imperfection: Christian Politics, Past and Present* (Grand Rapids, Mich.: Eerdmans, 2004), 48–72, and James W. Skillen, "Augustine and Contemporary Evangelical Social Thought," *The Reformed Journal* (January 1979): 19–24.

32. Robert D. Kaplan, *Warrior Politics: Why Leadership Demands a Pagan Ethos* (New York: Random House, 2002), passim.

33. The best discussions of Augustine on these matters are those of R. A. Markus, *Saeculum: History and Society in the Theology of St. Augustine* (Cambridge: Cambridge University Press, 1970), and Herbert A. Deane, *The Political and Social Ideas of St. Augustine* (New York: Columbia University Press, 1963), 78–153.

34. Deane, *St. Augustine*, 200.

35. See James Turner Johnson, *The Holy War Idea in Western and Islamic Traditions* (University Park: Pennsylvania State University Press, 1997), 52–56.

36. Pangle and Ahrensdorf, *Justice Among Nations*, 76.

37. Johnson, *Holy War Idea*, 54.

38. Johnson, *Holy War Idea*, 52–53. For a helpful brief overview of the Crusades, see Norman F. Cantor, ed., *The Encyclopedia of the Middle Ages* (New York: Viking, 1999), 139–41.

39. Johnson, *Holy War Idea*, 53.

40. Johnson, *Holy War Idea*, 150.

41. Johnson, *Holy War Idea*, 151.

42. William R. Stevenson, *Christian Love and Just War: Moral Paradox and Political Life in St. Augustine and His Modern Interpreters* (Macon, Ga.: Mercer University Press, 1987), 42.

43. Stevenson, *Christian Love*, 45–46.

44. "One may date the Papal Revolution from 1075, when Gregory proclaimed papal supremacy over the entire church and ecclesiastical independence from, and superiority over, the secular power, to 1122, when a final compromise was reached between the papal and the imperial authority" (Berman, *Law and Revolution*, 23).

45. Berman, *Law and Revolution*, 51.

46. For a good introduction to, and selections from, Aquinas, see Oliver O'Donovan and Joan Lockwood O'Donovan, eds., *From Irenaeus to Grotius: A Sourcebook in Christian Political Thought, 100–1625* (Grand Rapids, Mich.: Eerdmans, 1999), 320–61, and A. P. D'Entreves, ed., *Aquinas: Selected Political Writings*, trans. J. G. Dawson (Oxford: Basil Blackwell, 1970).

47. Russell Hittinger, *The First Grace: Rediscovering the Natural Law in a Post-Christian World* (Wilmington, Del.: ISI Books, 2003), xxiii. Much more than Ullmann and Pangle and Ahrensdorf, Hittinger emphasizes the close interdependence of nature and grace, of natural law and eternal law, of the human and the divine.

48. In Aquinas's view of the relation between the spiritual and the temporal authorities, say the O'Donovans, "the universal subjection of Christian kings to the Roman pope as Christ's vicar is balanced by a conception of papal direction as preeminently theological and moral (2.4: *ST* 2a2ae.60.6 ad 3). He [Aquinas] concurs with the opinion that the church may punish the apostasy of kings with excommunication, thereby releasing subjects from their oaths of fealty. He does not, however, allow the teleological subjection of temporal to spiritual rule to undercut the former's independent foundation in the *ius gentium* left intact by the 'law of grace' (2a2ae. 10.10; 12)" (*Sourcebook*, 323).

49. Ullmann, *Middle Ages*, 178.

50. Ullmann, *Middle Ages*, 177.

51. Ullmann, *Middle Ages*, 179–80.

52. O'Donovan and O'Donovan, *Sourcebook*, 324. For a careful assessment of medieval accounts of natural law, including that of Aquinas, see Jean Porter, "Reason, Nature, and Natural Order in Medieval Accounts of Natural Law," *Journal of Religious Ethics* 24, no. 2 (Fall 1986): 207–32. Also see Porter's *The Recovery of Virtue: The Relevance of Aquinas for Christian Ethics* (Louisville, Ky.: Westminster/John Knox Press, 1990).

53. Pangle and Ahrensdorf, *Justice Among Nations*, 83.

54. Pangle and Ahrensdorf, *Justice Among Nations*, 85–88.

55. Weigel, *Tranquillitas Ordinis*, 37.

56. Weigel, *Tranquillitas Ordinis*, 37.

57. Dawson, *Religion*, 137.

58. Ullmann, *Middle Ages*, 177. A. P. D'Entreves concurs: "No doubt the idea of the fundamental unity of mankind is preserved in the general outlines of St. Thomas's conception of politics. It survives in the very notion of a natural law, common to all men, from which the several systems of positive laws derive their substance and value. It survives in the conception of the *unus populus Christianus* [one Christian people], which embraces all countries and nations, and which finds its highest expression in the *Corpus mysticum Ecclesiae* [mystical Church]. But in the sphere of practical politics it is the particular State which carries the day" (*Aquinas*, xxv).

Chapter 5

1. Martin Van Creveld, *The Rise and Decline of the State* (Cambridge: Cambridge University Press, 1999), 58.

2. S. E. Finer, *Empires, Monarchies, and the Modern State*, vol. 3 of *The History of Government from the Earliest Times* (New York: Oxford University Press, 1999, 1997), 1261.

3. Paul Kennedy, *The Rise and Fall of the Great Powers: Economic Change and Military Conflict from 1500–2000* (New York: Random House, 1987), 16–30.

4. Kennedy, *Great Powers*, 29.

5. Van Creveld compactly summarizes the church's position as follows:

> From about A.D. 1100 on it possessed, apart from the power to lay down and interpret divine law, the right to nominate and promote its own officials; immunity from secular justice, also known as benefit of clergy; the right to judge and punish both its own personnel and, in cases involving the care of souls, laymen; the right to offer asylum to fugitives from secular justice; the right to absolve subjects from their oaths to their rulers; and, to support the lot, immense landed estates, a separate system of taxation, and, here and there, the right to strike money as well. Not only were higher prelates almost always noblemen but, like other lords, the church could both give benefices and receive them from others. Throughout much of Europe, ecclesiastical domains and even principalities existed side by side with their secular counterparts; the main difference was that the ecclesiastical succession, instead of proceeding from father to (necessarily illegitimate) son, often went from uncle to nephew. Thus the church became integrated with the feudal system, being supported by the latter and, in turn, supporting it. [*Rise and Decline*, 60–61]

6. Harold J. Berman, *Law and Revolution: The Formation of the Western Legal Tradition* (Cambridge, Mass.: Harvard University Press, 1983), 24. "The imposing structure of medieval Christendom," says Christopher Dawson, "which had been built up by the idealism of the reforming movement, the organizing power of the Papacy, and the devotion of the religious Orders proved powerless to withstand the determined attack of a handful of unscrupulous officials . . . who were the servants of the new monarchy and understood how to exploit the new techniques of power in a ruthlessly

totalitarian fashion" (*Religion and the Rise of Western Culture* [New York: Doubleday, 1950], 217).

7. Berman, *Law and Revolution*, 89.

8. Berman, *Law and Revolution*, 66. Even more important than Charles's inauguration as Augustus in 800, says Judith Herrin, was the church synod that he called in Frankfurt in 794, which

> established a breach not only between West and East, but also within the West. For the separation from Constantinople of the churches under Charles's control, encouraged by the example of independent Visigothic practice and theory, also reduced Rome's control over the West. The synod witnessed the end of an era of papal hegemony over the western churches. Thereafter, Frankish leaders assumed a less humble and more directive relationship with the papacy. They had discovered an autonomy that would structure subsequent Christian development in Europe. Although Rome would reassert its authority under more powerful ninth-century leaders, the Frankish initiative of 794 had created an alternative focus of religious expertise and judgment. It had set a precedent for secular rulers backed by their own ecclesiastics to challenge papal interpretations of purely theological matters, a dangerous threat to previous acceptance of Petrine supremacy. [*The Formation of Christendom* (Princeton, N.J.: Princeton University Press, 1987), 443–4]

9. According to Berman, Charlemagne and his successors were unlike Caesar in that they

> did not rule their subjects through an imperial bureaucracy. There was no capital city comparable to Rome or Constantinople—indeed, in sharp contrast to Caesar's city-studded empire, Charlemagne and his successors had hardly any cities at all. Instead, the emperor and his household traveled through his vast realm from one principal locality to another. . . . In an economy which was almost entirely local, and in a political structure which gave supreme power to tribal and regional leaders, the emperor had both the military task of maintaining a coalition of tribal armies which would defend the empire against enemies from without and the spiritual task of maintaining the Christian faith of the empire against a reversion to paganism. He ruled by holding court. [*Law and Revolution*, 89]

10. Van Creveld, *Rise and Decline*, 86.

11. Van Creveld, *Rise and Decline*, 86.

12. Van Creveld, *Rise and Decline*, 86.

13. Van Creveld, *Rise and Decline*, 103.

14. Van Creveld, *Rise and Decline*, 104.

15. Van Creveld, *Rise and Decline*, 115.

16. Van Creveld, *Rise and Decline*, 116. Simon Schama's *The Embarrassment of Riches: An Interpretation of Dutch Culture in the Golden Age* (New York: Alfred A. Knopf, 1987), gives a wonderfully rich picture of the culture from which the Dutch empire emerged and grew. Russell Shorto's new book on New Amsterdam, *The Island at the Center of the World* (New York: Doubleday, 2004), illuminates the importance of the Dutch contribution to the foundations of New York and the United States.

17. Van Creveld, *Rise and Decline*, 118.
18. Van Creveld, *Rise and Decline*, 119ff.
19. See Stephen A. McKnight's *Sacralizing the Secular: Renaissance Origins of Modernity* (Baton Rouge: Louisiana State University Press, 1989), for this explanation of the impact of the Renaissance humanism.
20. Finer, *Empires, Monarchies*, 1263.
21. On this point, see Daniel Philpott, "On the Cusp of Sovereignty: Lessons from the Sixteenth Century," in *Sovereignty at the Crossroads? Morality and International Politics in the Post-Cold War Era*, ed. Luis E. Lugo (Lanham, Md.: Rowman & Littlefield, 1996), 37–62; and John D. Carlson and Erik C. Owens, "Introduction: Reconsidering Westphalia's Legacy for Religion and International Politics," in *The Sacred and the Sovereign: Religion and International Politics*, eds. Carlson and Owens (Washington, D.C.: Georgetown University Press, 2003), 1–37.
22. For overlapping yet contrasting interpretations of the Renaissance and its inspiration of the Enlightenment, see McKnight, *Sacralizing the Secular*; Stephen L. Collins, *From Divine Cosmos to Sovereign State* (New York: Oxford University Press, 1989); Herman Dooyeweerd, *Roots of Western Culture: Pagan, Secular, and Christian Options*, eds. Mark Vander Vennen, Bernard Zylstra, and D. F. M. Strauss, trans. John Kraay (Lewiston, N.Y.: The Edwin Mellen Press, 2003, 1979, 1959); Basil Willey, *The Seventeenth Century Background* (New York: Doubleday Anchor Books, 1953, 1935); and Eric Voegelin, *From Enlightenment to Revolution*, ed. John H. Hallowell (Durham, N.C.: Duke University Press, 1975).
23. A few of the helpful texts and interpretations of the Reformation's contribution to political life include Harold J. Berman, *Law and Revolution II: The Impact of the Protestant Reformations on the Western Legal Tradition* (Cambridge, Mass.: Harvard University Belknap Press, 2004); Dooyeweerd, *Roots of Western Culture*; William R. Stevenson Jr., *Sovereign Grace: The Place and Significance of Christian Freedom in John Calvin's Political Thought* (New York: Oxford University Press, 1999); Ralph C. Hancock, *Calvin and the Foundations of Modern Politics* (Ithaca, N.Y.: Cornell University Press, 1989); William A. Mueller, *Church and State in Luther and Calvin* (New York: Doubleday Anchor Books, 1965, 1954); Oliver O'Donovan and Joan Lockwood O'Donovan, eds., *From Irenaeus to Grotius: A Sourcebook in Christian Political Thought, 100–1625* (Grand Rapids, Mich.: Eerdmans, 1999), 549–820; and Julian H. Franklin, ed., *Constitutionalism and Resistance in the Sixteenth Century: Three Treatises by Hotman, Beza, and Mornay* (New York: Pegasus, 1969).
24. This judgment will undoubtedly be contested because there can be no doubt about the significant impact of the Reformation on legal reform within the states. Moreover, everyone is aware of the impact of the Reformation on the shape of Swiss, Dutch, English, Scottish, and American polities in particular and on constitutionalism generally. My intention is not to deny any of this but rather to say that the Reformers did not contribute a distinctively new view of political community and of international relations that stands out strongly from other contributions to the development of the modern state. That is why scholars such as Ralph Hancock are

still trying to decide whether Calvin was medieval or modern. Though if one wants to identify Reformed emphases that were consequential, they would be in the support of constitutionalism and in the rejection of both the ecclesiastical control of government and the secularization of government (in the sense of cutting off government's accountability to God). See Hancock, *Calvin*; Stevenson, *Sovereign Grace*; Berman, *Law and Revolution, II*; and John Witte, Jr., *Law and Protestantism: The Legal Teachings of the Lutheran Reformation* (Cambridge: Cambridge University Press, 2002).

25. See Guenther H. Haas, *The Concept of Equity in Calvin's Ethics* (Waterloo, Ontario: Wilfrid Laurier University Press, 1997), and W. Fred Graham, *The Constructive Revolutionary: John Calvin and His Socio-Economic Impact* (Richmond: John Knox Press, 1971).

26. Finer, *Empires, Monarchies*, 1299.

27. Finer, *Empires, Monarchies*, 1298–99. "This central notion that the relationship of the government to the individual must be based on law, that the individual possessed certain inherent rights, and that consequently he could be deprived of these only by due process, marked the essential difference between these newly arisen European states and those of Asia," says Finer. Asian absolutism "knew almost none of the legal restraints that existed in Europe, and few if any of the practical ones. There were no natural aristocracies, no counterbalancing Church, no autonomous guilds, corporations, cities, and the like; in short, no *corps intermediaries* which formed the bulwark against absolutist pretensions in Europe" (1303).

28. For a more detailed argument about the differentiated, public-interest state that emerges with and makes room for the differentiation of nongovernmental institutions and organizations, see James W. Skillen, *In Pursuit of Justice: Christian-Democratic Explorations* (Lanham, Md.: Rowman & Littlefield, 2004).

Chapter 6

1. See Donald S. Lutz, *The Origins of American Constitutionalism* (Baton Rouge: Louisiana State University Press, 1988), and Donald S. Lutz, ed., *Colonial Origins of the American Constitution: A Documentary History* (Indianapolis, Ind.: Liberty Fund, 1998).

2. From the "Declaration of Independence," in *Major Themes*, vol. 1 of *The Founders' Constitution*, eds. Philip B. Kurland and Ralph Lerner (Chicago: University of Chicago Press, 1987), 9.

3. Daniel George Lang, *Foreign Policy in the Early Republic: The Law of Nations and the Balance of Power* (Baton Rouge: Louisiana State University Press, 1985), 9–10.

4. Lang, *Foreign Policy*, 10.

5. Lang, *Foreign Policy*, 35.

6. Lang, *Foreign Policy*, 35.

7. Mark A. Noll, *America's God: From Jonathan Edwards to Abraham Lincoln* (New York: Oxford University Press, 2002), 33.

8. I'm referring here to the picture Christopher Dawson draws of Christendom in his book, *Religion and the Rise of Western Culture* (New York: Doubleday, 1950), discussed earlier in chapter 4.

9. Arthur Herman, *How the Scots Invented the Modern World* (New York: Three Rivers Press, 2001), 15.

10. Richard M. Gamble, *The War for Righteousness: Progressive Christianity, the Great War, and the Rise of the Messianic Nation* (Wilmington, Del.: ISI Books, 2003), 8.

11. Gamble, *War for Righteousness*, 9.

12. Noll, *America's God*, 41.

13. Noll, *America's God*, 32–33.

14. Noll, *America's God*, 206.

15. Gamble, *War for Righteousness*, 10.

16. James E. Block, *A Nation of Agents: The American Path to a Modern Self and Society* (Cambridge, Mass.: Harvard University Belknap Press, 2002), 449.

17. Block, *Nation of Agents*, 449.

18. Wilfred M. McClay, "The Soul of a Nation," *The Public Interest*, no. 155 (Spring 2004): 9.

19. McClay, "Soul of a Nation," 13.

20. McClay, "Soul of a Nation," 17.

21. McClay, "Soul of a Nation," 18.

22. McClay, "Soul of a Nation," 19.

23. See James W. Skillen, *In Pursuit of Justice: Christian-Democratic Explorations* (Lanham, Md.: Rowman & Littlefield, 2004), and Skillen, *Recharging the American Experiment: Principled Pluralism for Genuine Civic Community* (Grand Rapids, Mich.: Baker Books, 1994), for the development of an argument that Christianity can contribute to strong citizenship while opposing all civil religions.

24. Block, *Nation of Agents*, 458.

Chapter 7

1. Lloyd E. Ambrosius, *Wilsonianism: Woodrow Wilson and His Legacy in American Foreign Relations.* (New York: Palgrave McMillan, 2002), 36.

2. See also Ambrosius's *Wilsonian Statecraft: Theory and Practice of Liberal Internationalism During World War I* (Wilmington, Del.: Scholarly Resources, 1991), and *Woodrow Wilson and the American Diplomatic Tradition* (Cambridge: Cambridge University Press, 1987).

3. Ambrosius, *Wilsonianism*, 37.

4. Ambrosius, *Wilsonianism*, 33.

5. Richard M. Gamble, *The War for Righteousness: Progressive Christianity, the Great War, and the Rise of the Messianic Nation* (Wilmington, Del.: ISI Books, 2003), 149.

6. Charles N. Cochrane, *Christianity and Classical Culture* (New York: Oxford University Press, 1944), 197.

7. Gamble, *War for Righteousness*, 153.

8. Gamble, *War for Righteousness*, 159.

9. Gamble, *War for Righteousness*, 177.

10. Gamble, *War for Righteousness*, 157.

11. Gamble, *War for Righteousness*, 155.

12. Ambrosius, *Wilsonianism*, 38. See also Niall Ferguson, *Colossus: The Price of America's Empire* (New York: The Penguin Press, 2004), 52–60.

13. Ambrosius, *Wilsonianism*, 41.

14. Ambrosius, *Wilsonianism*, 54.

15. Ambrosius, *Wilsonianism*, 59. The debates and negotiations over the League are covered by Margaret MacMillan, *Paris 1919* (New York: Random House Trade Paperbacks, 2002, 2001), 53–106.

16. Ambrosius, *Wilsonianism*, 129.

17. Ambrosius, *Wilsonianism*, 127. The discussion of Henry Kissinger is with reference to the latter's book *Diplomacy* (New York: Simon and Schuster, 1994). Also in consideration by Ambrosius is Tony Smith, *America's Mission: The United States and the Worldwide Struggle for Democracy in the Twentieth Century* (Princeton, N.J.: Princeton University Press, 1994), and Daniel Patrick Moynihan, *Pandaemonium: Ethnicity in International Politics* (New York: Oxford University Press, 1993).

18. Ambrosius, *Wilsonianism*, 130.

19. Ambrosius, *Wilsonianism*, 130–31. On the "mandates," see MacMillan, *Paris 1919*, 83–106. It is interesting that Niall Ferguson in *Colossus* calls today for something like the recovery of Wilson's idea of "mandates." "In vast swatches of Africa, Asia and the Middle East national self-determination has led to much grief," writes John Ikenberry in a review of Ferguson's book. "Ferguson argues without qualification that 'the experiment with political independence—especially in Africa—has been a disaster for most poor countries.' To Ferguson, the extension of liberal empire into these regions (even involving some form of colonial rule) is necessary." G. John Ikenberry, "Illusions of Empire: Defining the New American Order," *Foreign Affairs* (March/April 2004): 149.

20. Ambrosius, *Wilsonianism*, 2.

21. Lang, *Foreign Policy*, 35.

22. Ambrosius, *Wilsonianism*, 27. Benjamin Barber's book, *Fear's Empire: War, Terrorism, and Democracy* (New York: W.W. Norton, 2003), urges American leaders to forsake unilateral imperialism and to pursue a cosmopolitan order of universal law, something that sounds much like what Wilson wanted to achieve through the League of Nations.

23. Ambrosius, *Wilsonianism*, 27–28.

24. Andrew J. Bacevich, *American Empire: The Realities and Consequences of U.S. Diplomacy* (Cambridge, Mass.: Harvard University Press, 2002), 8.

25. Ferguson, *Colossus*, 78. In this regard, see Barber, *Fear's Empire*, 67–101.

26. Joseph S. Nye Jr., *Soft Power: The Means to Success in World Politics* (New York: Public Affairs, 2004).

27. Zbigniew Brzezinski, *The Choice: Global Domination or Global Leadership* (New York: Basic Books, 2004).

28. John Lewis Gaddis, *Surprise, Security, and the American Experience* (Cambridge, Mass.: Harvard University Press, 2004), 107–18; Ferguson, *Colossus*; and Charles Krauthammer, *Democratic Realism: An American Foreign Policy for a Unipolar World* (Washington, D.C.: The AEI Press, 2004). Gaddis is more cautious than Krauthammer and does not argue for the kind of unilateralism that the latter is comfortable with. He cautions against the sin of pride and states that "you can't sustain hegemony without consent" (*Surprise, Security*, 117). But global leadership for Gaddis is very much what the entire American tradition has stood for, and when he speaks of hope, he evokes the American exceptionalist vision of the world's destiny. "The key to American influence in the world has always been the hope for a better life that we still, more credibly than anyone else, have to offer. The Founding Fathers had hope in mind when they crafted the most durable ideology in modern history. Lincoln evoked that hope at what seemed a hopeless time for this nation. Woodrow Wilson and Franklin D. Roosevelt held out hope in what seemed to be a hopelessly war-torn world. We need to hang onto hope as we prepare for the new era of insecurity we've entered and as we remember the tragedy that brought it about" (*Surprise, Security*, 117–18).

29. Paul Kennedy, *The Rise and Fall of the Great Powers: Economic Change and Military Conflict from 1500 to 2000* (New York: Random House, 1987), 514–15. Emmanuel Todd believes that the American empire is already in serious decline: *After the Empire: The Breakdown of the American Order* (New York: Columbia University Press, 2003).

30. Clyde Prestowitz, *Rogue Nation: American Unilateralism and the Failure of Good Intentions* (New York: Basic Books, 2003), 284.

31. Prestowitz, *Rogue Nation*, 283–84.

32. Prestowitz, *Rogue Nation*, 284.

Chapter 8

1. Niall Ferguson, *Colossus: The Price of America's Empire* (New York: The Penguin Press, 2004), 10.

2. Ferguson, *Colossus*, 13.

3. Ferguson, *Colossus*, 13.

4. Ferguson, *Colossus*, 13.

5. Tod Lindberg, "The Bush Doctrine," *Hoover Digest* no. 4 (2002): 117.

6. Lindberg, "Bush Doctrine," 118.

7. Lindberg, "Bush Doctrine," 120.

8. Lindberg, "Bush Doctrine," 120–21.

9. John Lewis Gaddis, *Surprise, Security, and the American Experience* (Cambridge, Mass.: Harvard University Press, 2004), 90.

10. Gaddis, *Surprise, Security*, 100–101.

11. Walter Russell Mead, *Power Terror, Peace, and War: America's Grand Strategy in a World at Risk* (New York: Knopf, 2004), 198.

12. William Galston, "Perils of Preemptive War," *The American Prospect* (September 23, 2002); also available at www.prospect.org/print-friendly/print/V13/17/galston-w.html. The inner contradiction of the Bush strategy is also illumined by Hendrik Hertzberg:

> [The NSS] implicitly recognizes that national sovereignty is in many ways an outdated and dangerous doctrine, one that must increasingly give way to other exigencies. Is the sovereignty of the Iraqi state to be valued more than the right of Iraq's neighbors and the rest of the world to be reasonably free of the fear of being vaporized or sickened unto death by Iraqi weapons of mass destruction? Of course not. So the Bush doctrine, in spite of itself, recognizes the logic of something like . . . world government. But its idea of world government looks very much like a benevolent American dictatorship—a dictatorship of the entrepreneuriat, you might say. [Hertzberg, editorial, *New Yorker*, October 14 and 21, 2002]

13. Interestingly, and parenthetically here, the Bush administration evidently wants to reorient the responsibilities of the federal government at home so it will be better prepared for the global military role outlined above. The pattern was established by the Reagan administration. The federal government, budgetarily speaking, would become proportionately more responsible for military and security affairs and proportionately less responsible for the nation's social, welfare, health, labor, education, and environmental affairs. The states would have to take back responsibility for the latter if they are not relegated to the market. Massive increases in defense spending since 9/11, coupled with cuts in federal taxes, are evidence of the Bush administration's inclination in this direction. The fact that federal spending in some nonmilitary areas—such as education and drug subsidies for the elderly—increased during the Bush administration is probably due to short-term domestic political considerations. The consequential federal deficits and the approaching crises over Social Security and health care spending, however, will force Congress in the future to make decisions that will, in the Bush administration's view, almost certainly have to favor military and security spending while other concerns are turned back to the states and to the market.

Chapter 9

1. Robert D. Kaplan, *Warrior Politics: Why Leadership Demands a Pagan Ethos* (New York: Random House, 2002), 77.

2. Kaplan, *Warrior Politics*, 114.

3. Kaplan, *Warrior Politics*, 115.

4. Clyde Prestowitz, *Rogue Nation: American Unilateralism and the Failure of Good Intentions* (New York: Basic Books, 2003), 180–91.

5. Prestowitz, *Rogue Nation*, 284.

6. Kaplan, *Warrior Politics*, 109.

7. My aim here does not include a consideration of twentieth-century arguments about, and refinements of, the tradition of just war reasoning. For the most important of them, see Reinhold Niebuhr, *Moral Man and Immoral Society* (New York: Charles Scribner's Sons, 1932); Niebuhr, *Beyond Tragedy* (New York: Charles Scribner's Sons, 1937); Niebuhr, *Love and Justice*, ed. D. B. Robertson (Gloucester, Mass.: Peter Smith, 1967); Robert W. Tucker, *The Just War: A Study in Contemporary American Doctrine* (Baltimore: Johns Hopkins University Press, 1960); John Courtney Murray, *We Hold These Truths: Catholic Reflections on the American Proposition* (New York: Doubleday Image Books, 1964); Paul Ramsey, *The Just War: Force and Political Responsibility* (New York: Charles Scribner's Sons, 1968); Ramsey, *War and Christian Conscience: How Shall Modern War Be Conducted Justly?* (Durham, N.C.: Duke University Press, 1961); Michael Walzer, *Just and Unjust Wars* (New York: Basic Books, 1977); James Turner Johnson, "Humanitarian Intervention, Christian Ethical Reasoning, and the Just-War Idea," in *Sovereignty at the Crossroads? Morality and International Politics in the Post-Cold War Era*, ed. Luis E. Lugo (Lanham, Md.: Rowman & Littlefield, 1996), 127–43; Johnson, *Can Modern War Be Just?* (New Haven, Conn.: Yale University Press, 1984); Johnson, *Just War Tradition and the Restraint of War: A Moral and Historical Inquiry* (Princeton, N.J.: Princeton University Press, 1981); and George Weigel, *Tranquillitas Ordinis: The Present Failure and Future Promise of American Catholic Thought on War and Peace* (New York: Oxford University Press, 1987).

8. Richard B. Hays, *The Moral Vision of the New Testament: A Contemporary Introduction to the New Testament* (San Francisco: HarperSanFrancisco, 1996), 317–46. My discussion of Hays that follows depends in part on an earlier essay written jointly with Keith J. Pavlischek, "Political Responsibility and the Use of Force: A Critique of Richard Hays," *Philosophia Christi* 3, no. 2, Series 2 (2001): 421–45.

9. See, for example, John Howard Yoder, *The Politics of Jesus* (Grand Rapids, Mich.: Eerdmans, 1972), and Yoder, *For the Nations: Essays Public and Evangelical* (Grand Rapids, Mich.: Eerdmans, 1997); and Stanley Hauerwas, *In Good Company: The Church as Polis* (Notre Dame, Ind.: University of Notre Dame Press, 1995).

10. Hays, *Moral Vision*, 317.

11. Hays, *Moral Vision*, 332.

12. Hays, *Moral Vision*, 343.

13. Hays, *Moral Vision*, 342.

14. Hays, *Moral Vision*, 322, 337.

15. Hays, *Moral Vision*, 337.

16. Yoder, *Politics of Jesus*, 183–214.

17. My argument here is similar to Paul Marshall's in *God and the Constitution: Christianity and American Politics* (Lanham, Md.: Rowman & Littlefield, 2002), 169–70.

18. As William R. Stevenson explains, one of the concerns of Paul Ramsey about twentieth-century Protestant thought was the inattention to "just means." While

"claiming Augustinian realism as its ancestor," wrote Ramsey in *War and Christian Conscience*, Protestant ethics

> has given way to an ethic of political expediency. In concentrating its efforts on determinations of "the 'lesser evil' or perchance the 'greater good' among the supposed *consequences* of actions," it has "sought to find the path along which action should be directed in order to defend some sort of values at the end of the road toward which action reaches, yet never reaches." . . . For if "no more can be said about the morality of *action* than can be derived backward from the future goal" then "ethics has already more than half-way vanished, i.e., it has become mere calculation of the means to projected ends." Such an ethic therefore "produces some version of the opinion that the end justifies the means." [*War and Christian Conscience: How Shall Modern War Be Conducted Justly?* (Durham, N.C.: Duke University Press, 1961), 121]

19. Alexander F. C. Webster and Darrell Cole offer an insightful judgment in this regard in their book *The Virtue of War: Reclaiming the Classic Christian Traditions East and West* (Salisbury, Md.: Regina Orthodox Press, 2004):

> The pacifist rightly attacks [Reinhold] Niebuhr [and I would add, Robert Kaplan] for making Jesus's ethic an "otherworldly" ethic. Jesus's ethic is very much a "this-worldly" ethic. But the sort of theology we see at work in the early fathers, St. Thomas, and Calvin insists that Jesus's ethic be read harmoniously with God's "this-worldly" ethic as revealed in the Old Testament. Those adhering to classical just war doctrine, we suggest, would make one with Hauerwas and Yoder that Niebuhr's position is mistaken, but they part company on how to remedy the mistake. If by the term "responsible citizens" we mean what Niebuhr means (i.e., citizens who must leave the personal ethic of Jesus behind and get their hands "dirty" if they wish to be "responsible"), then the just warrior is solidly in the pacifist camp. The just warrior agrees with the pacifist that no deals should be made with the devil. The just warrior along with the pacifist refuses to get his or her hands "dirty." Just warriors nevertheless insist that they are responsible citizens in so far as they are willing to use force when the cause is just. They merely deny that using force means that we have to get our hands "dirty," and when we have to get our hands "dirty" in order to be effective politically, just warriors will remain "ineffective." That much again they have in common with pacifists. To sum up this last point: the just warrior is able to agree with the pacifist about "dirty hands" while disagreeing with the pacifist about what this means for being a responsible citizen. [178–79]

20. Jean Bethke Elshtain, *Just War Against Terror: The Burden of American Power in a Violent World* (New York: Basic Books, 2003).
21. Elshtain, *Just War*, 24.
22. Elshtain, *Just War*, 46.
23. Elshtain, *Just War*, 49.
24. Elshtain, *Just War*, 54.
25. Elshtain, *Just War*, 51.
26. Elshtain, *Just War*, 52.
27. Elshtain, *Just War*, 57–58.

28. Jean Bethke Elshtain, "Just War, Realism, and Humanitarian Intervention," in *The Sacred and the Sovereign: Religion and International Politics*, eds. John D. Carlson and Erik C. Owens (Washington, D.C.: Georgetown University Press, 2003), 96.

29. Elshtain, *Just War*, 155. In her essay "Just War, Realism, and Humanitarian Intervention," Elshtain says, "Just war thinking also requires sustained attention even after the shooting has stopped" (99).

30. Elshtain, *Just War*, 144.

31. Elshtain, *Just War*, 154.

32. Elshtain, *Just War*, 150–51.

33. Elshtain, *Just War*, 162.

34. Elshtain, *Just War*, 169.

Chapter 10

1. Michael Ignatieff, *The Lesser Evil: Political Ethics in an Age of Terror* (Princeton, N.J.: Princeton University Press, 2004), 156.

2. Walter Russell Mead, *Power, Terror, Peace, and War: America's Grand Strategy in a World at Risk* (New York: Knopf, 2004), 198.

3. Ignatieff, *Lesser Evil*, 159.

4. Mead, *Power*, 167.

5. Michael Ignatieff, "Why Are We in Iraq?" *New York Times Magazine*, September 7, 2003, 43.

6. Jeffrey Record, "The Bush Doctrine and War with Iraq," *Parameters* (Spring 2003): 16.

7. Record, "Bush Doctrine," 16, quoting John Ikenberry, "America's Imperial Ambition," *Foreign Affairs* 81 (September/October 2002): 45.

8. There is not a single school of "realism." I am generalizing here. A well-known example of realist thinking is Hans J. Morgenthau, *Politics Among Nations*, 5th ed. (New York: Knopf, 1976). A sophisticated realist who tries to take American idealism into account is Henry Kissinger; see his *Diplomacy* (New York: Simon and Schuster, 1994), particularly chapter 1, "The New World Order," 17–27, and chapter 31, "The New World Order Reconsiderd," 804–35. On modern realism from Machiavelli to Kenneth Waltz, see Thomas L. Pangle and Peter J. Ahrensdorf, *Justice Among Nations: On the Moral Basis of Power and Peace* (Lawrence: University Press of Kansas, 1999), 125–61 and 218–57. For a discussion of Hamiltonian realism see Walter Russell Mead, *Special Providence: American Foreign Policy and How It Changed the World* (New York: Knopf, 2001), referenced in Joseph S. Nye Jr. *Soft Power: The Means to Success in World Politics* (New York: Public Affairs, 2004), 139–41. I am indebted here and in the rest of this chapter to Justin Cooper's "The State, Transnational Relations, and Justice: A Critical Assessment of Competing Paradigms of World Order," in *Sovereignty at the Crossroads*, edited by Luis E. Lugo (Lanham, Md.: Rowman & Littlefield, 1996), 3–27.

9. See Douglas Johnston and Cynthia Sampson, eds., *Religion: The Missing Dimension in Statecraft* (New York: Oxford University Press, 1994).

10. George Soros, "The Bubble of American Supremacy," *Atlantic Monthly* (December 2003): 66.

11. Pangle and Ahrensdorf, *Justice Among Nations*, 31, 29.

12. Niall Ferguson, *Colossus: The Price of America's Empire* (New York: The Penguin Press, 2004), 258–302.

13. Ignatieff, "Why Are We in Iraq?" 71.

14. Ignatieff, "Why Are We in Iraq?" 71. "In stretching the evidence [about Saddam Hussein's weapons of mass destruction]," says Ignatieff, Bush and British Prime Minister Tony Blair "sought to manipulate democratic consent for war, and even those who supported them cannot feel that a desirable end justified such means. As it happened, the war does not appear to have had a preemptive justification at all, since no weapons or advanced programs have been found in the year since the regime's fall." *Lesser Evil*, 163.

15. Philip B. Heymann, *Terrorism, Freedom and Security* (Cambridge, Mass.: The MIT Press, 2003), 117.

16. Of help here on "idealism," its strengths, and its weaknesses, see Pangle and Ahrensdorf, *Justice Among Nations*, 162–217; John Hare, "Kantian Ethics, International Politics, and the Enlargement of the *Foedus Pacificum*," in *Sovereignty at the Crossroads*, 71–92; Cooper, "The State"; John D. Carlson, "Trials, Tribunals, and Tribulations of Sovereignty: Crimes against Humanity and the *imago Dei*," in *The Sacred and the Sovereign*, 196–232; Benjamin Barber, *Fear's Empire: War, Terrorism, and Democracy* (New York: W. W. Norton, 2003), 145–220; Stanley Hoffmann, *Duties Beyond Borders: On the Limits and Possibilities of Ethical International Politics* (Syracuse, N.Y.: Syracuse University Press, 1981); Saul H. Mendlovitz, *On the Creation of a Just World Order: Preferred Worlds for the 1990s* (New York: Free Press, 1975).

17. Quoted in Margaret MacMillan, *Paris 1919* (New York: Random House Trade Paperbacks, 2002, 2001), 86.

18. Anne-Marie Slaughter, "Leading Through Law," *Wilson Quarterly* (Autumn 2003): 39, 38. Jacques deLisle explains that "the international legal system lacks singular institutions with the capacity to determine authoritatively and effectively whether an act is legal or not. Because international law does not have a viable executive, capable of enforcing the legal rules, it depends instead on what international law calls 'horizontal enforcement'—that is, self-help (or other-helping) measures by those who in a more robust legal system would depend on police and prosecutors to redress or deter encroachments on legal rights" ("Illegal? Yes. Lawless? Not so Fast: The United States, International Law, and the War in Iraq," Foreign Policy Research Institute *E-Notes*, March 28, 2003, http://fpri.org/enotes.

19. Slaughter, "Leading Through Law," 41.

20. Jeb Rubenfeld, "The Two World Orders," *Wilson Quarterly* (Autumn 2003): 25.

21. Rubenfeld, "Two World Orders," 25.

22. Rubenfeld, "Two World Orders," 26. The contrast between European and American views of international law and order is the burden of Robert Kagan's argument in "America's Crisis of Legitimacy," *Foreign Affairs* (March/April 2004).

23. Ignatieff, "Why Are We in Iraq?" 85.

24. Michael Sandel, "America's Search for a New Public Philosophy," *Atlantic Monthly* (March 1996): 72. Almost twenty-five years ago, Stanley Hoffmann made a similar point: "One of our greatest present difficulties is that the transnational society which crosses borders and plays a vital role in economic affairs, communications, education, and science, as well as in the service of many good causes, does not coincide fully with the international system" (*Duties Beyond Borders*, 222).

25. The best detailed reflection on, and proposals for, European federal integration can be found in the study by the policy research center of the Dutch Christian Democratic Appeal (wi@bureau.cda.nl) titled, *Public Justice and the European Union* (The Hague, CDA, 1999).

26. On confederalism and federalism, see F. Parkinson, *The Philosophy of International Relations* (Beverly Hills, Calif.: Sage Publications, 1977), 143–66; Felix Morley, *Freedom and Federalism* (Indianapolis, Ind.: Liberty Fund, 1981, 1959); Daniel J. Elazar, *Covenant and Civil Society: The Constitutional Matrix of Modern Democracy* (New Brunswick, N.J.: Transaction Publishers, 1998).

27. John Kelsay, "Justice, Political Authority and Armed Conflict: Challenges to Sovereignty and the Just Conduct of War," in *The Sacred and the Sovereign*, 115.

28. Kelsay, "Justice, Political Authority," 116.

29. James Traub, "Who Needs the U.N. Security Council," *The New York Times Magazine*, November 17, 2002.

30. Ignatieff, "Why Are We in Iraq?" 85.

31. Ignatieff, "Why Are We in Iraq?" 85. For a similar proposal to reshape the UN Security Council, see Mead, *Power*, 201–2.

32. Ignatieff, "Why Are We in Iraq?" 85.

33. Ignatieff, "Why Are We in Iraq?" 85.

34. See Kelsay, "Justice, Political Authority," 121ff.

35. "The Responsibility to Protect," a report of the International Commission on Intervention and State Sovereignty (Ottawa, Ontario: International Development Research Centre, 2001); also available at www.idrc.ca.

36. Ferguson, *Colossus*, 296.

37. Heymann, *Terrorism*, 121.

38. Hoffmann, *Duties Beyond Borders*, 205.

39. Hedley Bull, *The Anarchical Society: A Study of Order in World Politics* (New York: Columbia University Press, 1977), 302ff.

40. Michael Walzer, "International Society: What Is the Best We Can Do?" *Ethical Perspectives* (Journal of the European Ethics Network) 6, nos. 3–4 (December 1999): 201.

41. Sandel, "America's Search," 73–74.

42. Walzer, "International Society," 206–7.

43. Walzer, "International Society," 208.

Bibliography

Ambrosius, Lloyd E. *Wilsonian Statecraft: Theory and Practice of Liberal Internationalism During World War I.* Wilmington, Del.: Scholarly Resources, 1991.

———. *Wilsonianism: Woodrow Wilson and His Legacy in American Foreign Relations.* New York: Palgrave McMillan, 2002.

———. *Woodrow Wilson and the American Diplomatic Tradition.* Cambridge: Cambridge University Press, 1987.

Bacevich, Andrew J. *American Empire: The Realities and Consequences of U.S. Diplomacy.* Cambridge, Mass.: Harvard University Press, 2002.

Barber, Benjamin. *Fear's Empire: War, Terrorism, and Democracy.* New York: W. W. Norton, 2003.

Berman, Harold J. *Law and Revolution: The Formation of the Western Legal Tradition.* Cambridge, Mass.: Harvard University Press, 1983.

———. *Law and Revolution, II: The Impact of the Protestant Reformations on the Western Legal Tradition.* Cambridge, Mass.: Harvard University Belknap Press, 2003.

Berman, Paul. *Terror and Liberalism.* New York: W. W. Norton, 2003.

Bloch, Ruth H. "Religion and Ideological Change in the American Revolution." In *Religion and American Politics: From the Colonial Period to the 1980s,* edited by Mark A. Noll, 44–61. New York: Oxford University Press, 1990.

Block, James E. *A Nation of Agents: The American Path to a Modern Self and Society.* Cambridge, Mass.: Harvard University Belknap Press, 2002.

Boffetti, Jason. "How Richard Rorty Found Religion." *First Things,* no. 143 (May 2004): 24–30.

Boman, Thorleif. *Hebrew Thought Compared with Greek.* New York: W. W. Norton, 1950.

Bronner, Ethan. "Collateral Damage." *The New York Times Book Review,* February 22, 2004, 11.

Brzezinski, Zbigniew. *The Choice: Global Domination or Global Leadership*. New York: Basic Books, 2004.

Bull, Hedley. *The Anarchical Society: A Study of Order in World Politics*. New York: Columbia University Press, 1977.

Buruma, Ian, and Avishai Margalit. *Occidentalism: The West in the Eyes of Its Enemies*. New York: The Penguin Press, 2004.

Cantor, Norman F., ed. *The Encyclopedia of the Middle Ages*. New York: Viking, 1999.

Carlson, John D., and Erik C. Owens, eds. *The Sacred and the Sovereign: Religion and International Politics*. Washington, D.C.: Georgetown University Press, 2003.

Cicero. *On the Commonwealth*, translated by George H. Sabine and Stanley B. Smith. Indianapolis, Ind.: The Bobbs-Merrill Co., 1976.

Clubb, O. Edmund. *China and Russia: The Great Game*. New York: Columbia University Press, 1971.

Cochrane, Charles N. *Christianity and Classical Culture*. New York: Oxford University Press, 1944.

Coll, Steve. *Ghost Wars: The Secret History of the CIA, Afghanistan, and bin Laden, from the Soviet Invasion to September 10, 2001*. New York: Penguin, 2004.

Collins, Stephen L. *From Divine Cosmos to Sovereign State*. New York: Oxford University Press, 1989.

Cooper, Justin. "The State, Transnational Relations, and Justice: A Critical Assessment of Competing Paradigms of World Order." In *Sovereignty at the Crossroads*, edited by Luis E. Lugo, 3–27. Lanham, Md.: Rowman & Littlefield, 1996.

Daalder, Ivo H., and James M. Lindsay. *America Unbound: The Bush Revolution in Foreign Policy*. Washington, D.C.: Brookings Institution Press, 2003.

Dawson, Christopher. *Religion and the Rise of Western Culture*. New York: Doubleday, 1950.

Deane, Herbert A. *The Political and Social Ideas of St. Augustine*. New York: Columbia University Press, 1963.

D'Entreves, A. P., ed. *Aquinas: Selected Political Writings*, translated by J. G. Dawson. Oxford: Basil Blackwell, 1970.

deLisle, Jacques. "Illegal? Yes. Lawless? Not So Fast: The United States, International Law, and the War in Iraq." Foreign Policy Research Institute *E-Notes*, at http://fpri.org/enotes (March 28, 2003).

Dooyeweerd, Herman. *Roots of Western Culture: Pagan, Secular, and Christian Options*. Edited by Mark Vander Vennen, Bernard Zylstra, and D. F. M. Strauss. Translated by John Kraay. Lewiston, N.Y.: Edwin Mellen Press, 2003, 1979, 1959.

Doran, Michael S. "Intimate Enemies." *The Washington Post*, February 18, 2004.

Dumbrell, William J. *The Search for Order: Biblical Eschatology in Focus*. Grand Rapids, Mich.: Baker Books, 1994.

Elazar, Daniel J. *Covenant and Civil Society: The Constitutional Matrix of Modern Democracy*. New Brunswick, N.J.: Transaction Publishers, 1998.

Elshtain, Jean Bethke. *Augustine and the Limits of Politics*. Notre Dame, Ind.: University of Notre Dame Press, 1995.

———. *Just War Against Terror: The Burden of American Power in a Violent World*. New York: Basic Books, 2003.

———. "Just War, Realism, and Humanitarian Intervention." In *The Sacred and the Sovereign*, edited by John D. Carlson and Erik C. Owens, 90–112. Washington, D.C.: Georgetown University Press, 2003.

Ferguson, Niall. *Colossus: The Price of America's Empire*. New York: The Penguin Press, 2004.

Finer, S. E. *The History of Government from the Earliest Times*. 3 vols. New York: Oxford University Press, 1999, 1997.

Fox, Robin Lane. *Pagans and Christians*. New York: Harper and Row, 1986.

Franklin, Julian H., ed. *Constitutionalism and Resistance in the Sixteenth Century: Three Treatises by Hotman, Beza, and Mornay*. New York: Pegasus, 1969.

Gaddis, John Lewis. *Surprise, Security, and the American Experience*. Cambridge, Mass.: Harvard University Press, 2004.

Galston, William. "Perils of Preemptive War," *The American Prospect*, September 23, 2002. Also see www.prospect.org/print-friendly/print/V13/17/galston-w.html.

Gamble, Richard M. *The War for Righteousness: Progressive Christianity, the Great War, and the Rise of the Messianic Nation*. Wilmington, Del.: ISI Books, 2003.

Gerecht, Reuel Marc. "The Gospel According to Osama Bin Laden." *The Atlantic Monthly* (January 2003): 46–48.

Graham, W. Fred. *The Constructive Revolutionary: John Calvin and His Socio-Economic Impact*. Richmond: John Knox Press, 1971.

Grant, Michael. *Constantine the Great*. New York: Scribner's, 1993.

Haas, Guenther H. *The Concept of Equity in Calvin's Ethics*. Waterloo, Ontario: Wilfrid Laurier University Press, 1997.

Hancock, Ralph C. *Calvin and the Foundations of Modern Politics*. Ithaca, N.Y.: Cornell University Press, 1989.

Hare, John. "Kantian Ethics, International Politics, and the Enlargement of the *Foedus Pacificum*." In *Sovereignty at the Crossroads*, edited by Luis E. Lugo, 71–92. Lanham, Md.: Rowman & Littlefield, 1996.

Harris, Lee. "Al Qaeda's Fantasy Ideology." *Policy Review* (August–September 2002): 19–36.

Hauerwas, Stanley. *In Good Company: The Church as Polis*. Notre Dame, Ind.: University of Notre Dame Press, 1995.

Hays, Richard B. *The Moral Vision of the New Testament: A Contemporary Introduction to the New Testament*. San Francisco: HarperSanFrancisco, 1996.

Herman, Arthur. *How the Scots Invented the Modern World*. New York: Three Rivers Press, 2001.

Herrin, Judith. *The Formation of Christendom*. Princeton, N.J.: Princeton University Press, 1987.

Hertzberg, Hendrik. "Editorial." *The New Yorker*, October 14 and 21, 2002.

Heschel, Abraham Joshua. *Moral Grandeur and Spiritual Audacity*, edited by Susannah Heschel. New York: Farrar, Straus and Giroux, 1996.

———. *The Prophets*. New York: Harper and Row, 1962.

Heymann, Philip B. *Terrorism, Freedom and Security*. Cambridge, Mass.: The MIT Press, 2003.

Hittinger, Russell. *The First Grace: Rediscovering the Natural Law in a Post-Christian World*. Wilmington, Del.: ISI Books, 2003.

Hoffmann, Stanley. *Duties Beyond Borders: On the Limits and Possibilities of Ethical International Politics*. Syracuse, N.Y.: Syracuse University Press, 1981.

Huntington, Samuel P. *The Clash of Civilizations and the Remaking of World Order*. New York: Simon and Schuster Touchstone Books, 1997.

Ibrahim, Saad Eddin. *Egypt, Islam and Democracy: Critical Essays*. Cairo: The American University in Cairo Press, 2002, 1996.

Ignatieff, Michael. *The Lesser Evil: Political Ethics in an Age of Terror*. Princeton, N.J.: Princeton University Press, 2004.

———. "Why Are We in Iraq?" *The New York Times Magazine*, September 7, 2003, 39ff.

Ikenberry, G. John. "Illusions of Empire: Defining the New American Order." *Foreign Affairs* (March/April 2004): 144–54.

International Commission on Intervention and State Sovereignty. "The Responsibility to Protect." Ottawa, Ontario: International Development Research Centre, 2001, vailable at www.idrc.ca.

Johnson, James Turner. *Can Modern War Be Just?* New Haven, Conn.: Yale University Press, 1984.

———. *The Holy War Idea in Western and Islamic Traditions*. University Park: Pennsylvania State University Press, 1997.

———. "Humanitarian Intervention, Christian Ethical Reasoning, and the Just-War Idea." In *Sovereignty at the Crossroads*, edited by Luis E. Lugo, 127–43. Lanham, Md.: Rowman & Littlefield, 1996.

———. *Just War Tradition and the Restraint of War: A Moral and Historical Inquiry*. Princeton, N.J.: Princeton University Press, 1981.

Johnston, Douglas, and Cynthia Sampson, eds. *Religion: The Missing Dimension in Statecraft*. New York: Oxford University Press, 1994.

Kagan, Robert. "America's Crisis of Legitimacy." *Foreign Affairs* 83, no. 2 (March/April 2004): 65–87.

Kaplan, Robert D. *Warrior Politics: Why Leadership Demands a Pagan Ethos*. New York: Random House, 2002.

Kelsay, John. "Justice, Political Authority and Armed Conflict: Challenges to Sovereignty and the Just Conduct of War." In *The Sacred and the Sovereign*, edited by John D. Carlson and Erik C. Owens, 113–36. Washington, D.C.: Georgetown University Press, 2003.

Kennedy, Paul. *The Rise and Fall of the Great Powers: Economic Change and Military Conflict from 1500–2000*. New York: Random House, 1987.

Kepel, Gilles. *Jihad: The Trail of Political Islam*. Cambridge, Mass.: Harvard University Belknap Press, 2002.

Kissinger, Henry. *Diplomacy*. New York: Simon and Schuster, 1994.

Krauthammer, Charles. *Democratic Realism: An American Foreign Policy for a Unipolar World*. Washington, D.C.: The AEI Press, 2004.

Kurland, Philip B., and Ralph Lerner, eds. *Major Themes*, vol. 1 of *The Founders' Constitution*. Chicago: University of Chicago Press, 1987.

Lang, Daniel George. *Foreign Policy in the Early Republic: The Law of Nations and the Balance of Power*. Baton Rouge: Louisiana State University Press, 1985.

Levi, Mario Attilio. *Political Power in the Ancient World*, translated by Jane Costello. New York: New American Library, 1965.

Lewis, Bernard. *What Went Wrong? Western Impact and Middle East Response*. New York: Oxford University Press, 2002.

Lindberg, Tod. "The Bush Doctrine." *Hoover Digest*, no. 4 (2002): 116–21.

Lutz, Donald S., ed. *Colonial Origins of the American Constitution: A Documentary History*. Indianapolis, Ind.: Liberty Fund, 1998.

———. *The Origins of American Constitutionalism*. Baton Rouge: Louisiana State University Press, 1988.

MacMillan, Margaret. *Paris 1919*. New York: Random House Trade Paperbacks, 2002, 2001.

Markus, R. A. *Saeculum: History and Society in the Theology of St. Augustine*. Cambridge: Cambridge University Press, 1970.

Marshall, Paul. *God and the Constitution: Christianity and American Politics*. Lanham, Md.: Rowman & Littlefield, 2002.

Marshall, Paul, Roberta Green, and Lela Gilbert. *Islam at the Crossroads*. Grand Rapids, Mich.: Baker Books, 2002.

McClay, Wilfred M. "The Soul of a Nation." *The Public Interest*, no. 155 (Spring 2004): 4–19.

McKnight, Stephen A. *Sacralizing the Secular: Renaissance Origins of Modernity*. Baton Rouge: Louisiana State University Press, 1989.

Mead, Walter Russell. *Power, Terror, Peace, and War: America's Grand Strategy in a World at Risk*. New York: Knopf, 2004.

———. *Special Providence: American Foreign Policy and How it Changed the World*. New York: Knopf, 2001.

Mendlovitz, Saul H. *On the Creation of a Just World Order: Preferred Worlds for the 1990s*. New York: Free Press, 1975.

Morgenthau, Hans J. *Politics Among Nations*. 5th ed. New York: Knopf, 1976.

Morley, Felix. *Freedom and Federalism*. Indianapolis, Ind.: Liberty Fund, 1981, 1959.

Mueller, William A. *Church and State in Luther and Calvin*. New York: Doubleday Anchor Books, 1965, 1954.

Murray, John Courtney. *We Hold These Truths: Catholic Reflections on the American Proposition*. New York: Doubleday Image Books, 1964.

Niebuhr, Reinhold. *Beyond Tragedy*. New York: Scribner's, 1937.

———. *Love and Justice*, edited by D. B. Robertson. Gloucester, Mass.: Peter Smith, 1967.

———. *Moral Man and Immoral Society*. New York: Scribner's, 1932.

Noll, Mark A. *America's God: From Jonathan Edwards to Abraham Lincoln*. New York: Oxford University Press, 2002.

Nye, Joseph S., Jr. *Soft Power: The Means to Success in World Politics*. New York: Public Affairs, 2004.

O'Donovan, Oliver, and Joan Lockwood O'Donovan. *Bonds of Imperfection: Christian Politics, Past and Present*. Grand Rapids, Mich.: Eerdmans, 2004.

O'Donovan, Oliver, and Joan Lockwood O'Donovan, eds. *From Irenaeus to Grotius: A Sourcebook in Christian Political Thought, 100–1625*. Grand Rapids, Mich.: Eerdmans, 1999.

Pangle, Thomas L., and Peter J. Ahrensdorf. *Justice Among Nations: On the Moral Basis of Power and Peace*. Lawrence: University Press of Kansas, 1999.

Parkinson, F. *The Philosophy of International Relations*. Beverly Hills, Calif.: Sage Publications, 1977.

Philpott, Daniel. "On the Cusp of Sovereignty: Lessons from the Sixteenth Century." In *Sovereignty at the Crossroads?* edited by Luis E. Lugo, 37–62. Lanham, Md.: Rowman & Littlefield, 1996.

Porter, Jean. "Reason, Nature, and Natural Order in Medieval Accounts of Natural Law." *Journal of Religious Ethics* 24, no. 2 (Fall 1986): 207–32.

———. *The Recovery of Virtue: The Relevance of Aquinas for Christian Ethics*. Louisville, Ky.: Westminster/John Knox Press, 1990.

Prestowitz, Clyde. *Rogue Nation: American Unilateralism and the Failure of Good Intentions*. New York: Basic Books, 2003.

Public Justice and the European Union. The Hague: Christian Democratic Appeal, 1999. <wi@bureau.cda.nl>

Pythian, Mark. *Arming Iraq: How the US and Britain Secretly Built Saddam's War Machine*. Boston: Northeastern University Press, 1997.

Ramsey, Paul. *The Just War: Force and Political Responsibility*. New York: Scribner's, 1968.

———. *War and Christian Conscience: How Shall Modern War Be Conducted Justly?* Durham, N.C.: Duke University Press, 1961.

Record, Jeffrey. "The Bush Doctrine and War with Iraq." *Parameters* (Spring 2003): 4–21.

Record, Jeffrey, and W. Andrew Terrill, "Iraq and Vietnam: Differences, Similarities, and Insights." Carlisle, Pa.: Strategic Studies Institute, U.S. Army War College, May 2004.

"Religion, Culture, and International Conflict After September 11: A Conversation with Samuel P. Huntington." *Center Conversations* (a publication of the Ethics and Public Policy Center, Washington, D.C., June 2002).

Richey, Russell E., and Donald G. Jones, eds. *American Civil Religion*. New York: Harper and Row, 1974.

Rodenbeck, Max. "Islam Confronts Its Demons." *The New York Review of Books*, April 29, 2004, 14–18.

Rubenfeld, Jeb. "The Two World Orders." *Wilson Quarterly* (Autumn 2003): 22–36.

Sandel, Michael. "America's Search for a New Public Philosophy." *The Atlantic Monthly* (March 1996): 57–74.

Schama, Simon. *The Embarrassment of Riches: An Interpretation of Dutch Culture in the Golden Age.* New York: Alfred A. Knopf, 1987.

Scruton, Roger. "The Political Problem of Islam." *The Intercollegiate Review* (Fall 2002): 3–15.

Shorto, Russell. *The Island at the Center of the World.* New York: Doubleday, 2004.

Skillen, James W. *A Covenant to Keep: Meditations on the Biblical Theme of Justice.* Grand Rapids, Mich.: CRC Publications, 2000.

———. "Augustine and Contemporary Evangelical Social Thought." *The Reformed Journal* (January 1979): 19–24.

———. *In Pursuit of Justice: Christian-Democratic Explorations.* Lanham, Md.: Rowman & Littlefield, 2004.

———. *Recharging the American Experiment: Principled Pluralism for Genuine Civic Community.* Grand Rapids, Mich.: Baker Books, 1994.

Skillen, James W., and Keith J. Pavlischek. "Political Responsibility and the Use of Force: A Critique of Richard Hays." *Philosophia Christi* 3, no. 2, Series 2 (2001): 421–45.

Slaughter, Anne-Marie. "Leading Through Law." *Wilson Quarterly* (Autumn 2003): 37–44.

Soros, George. "The Bubble of American Supremacy." *The Atlantic Monthly* (December 2003): 63–66.

Stevenson, William R. *Christian Love and Just War: Moral Paradox and Political Life in St. Augustine and His Modern Interpreters.* Macon, Ga.: Mercer University Press, 1987.

———. *Sovereign Grace: The Place and Significance of Christian Freedom in John Calvin's Political Thought.* New York: Oxford University Press, 1999.

Todd, Emmanuel. *After the Empire: The Breakdown of the American Order.* New York: Columbia University Press, 2003.

Traub, James. "Who Needs the U.N. Security Council," *The New York Times Magazine,* November 17, 2002, 46–51.

Tucker, Robert W. *The Just War: A Study in Contemporary American Doctrine.* Baltimore: Johns Hopkins University Press, 1960.

Ullmann, Walter. *A History of Political Thought: The Middle Ages.* New York: Penguin Books, 1965.

Van Creveld, Martin. *The Rise and Decline of the State.* Cambridge: Cambridge University Press, 1999.

Veyne, Paul, ed. *From Pagan Rome to Byzantium,* vol. 1 of *A History of Private Life.* Cambridge, Mass.: Harvard University Belknap Press, 1987.

Voegelin, Eric. *From Enlightenment to Revolution,* edited by John H. Hallowell. Durham, N.C.: Duke University Press, 1975.

———. *Order and History,* 5 vols. Baton Rouge: Louisiana State University Press, 1956.

Vos, Geerhardus. *Biblical Theology: Old and New Testaments.* Grand Rapids, Mich.: Eerdmans, 1948.

Walzer, Michael. "International Society: What Is the Best We Can Do?" *Ethical Perspectives* (Journal of the European Ethics Network) 6, nos. 3–4 (December 1999): 201–10.

———. *Just and Unjust Wars.* New York: Basic Books, 1977.

Webster, Alexander F. C., and Darrell Cole. *The Virtue of War: Reclaiming the Classic Christian Traditions East and West.* Salisbury, Md.: Regina Orthodox Press, 2004.

Weigel, George. *Tranquillitas Ordinis: The Present Failure and Future Promise of American Catholic Thought on War and Peace.* New York: Oxford University Press, 1987.

Willey, Basil. *The Seventeenth Century Background.* New York: Doubleday Anchor Books, 1953, 1935.

Witte, John, Jr. *Law and Protestantism: The Legal Teachings of the Lutheran Reformation.* Cambridge: Cambridge University Press, 2002.

Wright, N. T. *The Climax of the Covenant: Christ and the Law in Pauline Theology.* Minneapolis, Minn.: Fortress Press, 1991.

Yoder, John Howard. *For the Nations: Essays Public and Evangelical.* Grand Rapids, Mich.: Eerdmans, 1997.

———. *The Politics of Jesus.* Grand Rapids, Mich.: Eerdmans, 1972.

Zakaria, Fareed. *The Future of Freedom: Illiberal Democracy at Home and Abroad.* New York: W. W. Norton, 2003.

———. "Terror and the War of Ideas." *The Washington Post,* April 10, 2004.

Index

About the Author

James W. Skillen is president of the Center for Public Justice, which he has directed since 1981, and is the editor of its *Public Justice Report* (quarterly) and *Capital Commentary* (bi-monthly). He earned his B.A. in philosophy at Wheaton College, the B.D. at Westminster Theological Seminary, and the M.A. and Ph.D. in political philosophy, international relations, and comparative politics at Duke University.

He is the author or editor of seventeen books, including *In Pursuit of Justice: Christian-Democratic Explorations* (Rowman & Littlefield, 2004); *A Covenant to Keep: Meditations on the Biblical Theme of Justice* (2000); *Recharging the American Experiment: Principled Pluralism for Genuine Civic Community* (1994); *The Scattered Voice: Christians at Odds in the Public Square* (1990); and, as coeditor, *Welfare in America: Christian Perspectives on a Policy in Crisis* (with Stanley Carlson-Thies, 1996) and *Political Order and the Plural Structure of Society* (with Rockne McCarthy, 1991).

A frequent speaker in civic forums and on college campuses, Skillen has lectured on American foreign policy and international affairs at conferences and universities in Canada, Europe, Russia, China, Korea, and South Africa. He and Doreen are the parents of Jeanene and James. They live in Annapolis, Maryland.